WALKING UP & DOWN IN THE WORLD

WALKING
UP & DOWN
IN THE WORLD

Memories of a Mountain Rambler

SMOKE BLANCHARD

SIERRA CLUB BOOKS • SAN FRANCISCO

The Sierra Club, founded in 1892 by John Muir, has devoted itself to the study and protection of the earth's scenic and ecological resources—mountains, wetlands, woodlands, wild shores and rivers, deserts and plains. The publishing program of the Sierra Club offers books to the public as a nonprofit educational service in the hope that they may enlarge the public's understanding of the Club's basic concerns. The point of view expressed in each book, however, does not necessarily represent that of the Club. The Sierra Club has some fifty chapters coast to coast, and in Canada, Hawaii, and Alaska. For information about how you may participate in its programs to preserve wilderness and the quality of life, please address inquiries to Sierra Club, 530 Bush Street, San Francisco, CA 94108.

LIBRARY OF CONGRESS CATALOGING IN PUBLICATION DATA
Blanchard, Smoke, 1915–
Walking up and down in the world.

1. Blanchard, Smoke, 1915–   . 2. Mountaineers—
United States—Biography. 3. Mountaineering—
Anecdotes, facetiae, satire, etc. I. Title.
GV199.92.B58A38 1984   796.5'22'092'4 [B]   84–5380
ISBN 0–87156–827–6

Jacket design by Paul Gamarello
Book design by Wilsted & Taylor
Maps by Nancy Warner
Composition by Wilsted & Taylor
Printed in the United States of America
10 9 8 7 6 5 4 3 2 1

Contents

To my son, Robert C. Blanchard,
hero of this story from my notes of 1974:

As we walked home from town one evening, Bobbo pointed at a three-inch space between the buildings that house Dirty Duke's Tire Shop and Greasy Joe's Garage. "That's a great hand jam there, Dad. Like this."

"Oh yeah, have you climbed it?"

"Look at him grin," Su said. "Of course he has."

"Yeah, I got grabbed for that—Doug Robinson, Billy Albright, and I. They took us down to the station. Suspicion of burglary. The Chief talked to us. It didn't go so well at first. 'Just walking around,' we said. Finally we had to admit we were climbing buildings. 'Yeah, I thought so, Blanchard,' the Chief said. 'I've known you since you were that high. Why don't you go out on the rocks?' "

Foreword
by Doug Robinson

THE TEMPTATION is to lie. The question comes up innocently enough, but it always comes up. I could say that I make a living rewinding videotape, or staring out a window at the Rand Corporation, anything. Instead, I usually tell the truth: that I'm a professional climber. Guiding, writing, designing equipment, giving slide shows—anything to grubstake the next trip back over timberline. But it's a good bet that my admission has let me in for explaining everything my new acquaintance suddenly wants to know about climbing, even if he had never thought about it before. The list of questions is predictable too, starting with "How does the rope get up there?"

Smoke Blanchard, one of the finest mountain guides I know, has been carrying the sharp end of the rope up there for half a century now. In this book he sets out to answer, once and for all, those inevitable questions. I suppose he's hoping to buy time for himself and the rest of us to circulate a little, maybe find out what a hang-glider pilot on his way to an altitude record thinks as he eases his kite up into the jet lanes. In the process, Smoke has come perilously close to letting the cat out of the bag. I hurriedly turned to the chapter titled "Guiding Secrets" to see which ones he was giving away. What I found, there and elsewhere, makes this, among its other virtues, the book to recommend to apprentice guides.

But guiding is only part of Smoke's story. We first come upon him as a young climber escaping Portland and the Depression on the back of a motorcycle. He is bound for Mount Hood, which he will climb repeatedly: twice one day, in record time another, up by new routes, down on skis. Venturing afield, he rebounds from Yosemite to land in the Owens Valley, east of the Sierra Nevada, and stay. We share the maturing mountaineer's inevitable challenging of great northern ranges, with early climbs on Mount McKinley and first ascents in the Yukon. But just when one would expect a climber's reminiscences to begin snuggling into hearth and home hills, we instead find Smoke walking the Pacific shoreline of two states, or across California, or bicycling in the footsteps of the Buddha, or wandering the mountains of Nepal, Japan, or China with the correct local dialect on the tip of his tongue. He's hardly ever home anymore.

I met Smoke the same summer I began to guide, in 1966. We were introduced by Sheridan Anderson, the alpine cartoonist and timberline *bon vivant*, who took me by Smoke's house in the high desert town of Bishop, at the foot of the eastern wall of the Sierra. Smoke was not a professional guide then—not full-time, anyway. He was a truck driver by trade, hauling propane all winter to keep his summers free for mountains. But he was the only Buddhist truck driver I had ever met who memorized poetry to recite to himself on the road. I think he liked driving trucks partly because it was the perfect cover (Smokescreen?) for a climber.

Smoke learned early the art of downplaying mountaineering, and he got so good at it that sometimes he even fooled his family. When I met him, the tale of a conversation with his son Bob was already an old story. It seems he was returning from a Sunday excursion back when Bob was young and Smoke still smoked (no, that's not where his name came from . . .).

"Where have you been?" Bob asked.

"Up the Little Pinnacle," replied Smoke.

"Oh yeah—smoking pipes and reading books," Bob figured, easily imagining a little pinnacle to be at the limit of his father's ambition.

Actually, Smoke's "Little Pinnacle" is a looming hulk of granite well over a thousand feet high, little only by comparison to the enormity of the Wheeler Crest rising 7,000 feet behind it. Climbing it is no small feat either. Most people would want a rope, at least, to get up it. Smoke soloes, unroped, and the name he has chosen for this formation perfectly reflects his sense of humor. He has routes like that tucked up every canyon above Bishop.

Smoke always returns to his favorite spot—the Buttermilk rocks just outside of town—so it wasn't long before I found myself lacing on shoes at the foot of a maze of rocks that would do credit to a head-em-off-at-the-pass Western movie set. Smoke's Rock Course is the key to that maze, a subtle line that winds through subterranean passageways en route to a dozen summits. Fresh from years of training in Yosemite, I followed. Soon, however, I found myself high-stepping moves and panting hard just to keep up. The full course took all day, with no time spared to learn the route; in fact, Smoke is still the only person who can lead the whole thing. This conqueror of little pinnacles, though disguised in trucker's clothes and veiled by Buddhist self-effacement, was no mean rock climber.

So you have to read between the lines a bit in these pages. Smoke has perfected an "aw, shucks" style that is the absolute antithesis of Victorian climbing prose, where every casual scramble takes on heroic proportions. The well-turned phrases here bespeak a lot of work, yet Smoke put this book together in a hurry, between trips to the Orient. As I read, some of the stories began to have a familiar ring, and I realized that I've been hearing him polish them around campfires and across the kitchen table ever since we met. Now they can be shared by all.

On the other hand, when Smoke speaks of "mild mountaineering" he really means it as an invitation. Over the years he has introduced hundreds of people to climbing, more of them for love than money, even after he began buying groceries by guiding. In the early days he recruited friends, or even strangers off the street—who probably thought at first that they were going for a "stroll." Smoke's approach *is* mild mountaineering in the sense that none of them ever got hurt, and most came home ecstatic at mastering new and difficult terrain.

And difficult it becomes. Though they may start out "just scrambling," followers along the Buttermilk Rock Course soon find themselves thirty feet above the ground, wedged between the smooth walls of a two-foot-wide chimney. The technique is completely foreign, the means of staying wedged while moving up a mystery. Yet, just above, the master is absently clinging to the stone and giving advice, seemingly as a reluctant aside to the story he is telling: about the time Bob Thayer offered Smoke his Mercedes (but balked at the suggestion of throwing in his beautiful wife) as an inducement to get himself lowered from the summit of the outcrop they had just climbed. Smoke not only figured a way down from that first ascent, but named their climb the "Mercedes Boulder."

Meanwhile, the follower, having become so caught up in the story that he forgot his fear and chimneyed right on up in imitation of the master, has arrived at the top of another pinnacle and the apex of his hours-old climbing career. Coming along behind, I can't help but notice that the ascent is pretty difficult. But Smoke's teaching technique is so smooth that he regularly gets unathletic beginners up difficult rock and into the ranks of budding mountaineers.

In developing this strategy, Smoke was among the first to show his fellow guides that students could be propelled straight onto difficult climbing and into an immediate sense of accomplishment and confidence. That sort of gentle sandbagging has become a cornerstone of my own rockclimbing instruction. When the American Professional Mountain Guides Association was being formed recently, we couldn't interest Smoke in being "grandfathered" in as a charter member until we pleaded that young guides deserve a chance to learn from his teaching methods.

It was at Smoke's house that I had the privilege of meeting Norman Clyde, John Muir's successor as Grand Old Man of the Sierra. Ensconced on the couch, surrounded by books and yarning at anyone who came within range, he seemed like any old man beginning to come apart at the seams—until you noticed the gleam of alpine light in his eyes. Smoke was the closest friend of Clyde's final thirty years, and since Clyde wrote so sparingly, the portrait Smoke draws of him here is to be treasured.

I met Jules Eichorn at Smoke's place too. Eichorn had been with Clyde on the first ascent of Mount Whitney's east face, and it dawned on me that Smoke's friendships spanned the entire history of roped climbing in the Sierra. His perspective, that of the bemused soloist who nonetheless appreciates hard climbing, is a unique vantage on California's rise during that fifty years into the foremost venues of world mountaineering.

Because he is out there so often, Smoke runs into the modern climbers as well. He tells of meeting Galen Rowell one day at the foot of the Lemon Lichen Boulder in the Peabodies, a realm of the Buttermilk favored by the young and agile for its consistently hard climbing. Smoke was soon guiding Galen to an owl's nest he knew of on a nearby cliffside. The resulting photos have been widely published. But I've often wondered how Smoke, who publicly eschews the cult of difficult climbing, happened to be wandering around the Peabodies that morning in his climbing boots.

Later, Smoke took Galen and me on a climb up on the Wheeler Crest, a 7,000-foot hillside bristling with exposed granite buttresses, like the Little Pinnacle. We went to Wells Peak, which turned out to be fine white granite, its summit guarded by a sequence of airy ridge moves that were only climbable as if riding horseback.

Maybe it was going there first with Smoke—casually scrambling over breathtaking terrain without a break in the running commentary—that led us to underestimate the place. But when we went back up later, the smooth granite of the buttress turned us back after only 200 feet. Returning again with hardware and greater respect, we did eventually climb that thousand-foot tower flanking Wells Peak and named it the Smokestack in his honor. Purity of line and difficult climbing have made it a modern classic among the scores of technical routes now found along the Wheeler Crest, thanks to Smoke's lead.

In 1979 I went on expedition to Nepal. I was crossing a bridge over the Dudh Khosi one day, filled with a sense of the remoteness, the esoteric adventure of it all, when I looked up to see Smoke coming down the trail. These days, you're more likely to run into him in Asia than in the Sierra. Leading treks or poking around on his own, Smoke is at home in Nepal, China, Tibet, Bhutan, Sikkim, and Japan. Every year he's gone longer; this year he'll be home only three months. "Uphill or down, it's all the same now," he said that afternoon. It's not surprising that the Sherpas have grown so fond of *Gaga Esmoke*, or that his friends there include Tenzing Norgay, who shared the first ascent of Mount Everest with Sir Edmund Hillary. Smoke says his favorite famous climber is Nawang Gombu, who has climbed Everest twice and narrowly missed a third ascent. Together they've been mild mountaineering in Bhutan and India, with what even Smoke calls "a very rough storm on one trip and a difficult rescue on another."

I won't be surprised if one day Smoke just quits coming home. I can see him fixing up an old stone hut in the Himalayan backcountry, one that the Sherpas considered too high for anything except summer herding. But Smoke would move right in, a blue-eyed Buddhist with odd cheekbones living high on a mountainside—but not a hermit. No, he'd want to be able to walk down the hill to joke with Tenzing, stop in to a tea house for a ration of local homebrew, and cruise the bazaar with an eye for the younger women.

How many can say that they have fully inhabited their fondest dreams? We'll miss Smoke in the Sierra, in his absence valuing this book all the more.

Preface

THE PEOPLE who follow me around in the mountains of California, Alaska, Nepal, and Japan always ask questions. The adventure travel companies I work for say we should call our customers by the standard travel-business term: passengers. Passengers have a way of becoming friends. And friends also follow me around on noncommercial trips in the Yukon, Europe, Oregon, or India. They all ask questions, and if they don't, I tell them things anyhow. I try to entertain or instruct them, or to bemuse them so that they will not think the big hill we are climbing is all that monotonous.

Often my stories, anecdotes, and incidents are not innocent. During my several years here and there I have developed hardened prejudices. I have axes to grind.

For a half century I have tried to promote the idea that mountaineering is best approached as a combination of picnic and pilgrimage. Mountain picnic-pilgrimage is short on aggression and long on satisfaction. I hope that I can show that mild mountaineering can be happily pursued through a long lifetime without posting records. Can a love affair be cataloged?

Here are the answers to some of the many questions I'm asked when guiding, and some of the stories I tell my friends. The anecdotes are all true and related as accurately as a one-cylinder memory can revive them. I hope that a broad spectrum of outdoor-oriented readers can find something instructive or entertaining.

I trust that armchair travelers may be able to cope with technical mountain terms such as *bergschrund* and *puja*, and that the odd 5.14 big-wall climber can read manila-rope, tricouni-nail prose.

Having dashed off the above paragraph, I suddenly realize I don't know what a 5.14 big-wall climber is, except that he seems a little odd. Years ago the Sierra Club classified climbs by their difficulty in an effort to ease mountaineers' selection of routes consistent with ability. Rockclimbers attempting to apply a decimal vernier to Class 5, the most difficult climbs attempted without mechanical assistance, ran off the scale. Perhaps climbers making multi-day ascents of huge cliffs have not yet reached a grade of difficulty classed 5.14; still, I hope that even world-class climbers will find amusement in an old-style mountain walker's experiences. I also crave communication with those whose mountain experience is entirely vicarious, so I hasten to add that a bergschrund is the crevasse or crack at the top of a glacier that separates the flowing ice stream from the headwall of its carved valley, and *puja* is a general term used in India for any kind of religious exercise.

I beg indulgence for two semantic peculiarities. Neither Japanese nor Nepali has a special word for *trail*. They both use words which translate as *road*. More than a decade of talking of, and walking on, their "roads" has ground this term deep into my vocabulary. Our English word *hiking* has sneaked into Japanese, but, I note with satisfaction, they speak of anything more serious than a stroll as *tozan*: climbing. I'll be talking a lot about *walking* on *roads*.

Building a book is like organizing a twelve-year expedition. Among the people who inspired or urged me to take such a long trip I must mention Cheryl Arnold, Bob Swift, and Don Wobber.

Jerry Goodwin played an essential part in helping me to decide just what peaks I really wanted to climb along the way. Tom Cole, John Pollock, and especially Galen Rowell set me on the correct approach march. Mithoo Baxter loaned me a base camp for packing. Even after Jerry Goodwin's ruling that half the baggage should be left behind, I found the remaining equipment too heavy. Gordon Wiltsie and Pamela Naylor and, mainly, Joe Kelsey helped me to pare pounds. Diana Landau went over the equipment list line by line to the inexpressible benefit of the expedition.

And the Lord said unto Satan, Whence comest thou?
Then Satan answered the Lord, and said,
From going to and fro in the earth,
and from walking up and down in it.

JOB I:7

The path up and down is one and the same.

HERACLITUS

(C. 540–480 B.C.)

Fragment 60

Mount Hood

CAMP BLOSSOM CABIN

I recently had a curve-ball question thrown at me: "What is your favorite mountain?"

I fumbled and found the answer too late. I should have said that I once heard this question asked of the famous Sherpa Dawa Tenzing. The wily seventy-year-old "Tiger" of many early Himalayan expeditions paused for dramatic effect, as if searching his memory, and then answered solemnly, "All mountain good."

I was then asked what mountain had influenced me most. My friend already knew the answer—he was fishing for stories of Mount Hood. Any mountaineer from Oregon probably had his climbing career, and maybe even his character, molded by the mountain that is almost a symbol of the state.

The fifty miles between Portland and Mount Hood represented a fairly formidable separation in the Depression years. I usually hitchhiked. On speedier rides, I wobbled behind Joe Daniel on his Harley Davidson. I first met Joe Daniel high on Palmer Snowfield and talked him into following me up the Zigzag Route. This nar-

I

row defile between Crater Rock and Castle Crags subjects any climber dumb enough to choose this way to a bombardment of rocks and ice. Joe's mountain climbing was as incautious as his motorcycling, and I'd found a pal. We must have been a sight, weaving up the rain-slick highway toward the mountain, two parka-clad figures festooned with packboards, ice axes, ropes, and skis.

In the mid-1930s my equipment had yet to evolve to the modern laminated-wood, steel-edged skis that stand by my door today. Safety bindings (invented by Hjalmar Hvam to be worn with real ski boots) had not yet become part of my gear. When Joe and I emerged from Rafferty's Lodge to begin our uphill struggle to timberline, I mounted a pair of 7½-foot, double-grooved antiques, with leather bindings which accommodated arctic overshoes. For traction we wrapped half the length of our skis with clothesline. Our packboards groaned with the weight of food we brought to add to supplies we cached at timberline.

Even when the trail lacked tracks, we could find our way by using the light of Joe's kerosene lantern and watching for wide places in the snow-coned trees. After two hours, wider spaces in the trees signaled the left turn where we traversed, heads down against the prevailing cold west wind. Even in wind-swirled flakes, we could accurately count the snowdrifts and find the one where the cabin stovepipe stuck out of the snow like a U-boat's periscope. The top floor had a door hinged to swing inward just under the ridge. We could dig down with a ski, shoulder the door in, and reach a shovel with which to fashion a proper entrance.

The United States Forest Service Camp Blossom Shelter Cabin was open to all, but, because we came regularly and had boarded up corners (illegally) to make lockers for primus stoves and food, we thought of the cabin as ours. So did a number of other frequent visitors, many of them famous in Hood history.

Members of the elite Cascade Ski Club stopped by on their long-ranging tours. They included such fine skiers as Hjalmar Hvam, a national four-way champion, and Ole Langeraud and Einar Hermanson, both of whom skied down Hood long before the "man who skied down Everest" was born. Olaf Rodegard practiced in the cabin glade for the role he had skiing the part of Sonja Henie in the movie *It Happened in Sun Valley*. Haughty Wyeast Clubbers, both before and after they built their own timberline cabin, dropped around. Ralph Calkins and Joe Leuthold used the old cabin as base for many of their record climbs. Everett Darr got so turned on by snowy trips to timberline that he went into the ski business and spent his whole life in Government Camp, in close sight of the great peak.

I'll not neglect the nonclub "outlaws" either. A regular cabin camper was my schoolmate and ski partner Walt Johnson. Walt manufactured his first skis in his basement with a draw knife and homebuilt steam box. He still skis actively fifty years later.

My buddy Hubert North did not last to middle age, as Walt has. Hubert commanded longshoreman's wages in the late thirties and had the money, time, and loose lifestyle to motor to the mountains almost any time the mood moved him. I must explain this modern cliché, loose lifestyle, which crept into Hubert's description. His high school class would not recognize in this phrase the shy, sober, hard-working, straight-A student they knew. Hub's few friends would spot this phrase as a euphemism for longshoring hours made even more irregular by bouts with the bottle. Hubert's father made home hell by beating his mother during drunken rages. Hubert and his older brother, Henry, swore abstinence. Sometime after the father's dry-eyed funeral, when the widow North began to date again, a rejected suitor revengefully struck back by turning the pathologically shy, neurotic, younger boy to alcohol.

Hubert lusted less after the siren winter than some of us, but I could nearly always count on him for a summer ride to the mountain. I had only to look through the window of the brightly lit Blue Bell Tavern for a slim figure in white cap, hickory shirt, and heavy-duty black Frisco jeans. My own shyness precluded my slapping him on the back; had I done so, a fine white powder would have drifted ceilingward. He "worked flour" and came straight from the docks to his second home. I could never match him beer for beer, but enjoyed batting jokes in perfect understanding of his wry and dry humor.

If he had only one night off, he would drive the round trip to Government Camp to talk to Gary Leech. Hubert's mother worked for Grace Line, and Gary, Hubert, and I dreamed of getting a pass on a ship to go climbing in Peru. (My Christmas, 1981, climb of the Mexican volcano Popocatepetl was the first time any of us got to Latin America.) Hubert had a convenient itch for adventure and a Ford car; I could easily talk him into taking a month off. For these important trips, he would go on the wagon in both ways.

Hubert fixed up a converted, decked, and cabined lifeboat with a one-lung motor barely capable of one knot against the current, as a haven for serious drinking. When his brother, Henry, heard a report of the crewless boat found drifting down the Columbia River, he drove all the way to my home in Bishop, California, on the extremely slim chance that Hubert had docked and driven there to go climbing. We both knew he hadn't. I like to think Hubert floated out into the Pacific, bottle in hand, shouting ribald remarks to the waves before he sank under them.

Of the many colorful, eccentric characters who hung out at the cabin, the prize for least conventional went to Gordon Bennett Dukes. Dukes said, "Say, Blanchard, old chief, old chesty, old boy, if any of those damned women come up here this weekend, let's just strip to the waist and sit around and drink tea. Do you know those society women down in Portland? They take a bath every day, but they're dirty! They never come up to old Doc Hood and shee and schwet and clean out their pores!"

Dukes pronounced skis, poles, and wax as "shees," "shticks," and "shmeer." He wore genuine European knickers and a flat cap complete with badges, sported a mustache, and had his rucksack fitted with an interior frame on which he racked his suit jacket and necktie.

We thought Dukes was just a bit out of the ordinary. He was

fond of telling us why, too. He told us often and in detail about his seven ski tours the length of Europe. About how he made a fortune selling cars in Buenos Aires and married the heiress to a cattle ranch, "but she got fat, so I had to leave her. Hell, I was a trim athlete." Of how he found "powder snow at four thousand feet in southern Patagonia," and was still a member of the Club Chuquimata de Ski. He was born and raised in Kobe, Japan, and graduated from Cornell. He told us he had won a medal in the single-man scull in the 1912 Stockholm Olympics. We suspected we were getting a heavy dose of bull, but we listened. (Someone found out that he was, indeed, once a teacher of French literature at a private school for rich girls in Hollywood.)

Dukes was an older man. "Blanchard," he would ask, "you are very young, aren't you? Only twenty-one, twenty-two?" Since I was eighteen at the time, he instantly puffed out my chest and made me believe. "Your legs must be very strong. You know, confidentially, I'm forty-six!" Well, he really did not look or act ancient. In spite of this startlingly high number, he managed to teach us how to christy on a slalom course marked out with fir bows in the cabin glade.

Dukes always had a way of whipping up enthusiasm, one way being his Nudist Ski Club. The Nudist Shee Club, as he pronounced it, had no organizational structure whatsoever, except for its initiation, which involved skiing a gantlet, attired only in jockey strap, dodging snowballs thrown by previous inductees.

He had all sorts of skiing techniques. When we were preparing to run the four-mile trail to the village, he advised that "a half pint of cognac, neat, guarantees against sitzmarks." And, "Skiing up the mountain, one should carry a ski barometer. A ski barometer is a mason jar filled with hot tea and fitted with a cord that attaches to the belt. One climbs up the mountain with one eye on the tea; the first ice crystals signal the proper altitude has been reached to remove the skins and begin the down-go."

Dukes supported himself at the mountain for weeks by exchanging stories for stores. He was a bum, most people said. In the city, he supported himself through his facility with foreign languages, selling phonograph records, razor blades, fountain pens, and "men's accessories" (condoms) to sailors on foreign ships in Portland Harbor. He made enough money to fuel his Maxwell touring car (with sky-blue paint inside and out, dashboard covered with ski photos, and sailboat rack on the side) for regular trips to the mountain.

By this time, Joe Daniel might have to get back to work, the cabin would clear of skiers and climbers, and I'd have a day or three of solitude to listen to Brownlee's ghost moan in the wind. Long ago Al Ferrabin and Leslie Brownlee got separated in a storm while coming down from a midwinter ascent. Only Ferrabin reached Camp Blossom Cabin. Probably the strong west wind pushed Brownlee out onto the White River Glacier, and a crevasse ate him. It's been more than fifty years now; nothing is remembered of Brownlee among the plastic-wrapped snow players around the modern Timberline Lodge. Ah, but if you bivouac far from the crowds, the old men say, on a rough stormy night at some lonesome spot at tree line, you may still hear Brownlee's ghost searching for the right way down.

The way down can puzzle the toughest expert after he's fought a blast of stinging snow on the summit ridge only to be hassled off the mountain by a rising storm. Weary, wind-buffeted, half blind from staring into a froth of white nothing, he stumbles down the long snowfields into the evening dusk. Hard storms batter him for too many hours, and the body cries for rest. He can stop only to turn the feeble glow of his cold-dimmed flashlight onto a rime-crusted compass and clamp his jaw, determined to escape a rendezvous with Brownlee.

I took care to wait for a day of nearly guaranteed clear skies before setting out, solo, for a winter-guarded summit. Or I waited for Ole Lien to show up. The cabin knew no single-minded southside plodder more faithful than Ole Lien, and sooner more often than later he'd come snowshoeing into the glade to prepare for yet another climb. If I grew impatient for company, I might ski east and

slightly down through open timberline glades to the Wyeast Cabin
to see if Russ McJury was in residence. When weather was marginal for climbing, we'd make the round trip to Government
Camp, skiing our own cross-country route down through fifty-
foot snow-coned trees. Snow—deep, soft, silent, clean, and beautiful, the epitome of sacred wilderness—could anything be better
than gliding effortlessly through snow on magic hickories?

Marginal weather meant little to Gary Leech, and around three
in the morning I might be awakened by Gary clattering into the
cabin with "Shake out, Smoke, let's go up the mountain."

After all this talk of Camp Blossom Cabin and its denizens, I
should describe going up the mountain. That was primarily what
we were there for and what we did often during the old days. The
several-score climbs, in all seasons, by all routes, through all
weather, at all times of the day or night, make Mount Hood the
mountain that influenced me most.

OVER THE MOUNTAIN

My after-dinner Hood climb of July 19, 1938, was one of those
flash decisions that are often rewarded with the richest experiences. Two chance acquaintances had barely mentioned requesting a ride from Government Camp to Cloud Cap when a rare idea
exploded in my head. I would climb the mountain from Cloud
Cap, on the north side, then descend back to the south-side village
of Government Camp! An excellent idea! The only problem was
the car. When Gary Leech offered to drive it back, there was nothing in the way. "Jump in," I yelled to my acquaintances, "here we
go!"

My ice ax and rucksack were already in the car. In those days my
rucksack housed only sweater, parka, mittens, goggles, crampons, and warm cap. With Gary stowed across the ice ax in the
rear, we were soon hurtling down the highway. I turned onto the
narrow, winding Loop Road, and kept the Plymouth roaring in an
effort to make Cloud Cap in the shortest possible time. Every

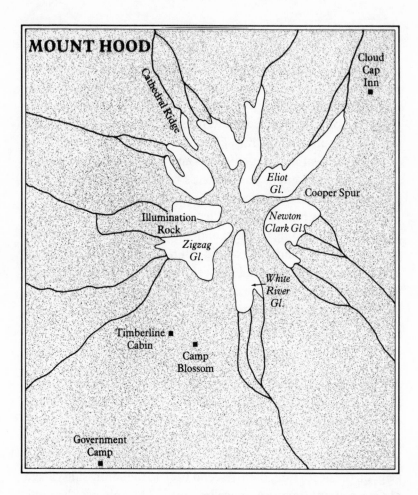

curve being familiar, I was able to extract the utmost speed from the tortuous twists. From Buzzard Point, Hood River Meadows, and Bennett Pass we caught fleeting glimpses of different aspects of the mountain, as the car dashed through the clearings and into the trees again.

Down through the canyon of the leaping Hood River we roared. We began to search for the first view of the majestic ice-draped Northeast Face. There it was: a 5,000-foot cold-snow wall. It disappeared while we wound up the tree-lined switchbacks, but we arrived at the turnaround at Cloud Cap in full view of the glory of the mountain.

Gary was in a hurry to get back. With a wave of his hand, he threw in the clutch and sped off toward Government Camp. Just then I thought of the flashlight. "Hey!" I yelled, and ran down the road. A cloud of dust rising from the switchback below indicated that my flashlight was on its way home. There was nothing to do but climb without it.

I dined in lonesome dignity on the glassed-in sun porch at Cloud Cap Inn. I looked out on the great snowy mountain. The eastern slopes were already in cold, blue shadow, while the western slopes of rock and green-hued ice reflected the gold of the evening sun. I seemed to be alone in the world, sitting in a box, as in a darkened theater. Behind me was nothing. Before me was everything: the sun-filled world of rolling, forested ridges, culminating in the ice- and rock-ribbed peak. My reverie was interrupted by the waitress emerging from the swinging door with a trayful of biscuits. "Soon," I told her with a dramatic sweep of the arm, "I shall enter these mountain fastnesses!"

"Oh, so you're that mountain climber," she replied without emotion.

I munched biscuits and reflected on the insensitivity of waitresses. Maybe I'm crazy, I concluded. At six P.M. I pushed back the table and thanked my hosts for the meal, which was on the house.

I left the Inn at a half-gallop. Once into the trees, I could have slowed to a walk without anyone knowing, but stubbornly, and a bit ashamed, I continued to jog up to timberline. I began to walk on the narrow-crested moraine, on a path that leads from the last stunted trees into the wide-open world above. I was so charged with energy that I fairly flew along with giant strides. I felt almost disembodied, with no sense of fatigue, free to look around at the beauties of the evening.

Gary had patiently endeavored to pound some pacing wisdom into my skull for years, but I was violating all his rules. "Start slow and warm up gradually," he always said. I had started on the run, now slowed to a fast walk. If lucky, I would finish at a crawl. I knew better, but I was full of youth, and my well-trained body drove my legs like a machine. I felt I was on a train, and the hurrying click-click-click of my ice ax on the stones was the sound of the wheels on the rail joints. In this fashion, I chugged along to the head of the moraine.

As usual, I detoured from the standard Cooper Spur Route so that I could walk on Eliot Glacier. One must always walk on a glacier if there's one around. Some people say it is counterproductive to walk up a glacier, but my pace had not slowed that much, in spite of breaking Gary's rules. I strode up the rough ice to the cliff of Cooper Spur. I stopped only once—for a snapshot of my shadow outlined against a snowbank.

I hastily installed crampons for the steep wall of snow that I would have to surmount when I left the glacier to regain the proper Cooper Spur Route. I chose this variation to avoid the unending pull over the soft ash of Cooper Spur. I glanced to the west and stopped, entranced by the view. Beyond the tumbled seracs of the Eliot Icefall, the setting sun spread a misty gold tinge along the blue, forested ridges of the Cascades.

I had to cross a bergschrund and ascend a medium snow slope above. This was one of the most interesting bits of the route, and I set to it with a will. I prodded the snow bridge that spanned the bergschrund with my ice ax, and gingerly clambered across the dark abyss. The sun's rays had just left the slope above, leaving the snow mushy and clumsy for crampons. I was still in a mood for speed and, fearing I would lose it, did not stop to remove the crampons. I continued clawing upward at a rapid pace. As the slope eased back to the gentle gradient of the regular route, I passed over snow that had lain in shadow since afternoon. Despite the firm footing, the pace began to tell, and I dropped into a much slower walk.

For the next hour I climbed steadily upward as the evening grew colder and darker. At last the toe points of my crampons grated on ice, and I paused with a sigh of relief. Black splotches of rock hemmed me in. I was in the upper trough, at the bottom of a rope fixed in place. This rope wears a groove in the snow on summer Sundays. Pride prohibited me from using the rope, while prudence cautioned me to stay out of the groove, which was made icy by evening frost. The peak blocked half the sky; the visible half was black and blinking with stars.

I reversed my ax and cut nicks for my feet. Step-cutting wore on my patience, but I found I could climb safely using the "Leech Crawl." That was Gary's name for the tripod stance over toe-points and ax-pick. Sun cups facilitated my climb up the forty-five-degree slope. Then I was over the wall and onto a small rib that juts down from the summit at an easy gradient for some 300 feet before plunging to the glacier. My pace had slowed to almost nothing, but the going was easy, and the faint line of summit snow against the sky cheered me on. Soon I was on the ridgeline, walking toward the highest point a short distance away.

Once on the top, I checked the western horizon. Yes, there was a faint line of yellow. I carried no watch but estimated the time as nine o'clock; I had taken three hours for the ascent from Cloud Cap. I pulled on a sweater and sat with my back against the east wall of the abandoned lookout cabin. All was dark and gloomy below; overhead the stars gleamed so brightly I thought I could scoop them up and stuff them in my rucksack. Unlike the sky seen through the haze of the valley, it contained no empty spaces—it was literally powdered with stars.

I lit a couple of "gopher" matches (strike one and go fer another) so I could scan the register book. The matches' flash, reflected on paper, blasted my night vision. When the matches sputtered out, it seemed darker than ever.

I slung my rucksack and grabbed my ax. I peered hard into the gloom at my feet, trying to follow the dark-rock summit ridge westward to the head of the South Chute. Once on the friendly rough snows of the Chute Glacier, my crampons found ample support. The angle of the South Slope was gentler than the North Face

I had come up, and I ambled as if on a sidewalk. I thought again of Gary's pacing ideas: slow start, gradual warm-up, increasing speed, stopless sprint to the summit, and all-out run down. I had reversed the order, and now I paid for it. My legs would hardly move, and often they stopped.

It was warm and balmy. I sat on my ax head and gazed languidly at the close stars and friendly dark rock cliffs. I felt an occasional warm breeze on my cheeks, and wondered why I should go down. Was this not the abode of peace and beauty and silence? Why should I leave it? I only wanted to be part of this peace and sit on my ax head indefinitely. I wasn't really asking too much.

But I lunged to my feet and slogged on down. Suddenly the ax point pinged on ice, alerting me that it was time to shake off my droopy mood and tend to business. A few feet of ice remained where melting snow had frozen, and then my crampons scratched and twisted on hard rock. In spite of the discomfort, I kept the irons on, because of the possibility of hard snow on the hogback below. While crossing a patch of cobbles, I was surprised by a fine shower of sparks, which completed my return to the real world. The real world, I remembered, included work in the morning, sleep to prepare for it, and another 5,000 feet of mountain to descend.

I moved rapidly down another crampon slope, which could have contained a few small crevasses. But no crevasses gobbled me up, and I shucked off the hooks at the lower fumarole rocks. I walked light-footed down the snow of the White River Glacier. At the steep breakover, I was careful to keep on rock, but from there it was all easy going. I trudged slowly down the long, dark expanse of the big snowfield, incapable of speed.

At Lone Fir Rock Lookout Station, just above treeline, I woke Boyd French to ask the time. It was 11:10—five hours and ten minutes for the trip over the mountain. Not bad for an evening stroll. I hurried down into the trees to catch a ride with the laundry man from Timberline Hotel.

At Government Camp, where the pinochle games were just breaking up, my friends lingered over their coffee and a final argument.

"Where have you been?"

"Oh, I got a quick ride to Cloud Cap after work, and walked back over the mountain." I passed it off casually, but I felt inside as if for one evening I had climbed far out into starry space on a wider orbit than my fellow man.

ILLUMINATION ROCK

In almost any photo of Portland, Oregon, the city is shown with its trademark backdrop of Mount Hood. Not only is the volcano pointed, lofty, and white, but its rugged features are glacier-chiseled as well. Portlanders so enjoy their every-clear-day sight of the jagged pinnacles of the mountain that one of the principal pinnacles, one night long ago, was illuminated with fireworks for nighttime viewing. Since then the U.S. Board of Geographic Names, as well as legions of south-side Hood trompers, has referred to this landmark cleaver as Illumination Rock. Of the multitudes stomping up the gentle snow slopes, only an insignificant few have committed the heresy of going "off-trail" to pay decent respect to this particular peak.

A very particular peak, according to Gary Leech. We had once just started across the Reid Glacier when he dramatically gestured with his ice ax, pointing at the winter-glistening bulk of Illumination's East Arête, and announced, "There is my personal deity."

It took awhile for me to pay proper respect. For some time my memory remained polluted with the anxiety felt on my first ascent. In later years more than a score of ascents, over every angle and face of Gary's god, made me an authentic devotee also.

What is this religious talk about piles of pyroclastics? Is there anything sacred about a pile of blocks whose hardness temporarily allows them to ride a ridge of glacier-gouged volcanic ash? Can erosion deify by sculpturing a pinnacle into a fantastic triple-peaked gem, with the highest summit overhanging spookily?

I thought of Illumination Rock as an oversized jungle gym when Gary and I skittered freely over its walls and ridges. Maybe Illumination was an icon for Gary, representing the larger god Hood. Now there is something I *can* believe in. The best proof of Hood's divinity is its power over nonclimbing heathen. Anyone who has ever lived in proximity to the mountain remembers how its mighty presence can be felt even through the clouds of a snowstorm. Mountains are mysteriously potent.

Here is Gary, introducing one of our most memorable climbs:

> The ensuing story was written by my lifelong friend Smoke Blanchard, who was my companion on most of the exploratory Illumination Rock climbs in the mid-1930s. Together we climbed all four of the towering ax blade's walls, found all the known routes and also the many holes and fissures that pierce this glacier-encroached peak, naming them as we found them, and reveling that this gaunt and splintered rock was more truly ours than anyone else's. The climb about to be described by my friend has several notable aspects, inasmuch as the bleak rock had never been climbed so late in the autumn before, much less in total darkness, with a foot of fresh snow covering every ledge and crevice.

OCTOBER 8, 1938 Clouds hid the mountain all day and only began clearing about quitting time. Gary and I stopped nailing shingles on the roof to watch the last storm banners draw back to reveal newly whitened slopes. "Let's take a walk," we both said at once.

We needed no destination. After dinner we threw ice axes and rucksacks in the turtle deck of the coupe and headed for timberline. As we started walking, the moon rose and lit up new snow on the upper half of the mountain. It was about nine o'clock when we plodded above the last trees, so we figured we could make a round trip to the summit and still get a couple of hours sleep before breakfast and carpentering.

Plodding was the problem. Gary set the usual slow warm-up

pace, but when it came time to open up, we still plodded. The ambition of this spur-of-the-moment expedition sagged like a seventy-pound rucksack. The frosty air and crunchy, frozen ground should have added wings to our feet, but our leather soles slipped on the frozen ground, and stones jumped up to trip us. We glanced apprehensively at small black clouds cruising innocently over the summit and silently felt sorry for ourselves. We agreed to turn back in case of storm. I think both of us secretly hoped for a storm.

Somewhere on the Palmer Snowfield, we began to look up and appreciate our surroundings. We told each other how fine Illumination looked in the moonlight with its overhanging summit block crowned with new powder snow. We fell to jabbering about the old climbs on Illumination's edges and faces, and automatically changed our itinerary. Our moods turned bright as the moonlight. We had just chopped sixteen hundred vertical feet from our work and had added some sparkle to our night's outing.

On the edge of the Zigzag Glacier, we stopped to munch cookies and talk about our gear. Leather soles don't grip rock the way rubber does, but the rock looked snowed up. Our rope was only half-length, which meant short leads.

The Zigzag Glacier is ridiculed by mountaineers—they pooh-pooh its gentle lap—but we were pleased to discover a couple of crevasse lips showing in the moonlight. I've never heard of anyone roping on this almost dead glacier, but I suppose one day I'll hear of someone falling in a schrund.

New snow had avalanched off the steepening slope. Edging up in our boots was too much work, so we stopped to put on crampons. We were dumping out our sacks on the ice in search of the unwieldy iron, complaining of the unnecessary weight we had carried, when a howl of woe broke from my companion's lips. Fearing the worst, I whirled around to see if Gary had disappeared in some hidden crevasse. The moonlight disclosed him enmeshed in a tangle of steel and straps, muttering crazily, "Two pair, oh, my God, two pair!" The poor fellow had neglected to remove crampons from his rucksack after a previous trip, and had shoved another pair in for this journey. Unwittingly carrying that extra weight this far had shaken him. To understand my partner's plight, one must realize that he was a fanatic on the subject of rucksack loads and made a fetish of going light. I doubled up and sank to the ice in a fit of mirth. Rude, but as the excess weight I carried had often been the butt of Gary's jibes, I took this opportunity to even the score.

"I say, Gary," I twitted him, "have you an extra ice ax in your sack? I only brought one."

An ominous growling warned me to keep quiet on the long glacier crossing but the sight of the erudite mountaineer ahead of me wearing one pair of crampons on his feet and dangling another pair on his back was too much for me, and many an indecent chuckle escaped from the rear.

Our climb began to take on interest when we set our course to avoid a group of crevasses that we knew lay between us and the Illumination saddle. The musical tinkle of ice chips loosened by our crampons, the secure crunch when points bit into the snow, the frosty air in our lungs, the silent watchfulness of the icy crags about us—all revived memories of previous winter adventures. We met a few crevasses near the saddle, but they were easily outmaneuvered, so that in a short time we reached the base of the rock.

We stared in shock at Illumination's sheer prow. It looked so unfriendly now: black and menacing in shadow, cold and aloof in moonlight. We had never seen so much snow plastering everything, and we had never thought of going rockclimbing at night.

The roping-up place is, by definition, the place where the ropes are laid out. It is also where the equipment rack is sorted, bellies stoked, plans firmed. During the ten-minute pause slack must be cinched out of the nerves to ready them for the job ahead. It was time for our standard mountain ration: King Oscar Royal Norwegian Kipper Snacks. At two cans for a nickel they made affordable fare for climbing carpenters. But haste makes waste. Greed can overcome a climber's caution and trick him into flubbing the critical first twist of the kipper-can key. A wrong move can result in a frustrating pinhole and necessitate mayhem on the can by the all-purpose ice ax. Gary and I passed the test. We omitted all but the main course, and dinner was soon over.

We tied on with bowlines, juggled our headlights into position, and moved off toward the rock. Instead of the rolling, sliding ash usually found on the preliminary ridge, we encountered a frozen substance that was as easy as concrete to edge boots into. We moved gingerly for the first rope length, experimenting with the solidity of rock nubbins jutting from the frozen surface. Fortunately, they seemed to be well frozen and enabled a safe if slow ascent. As I was making the traverse above a small crevasse, Gary's quaint warning echoed my own thoughts: "That's a good place not to fall off."

When we reached the crest of the ash ridge, Gary cried out, "Look at Illumination's shadow on the glacier!"

There it was: the black silhouette on the glistening new snow in the Reid Glacier gorge included the outline of every spire and pinnacle.

The hard, frozen ash crest was much easier to negotiate than it is in summer, when it's soft and crumbly. We attained the beginning of the rising andesite arête more rapidly than on former climbs. Gary led the first pitch. The short rope did not allow him to reach the usual stance, so I had to move up against the wall to a less-secure belay. In summer we would have climbed this pitch by a chimney, which was now all iced. Gary went over the initial block by an outside wall; so did I, on my turn, but I found it difficult. The holds were icy, and the view between my legs extended all the way down to the Reid Glacier. I didn't like it, but I wasn't required to enjoy it. My job was to sweep away the powder snow Gary hadn't brushed off and grunt, pull, and lever my way up. When I reached Gary, I moaned that even snow-free rock bothered me, that my leather soles were almost frictionless. Of course, his leather soles were no better. Then I cried that my stomach was nauseated from the greasy fish. The fish weren't greasy. Reflecting on my situation—teetering dangerously over snowy rocks, strung high in the air between two glaciers, in the middle of the night long past bed-time—had precipitated a psychosomatic attack.

The crest of the andesite arête is composed of huge tottering blocks with unhealthy deep cracks between them. We had entered the moon's shadow, and our lights disclosed only a smooth blanket of foot-deep powder snow concealing rock and precipice alike. Obviously this section called for much probing with the ax. The lower ridge abuts the vertical faces of the main ridge at the base of Overhanging Tower, where I gave Gary enough line to explore the route up to the Keyhole. In testing a stone, he accidentally loos-ened a large boulder that rolled over the edge, whistled through space, and crashed on the Reid Glacier. We treated the incident ca-sually, but it was not without its effect on us.

Floundering through the floury powder, Gary at length reached the head of a slab-lined chute. The prospects were dismal. Snow lay deep not only in the bed of the chute but also upon its far wall. Gary made several attempts to find a crossing, while I cheered him on with discouraging grumbles about the snow and my ailing stomach.

Suddenly he shouted, "Watch my belay, I'm going across!" Slowly at first and then more rapidly, the line jerked out. The fee-ble rays of my headlight did not pierce the gloom as far as Gary; the movement of the rope and ring of his ax point on ice were my only clues to his progress. At length he shouted that he had reached the Keyhole.

"Okay, I'm coming," I yelled.

"No, stay where you are until I crawl into the Keyhole."

Glaciers attack the soft ash on which Illumination is perched and have reduced the big pile to a holey state. The previous sum-mer we had taken advantage of this porosity and made a route through holes, tunnels, and a four-sided chimney. The knowledge of these snow-shed passageways gave us courage to attempt this night climb in wintry conditions. In July the Keyhole had been an impassable slot through the rib of a vertical tower. The key had been in the Keyhole, barring the slimmest of lock picks. Using a long, thin, fifty-pound boulder as a battering ram, Gary and I had broken the key out of the lock. The Keyhole would then admit one wriggling man, who passed right through the rib.

I beat my hands warm and looked at the iced crags of Yokum Ridge, wondering why Gary had called for me to wait. I was glad when he finally called and I could be off. I climbed with bare fingers for better grip. Gary had chopped ample footsteps through the snow into firm ice. The far wall proved to be steep and holdless, but a ticklish maneuver with my hands balanced against the smooth wall of the tower soon placed me upon the small platform at the Keyhole entrance. I saw immediately why Gary had moved past this summer belay stance. Snow and ice had plastered the precariously perched rocks, demanding that the belayer work from the uncomfortable but safe Keyhole.

Gary immediately moved on through the fissure, bidding me follow, so I inserted my shoulders into the Keyhole, wrestled with parka, ax, and rope coil, and squeezed through the narrow aperture. I was startled by the noise of sliding snow and, glancing behind, caught sight of my entrance platform disappearing in a whirl of snow, well on its way to the glacier.

We were now in the dark passageway aptly called the Fatman's Fissure and for the first time were able to relax. Watching our flashlights play on the smooth walls of the fissure, we marveled at our audacity—high above the sleeping world, crawling through the bowels of a rock peak, hidden from the moon itself! We speedily pushed out of the fissure's narrow exit onto the moonlit South Face of the mountain, high above the Zigzag Glacier. A tiny shelf we had named the Zigzag Balcony was crossed in only a few cautious steps. Turning into the Elevator Shaft, we plunged back into the vitals of the weird peak.

The Elevator Shaft ranks among the strangest of the architectural oddities of Illumination Rock. The chimney starts halfway up the tapering ax blade of Illumination and emerges on the North Face, just a long reach below the blade's cutting edge. It is a four-sided, vertical shaft, suitable, were it less angular and scratchy, for an elevator car.

No car existed, so Gary bridged across the walls with his back and knees. The first thirty feet went easily, but above, the chimney narrowed, and Gary's boot soles swung in my headlight's rays. Cursing and grunting accompanied the clang of falling stones; his sweater and bulky parka prevented his exiting from the narrow portal. I was treated to an impromptu but eloquent discourse on the blankety-blank size of the opening. Gary soon ran out of breath, made himself as small as possible, and forced himself out onto the North Face.

Then it was my turn to scramble, puff, and curse. I've heard that Santa Claus rises up chimneys by laying his finger alongside his nose, but it has never worked for me. Twice I jammed my body across the chimney and searched desperately with my headlight for holds that I knew existed somewhere, eventually finding them in front of my face. Clambering out, I stood with Gary on a snowy ledge and admired the icy spires of Yokum Ridge across a thousand feet of nothingness.

A short chimney brought us to the crest of the East Arête. First was a short but nervous traverse with great exposure and loose footing, but our lights only illuminated our immediate vicinity and left the precipice an ill-defined, hazy mystery that did not concern us. Beyond this delicate traverse the ridge steepened for a few exposed feet.

Above, the route attained the crest, then swung back onto the southern side of the arête. Here I met a great boss of snow with steps fashioned in it, leading around an edge. Rarely had I seen Gary cut an unnecessary step, and these were no exception. I would have chopped the snow completely away.

Turning the last bulging gendarme, I looked over Gary's shoulder at the awe-inspiring knife edge. On a peak like Illumination the climber finds much eerie architecture but still must gasp in amazement at this rapier thrust of arête toward the fantastically overhanging summit block. No warm, rich brown coloring of day showed cracks and rugosities; in the moonlight a smooth black was etched with silvery ice. The very edge of this ridge is so sharp it could draw blood.

Gary's advance was a slow and methodical crawl. Still, it seemed to me he almost jumped to the work; on this tight line in the sky, any move seemed rash. Gary patiently straddled the edge and carefully inched toward the far end, while I niggardly paid out rope. Scuffing ice off with his boots, rising to his knees, and then to his feet, he embraced the overhanging summit block. Very, very slowly he dragged himself up. With hands cupped over the crest and his clothing providing additional friction, he crawled to the ultimate summit. He quickly made ready the rope and I began my creep at the other end of the sword. I'd been here many times in sunny summer, but this was different. I took the time to make each move perfect. At last I crouched with Gary on the tiny point of the summit block. We had climbed Illumination by moonlight!

Our first act upon reuniting was not a solemn handclasp or a lusty cheer but a hungry stare toward the pinpoints of light in the village 5,500 feet below which signaled our next meal. We had to make our summit sojourn brief and descend quickly before we were forced to chew on our boots. Resting for a moment, we talked of other trips when we had ascended this weird ax blade from all directions, even scaling the terrible North Face, which was now underneath our dangling feet. We agreed that this must be the greatest of all trips: to sit upon the ultimate spire of a glacier-bound rock peak in the still moonglow of an October night.

Finding the summit register (perhaps the last I ever signed) in bad condition, we left a few papers in the tube and took the main book down for repairs.

Back along the crest of the East Arête we hurried as fast as we could. I rapidly lowered Gary into the tomblike interior of the Elevator Shaft; he made the squeeze more easily this time. On my squirm I got a taste of Gary's difficulty on the ascent; I had stupidly crammed the register book into a pocket and forgotten about it until it jammed in the narrow part. By tugging, groaning, cursing, and straining, I eventually worked free and slithered down to Gary. My leather soles helped by lubricating my downward skid. Back through the Fatman's Fissure and out of the Keyhole onto the dark, snowy North Face we rushed. I was relieved when I had eased my toes down to the bottom of the snowy pitch that had troubled me on the way up.

We quickly coiled the rope in the saddle and struck off across the glacier, or rather Gary did, for I lingered for one last view. Light from the westering moon just tipped the overhang of the Giant Tower, above which we had traversed. Reaching in my rucksack for my oldest and mellowest pipe, I filled it with tobacco and puffed an offering of smoke to the gods of the rock and ice and moon. The flame of the "gopher" match burned without a flicker—such a wonderful night!

I saw that Gary was becoming a smaller and smaller speck on the glacier. Still smoking my pipe, I zigzagged around some crevasses, whose snowy lips sparkled in the light, then bounded with long strides down the open glacier. On the middle slopes of the mountain we found excellent glissading and made much sport of it.

Not a word was spoken on the drive down from the hotel. Not until we stood blinking in the tavern lights did we find energy to speak, and then only to mutter something about eating. The first pale light of dawn showed in the east as we sought our beds.

Later in the day two night-prowling carpenters finished shingling the roof.

2

Innocents in the
Incomparable Valley

DURING our two days in Yosemite Valley in the summer of 1937, Hubert North and I concentrated on loafing. Gary Leech's enthusiasm for trail walking only tired us. Not till the second day in "Los Angeles in the Mountains" did we crane our necks to observe the perpendicular scenery of the canyon walls.

We found it hard to get used to so many people. We had seen only one set of tracks and no people during almost the entire month of June, which we spent in the backcountry. (Later we learned Norman Clyde had made those tracks.) We hesitated to drag our weary bones from the campground sanctuary, lest we be trampled by the multitude. We kept to our six-by-eight-foot plot of ground, only emerging at intervals, like a couple of toads from under a flat rock.

When we felt brave enough to leave our assigned corner, we scuttled to Camp Curry, where we cowered behind trees, hiding our wilderness beards, to watch the swarms of well-dressed people. By well-dressed I mean, of course, girls in shorts; thousands of them it seemed: all, to our snow-blinded eyes, beautiful.

Hubert struck up an acquaintance with a neighboring camper who shared our demophobia. He wanted to go fishing in Oregon, but his wife voted for Yosemite, so they "compromised" and came to Yosemite. He had other family problems, too. He complained to Hubert: "I've got my mother-in-law along; it's a son of a bitch."

In the morning, when we took our jug and stood in line for water, he would shout as we passed his camp, "Hey, you mountain climbers, where are you going with that jug?" He kidded us about professing to be climbers but seldom leaving camp.

I found a photographic studio and pounced on any postcard that suggested the High Sierra, no matter how homely. Hungry for scenes of solitude, I devoured all the dusty postcards of Clark, Vogelsang, and the upper Merced peaks that the clerk could dig up. Photographs by the master, Ansel Adams, shone forth among the drab contemporary examples as if illuminated.

On the way back to camp, I followed the busy roads to the Old Village, metropolis of the Valley. Here I got lost in a clamoring mob of shoppers rushing in and out of the ten-cent store, the confectionery, the pool hall, and the department store. I got so caught up in the swirl of colors and beehive of noises that I emerged in a drizzle having forgotten that this throng was in a national park. Yosemite Valley, California's mountain wonderland! I turned up my coat collar and shuffled through the trees to catch a glimpse of the granite walls. Yes, there they were, serenely unaware of the babble of mountain worshippers below.

In the afternoon, I drove Gary to the start of the Nevada Falls Trail and then, bragging to Hubert how I was going to walk to the top of Yosemite Falls, drove across the Valley. The sun bore down on the still, canyon-imprisoned air; the heat seemed stifling to one recently come from the cold high country of the upper Sierra.

"I'll work up a good sweat this afternoon," I thought. As I crawled out of the car at the end of the road, the thought occurred to me again. "Yes, I *will* work up a sweat; maybe the top of the first falls would be high enough."

At the bottom of the falls, I paused to admire the frothing pillar of water. "Ah, a truly noble sight—damn you little brats, why don't you watch where you're going with that velocipede?"

Uh, oh! Around the bend appeared mother: beefy, irate, and attired with a heavy walking stick. Where was my ice ax? The brave mountain climber departed into the brush. Here was no view of the falls, but neither was there an outraged mother to contend with.

"Oops, excuse me." More people! I fled to the sanctity of the car where, in a moment of daring, I hopped out and photographed the falls from the middle of the road. Somehow all the cars missed me.

Before returning to camp, I drove down the walled Valley to the base of El Capitan. A side road through the woods took me to a little sun-filled clearing close to the 3,000-foot face. There were no people, and I gazed open-mouthed at the stupendous precipice. The Cathedral Spires, 2,600 feet above the meanders of the Merced, were my next camera target. I gave a silent cheer for the gallant piton artists (Jules Eichorn and company) who had ascended these twin obelisks. Then, unkinking my neck, I climbed back in the car and returned happily to camp.

In the evening Gary came into camp dragging a young fellow he'd met on the trail who claimed to have climbed Mount Clark. When he hinted of brandy in his camp, we followed him. How the good stuff snuggled in our rusted stomachs.

"Take another quick one," said our new friend, whom we called Jack.

Just then his mother bellowed from the other tent, "Don't you be giving away that liquor to every Tom, Dick, and Harry. You know the old man wants a snort in the morning!"

Tiptoeing to the safety of nearby trees, we patted our pal on the back and listened to his description of the Camp Curry dance. Our brandied spirits cheered a chance to socialize. Lights and music, that's what we wanted. We agreed to meet Jack and marched off to find the Ford and descend on the shindig.

Jack had found a girl, so we stood in the door watching the crowd, wondering if that was what we wanted after all. The longer we watched the revelers, the more out of place we felt.

The image of a cold, aloof mass, high against the blue sky, kept appearing in our mind's eye. Shasta! Now we were watching the clock, its minute hand creeping toward the hour we'd scheduled for departure. At ten o'clock, we joyfully mounted our chariot to fly away to the Cascades.

3

Gary Denzel Leech

"GARY LEECH, Gov't Camp, Outlaw."

This entry in Mount Hood's summit book repeated itself with monotonous regularity on every page. As I returned again and again to sign the summit register, I looked forward to meeting the owner of that famous signature.

We first met at the small village of Government Camp, although Gary said he saw me earlier through the big telescope at Hill's Place. Some tourists trained the scope on Hood's summit, and, seeing a black speck on the gleaming snow of the Chute Glacier, asked Gary if there was a climber on the mountain. Gary took a quick look through the instrument and declared, "Naw, that's a rock. It's moving too slow to be a man!"

A couple of days later, the rock, which had been wallowing waist deep in soft new snow, walked down the main and only street of Government Camp and saw a tall, sandy-haired, hatchet-faced, deeply tanned fellow working on Hill's new waterpower plant.

"Are you the Government Camp Outlaw?"

He admitted it, although I had neglected to include commas in the address. The commas were vital. Summit register custom was to list name, address, and climbing club affiliation. "Outlaw" was the Mazama Club's designation for any climber who did not belong to one of the recognized mountain clubs. It also came to be a term of opprobrium for anyone, member or not, who joined unauthorized parties, strayed off route, or committed the ultimate sin of climbing alone. I'd found a kindred spirit and a title.

It was the start of an auspicious friendship. Gary became my hero and tutor. He taught me to cross those black-ice, rock-polished debris chutes we called "rifle ranges" on a slightly downhill course at a dead run. He advised me to discard my Swiss edge-nailed logging boots in favor of three-dollar work shoes, whose rock-gripping rubber soles could be improved for glissading by filing the forward edge of the heels. He made me keep my neck achingly upward with ears cocked for the first tinkle of falling rime ice and muscles tensed for an instant side-spring when eyes spotted the down-whirling knobs. He drilled me on the use of the ice ax for self-arrest, cutting steps, and probing for hidden crevasses. He demonstrated how to stand upright, in balance, over toeholds and showed me stemming and jamming tricks for rockclimbing. When I floundered in a snowdrift I thought steep, he lashed me with a criticism whose sting is with me yet: "Don't act like that was hard for you, Blanchard!"

"Grab, grab, grab," he counseled me; "don't ever give up, reach low and grab hard; if you slip off you can still save yourself." Yet this lifesaving reaction that he'd mentally trained for killed him, as I shall tell.

When Gary lived in Colorado, we could climb together only occasionally. I had been living in Bishop, California, at the foot of the Sierra's eastern slope, since shortly after our 1937 expedition demonstrated the town's advantages as a strategic mountain base. On returning to my home in Bishop from our latest climb, Gary was reluctant to leave. He stood up to go, and we shook hands. As a final thought I said, "Just a sec, Gary, I want to recite a poem. Oh, don't be alarmed, it's not one of mine. This is from a real poem. I forget the author, but it goes like this:

You to the east and I to the west,
For the ways of men must sever,
And it may well be for a day or a night,
And it may well be forever.

Gary walked back into the kitchen, poured himself a cup of tea, and said, "Sit down. That's something I want to talk to you about. We're going to climb together the rest of our lives. We've got this British Columbia trip next summer. We've got a lot to do. I'm going to retire here in Bishop, and I want to sit out on your front porch and review all the peaks we've climbed."

He waggled his long finger in front of my face. "We've got to be careful. I mean it. We've got to be careful in everything we do: walking across the street, working, and driving. Did you notice how I drive now? Defensive driving, our company calls it; we've got to practice defensive driving all the time. What a shame it would be for one of us to get killed in some silly accident. We've got a lot to do, boy; let's be careful."

He walked out the door, got in his car, and drove away.

As fall deepened into winter, Gary's letters began to breathe the urgency of the coming climbing season. He told me of making schedules and buying equipment and raved about what we would do, come summer. I studied maps and went around with my body in Bishop and my mind high on a glacier, wrestling crevasses with Gary.

On the afternoon of January 20, 1954, I walked down to the post office to mail a letter to Gary. On the way back, as I turned up the little dirt road to our house, I thought to myself, "Gary will never know the old place now, since the grader has been through."

When I came in the door, the phone was ringing. My wife, Vi, called, "It's Vernal, Utah, but it doesn't sound like Gary." A cold feeling went through me as I reached for the instrument.

A voice announced, "This is Frank Gruver, Stanolind Oil and Gas Company, Vernal. Gary Leech had an accident. He was seriously hurt."

"How serious?" My mind leaped ahead: Gary fallen from an oil derrick, back broken, needs help, check oil in car before leaving for Utah.

"He was killed. He was electrocuted on a power pole."

A day later I stood under that power pole in the Ashley Creek Oil Field near Vernal. With me was a little group of people—friends of Gary's, fellow workers, his Colorado climbing partner, executives of his oil company. A dark, gray overcast covered the sky and partially obscured the cliffs of Gary's Merkely Rock in the distance. We stood and stared at the pole, while each man contributed his part of the story and his opinion of Gary's final climb.

Gary, on duty as production maintenance man for the small field, had heard that a floodlight over an oil pump had burned out. Trucks used this pump at night to load crude oil. The company said Gary should have called an electrician. It was not like Gary to call an electrician to change a light bulb. He walked a half-mile to where two laborers were working and asked to borrow their ladder. They had only a fifteen-foot one. They said he could get a long ladder in the morning, but, no, Gary wanted to fix that light now so the drivers could load. He carried the fifteen-foot ladder back, leaned it against the pole, climbed up, and wired it on according to approved safety practice. There was still another fifteen feet of pole to climb, sans ladder, spikes, or anything. Gary shinnied up and balanced himself at the floodlight by bracing his muddy boots between a guy wire and a bolt head. He must have slipped and grabbed—just as he used to tell me, just as he had told himself over the years on high cliffs—grabbed a wire. It carried 7,200 volts.

After the knife of grief dulled, I caught myself opening old wounds by quarreling with fate. I had lost a climbing partner of two decades; the world had lost a talented sculptor and painter. A quarter of a century later, I sometimes think of the cruelty: Gary, whose love of mountains exceeded even my own, denied Himalayan fulfillment.

I always meant to do something with his writings. To prepare this chapter, I dug into a footlocker of Gary's writings, sent to me twenty years ago, when his last relatives died. The writings seem strange to me now. I read the long chapter analyzing the formation of Hood's buried forests and his theory of Hood's pulsating inner fires, which so affect its southern glaciers. I skipped his monograph on "The Geologic History of Umnak Island." The book-length story of his army career, full of humorous anecdotes about his horseplay and escapades, seemed irrelevant. The climbing journals of Rocky and Sierra trips were painstakingly detailed. Did we really climb all those pitches? Stories of our jokes and games on forgotten Montana peaks read like the ancient history of an alien people. I'd forgotten earning a steak dinner for participating in a rescue on Rising Wolf Mountain.

Finally, the climbs of Hood, although described in the same verbose, archaic style, found an audience. I read all afternoon, and, as clouds dropped like a blanket over Bishop and snowflakes whirled in a Sierran winter version of an Oregon storm, Gary's stories unstoppered a long-sealed jug. The djinn towering out of the memory bottle was a tall mountain, the "chill sentinel" Gary spoke of with such reverence. Soul-flooding recollections washed over me; the room seemed to grow cold, its walls faded away, and I was out on a vast slope feeling the sting of sleet, the power and push of a storm. I relived the deep snows, the probing of cornice and crevasse, the forcing of skis through thigh-deep powder, the crunch of crampon steps.

Here are a couple of typical Gary paragraphs:

I thrust my horizontal ax deeply in the brittle ice-feathers of the far depths of the cavity, flung my weight on the handle, kicked my toes into the smaller steps, and raised my body into a kneeling position on top of the handle of the ax. This accomplished, it was not difficult to shift my weight from the handle to the bed of the cavity, then release my ax and thrust it again into the ice just over the top of the spire. Of course, with the overhanging brittle ice, and with the threat of tumbling a hundred feet or so, it was not too ridiculously simple, but the blessed old ice ax held, and in a moment or two I clambered to safety on the very limited and fragile top of the pinnacle.

We both knew that many men had died in the three miles between us and timberline, yet in our little fortresses of ice-encased clothing we both felt a quiet confidence. It was a good feeling. Nothing short of extremely bad fortune could bring us harm now that we had descended the howling inferno of snow of the Crater Glacier and won our way about the avalanche-threatened sides of Crater Rock. Certainly our compasses could see in the dark quite as well as in the day, provided that we had the courage to believe them.

When Joe Daniel and I planned our Newton Clark Glacier–Cooper Spur climb, we did not include Gary because he had to work the night of our timberline bivouac. He decided to join us anyway, left Government Camp on completion of his shift at 3:23 A.M., and walked up 4,000 vertical feet—to within hailing distance of Joe and me as we sat at a second breakfast on the far side of the White River Glacier. His journal reads: "I told them to proceed and not wait for me." Over forty-five years later, the details of the great climb we three made that day are dim, but I can still recite the cross-glacier dialogue.

Smoke: "Hey, Gary, come join us. We'll wait for you."

Gary: "Good. I'm coming. Don't wait. Get up and go as fast as you can!"

Gary could shout so confidently across the great gulf of the White River Glacier because he had mastered pace. He used to drum it into me so regularly it got to be like the ticking of my heart. "Your heart is an engine. You must treat it well. Warm it slowly. Gradually increase the speed. Never, never stop. Speed up on easy ground, slack back on the steeps, keep your heartbeat the same, run the downhills. A mountaineer always runs all the way back down." I never did follow the last sentence. I always suspected it had to do with the necessity of Gary's getting back to his job at Government Camp. Although I was often a failing pupil, enough of this training stuck with me to get me and my party up the 7,000 vertical feet of the Shozuone route to Mount Shirouma in the Kita Alps in good shape one recent summer.

Gary didn't leave an autobiography. His journals, stuffed full of notes on glaciology, are not even complete for his climbs. He was born in Los Angeles and became interested in "those so very untouchable distant blue ranges of the Sierra" when his father worked in the San Joaquin Valley oil fields. Gary worked on the construction of Boulder Dam and worked a year or more on a ranch near Dupuyer, Montana. Perhaps it was en route to or from Montana that he first climbed Hood, over the Cooper Spur, in 1927.

Here is how Gary describes coming to live at the little village on the south side of Mount Hood:

"The magic name of Government Camp, the resort village at Mount Hood's southern base, came to my attention when I first arrived in Oregon and started work cutting pulpwood near Cherryville. To my intense disappointment, the deep hemlock forest prevented a view of the mountain, and I fretted much until I discovered I could clamber up a staircase of boughs on a tall Douglas fir that overtopped its fellows. Here I could pay homage to the noble mountain, for the frozen monarch soared a full ten thousand feet above. In this shaky grandstand, I spent many hours in aesthetic reverence, for my eyes never tired of studying the details of the long snowy slopes or the play of light on the upper crags. My economic condition might not allow me to track those mysterious heights, but miles were no bar to my fancy. Government Camp became synonymous with Mount Hood, and my heart ached to reach the village, roam its streets, and become friends with the frozen pile of earth at its back.

"In February, 1933, I walked the twenty-six miles up to the town, quite without fatigue, and would have walked back that winter night had not a kindly motorist offered me a ride. Fully a thousand vehicles passed me on the climb above Rhododendron, but I had not minded this at all, for I loved to walk. During my visit, I reveled in the town's atmosphere, reveled in the fifteen- or twenty-foot snows lining its streets and covering its cabins. I dreamed that one day I would live in this quaint community and know all the skiers and climbers.

"My hard and oftentimes hungry life in this lumber camp dragged on until June 11, 1933, but on that memorable date I placed my entire savings, seven or eight dollars, in food and camera film, and started walking across the Cascade Range. I would go mountain climbing and worry about eating afterwards, even though the Depression stood at its worst, and I was friendless in a strange state.

"Four days later, with five small summits and some eighty-one miles of continuous snow behind me (it was the heaviest winter on record), I found myself on a paved highway leading up the broad glaciated canyon of the Salmon River, with the massive white slopes of Hood directly in front of me. My course had been circuitous, to pick up the small peaks, but now I aimed directly for my goal. My plan was to sleep in Government Camp, a half-dozen miles, more or less; I could have walked it on stumps. And the next day I would climb the mountain!

"Fate had other ideas. I did not get to climb the mountain then. Instead, I got a job! Out of the clear sky, a man offered me the incredible sum of $2.50 a day for working on a rock crusher. My acceptance was immediate, for then I could live in Government Camp and climb the mountain whenever I wished. A wonderful life opened to me. Workers at the crusher boarded at the Battle Axe Inn, owned and operated by Mr. and Mrs. Henry Villiger, so I sought and obtained permission to board there also. This was living. It was spring, and I dwelled in a mountain world, able to touch the untouchable. I had found the pot of gold at the end of the rainbow.

"Naturally my greatest desire was to scale Hood as soon as possible, but my work at the crusher and other details kept me busy for a day or two. On June 18th, my chance came. After early breakfast at Battle Axe Inn, I casually remarked to the assemblage there that I would return in time for midday lunch."

Thus began a career on the mountain that doubtless will never be matched. When the crusher shut down, Gary got a job on the night shift at Hill's Place and climbed days. He would let a week or three go by and then climb every day. He did long strings of climbs faster than existing speed records. Many of them he made by new or different routes, often almost completely circling the mountain. Sometimes he scaled previously unascended pinnacles along the way. All of these trips began from the low base of Government Camp, which added 2,000 vertical feet to the climb and eight extra miles beyond that traveled by the timberline-based climber. The extra effort needed to overcome this added distance and vertical gain are difficult to appreciate in these days of automobile approach to timberline.

Let me lift from Gary's journal a few pieces that describe a climb during the early days of his Hood career:

"My thirty-first climb on Mount Hood was one of the most difficult, speaking of both hazard and labor. No less than nine hours of intensive labor were required to place me on the frigid summit, at a time when my average from Government Camp to the top was less than half that, four hours and nineteen minutes to be exact. Not only that, but once on the summit I was assailed by the wildest storm I had yet seen on a mountain.

"I had left Government Camp at 7:25 A.M., rather early for me. No sooner had I started than I regretted ever having made plans for climbing on this day, for the weather was none too favorable. For some time I wavered on the decision to give the trip up for a bad job, but hated to spoil my year's perfect record of no rebuffs. (If I had quit here, as it later developed, I would have spoiled a better record of climbing Hood 116 times without turning around for any reason.)

"I made myself go about the task. I attacked the step-cutting in a furious manner, hacking at the blue ice. I was not very cold, not with the alpenstock whirling like an idling propeller. My time to the lookout was over nine hours, with about four hours being used to negotiate the Chute, which I had several times previously climbed in fifteen minutes. It was then about five o'clock.

"I set off back across the rim top, truly the battleground of the elements. Along its narrow portion, the relentless wind upset me several times, causing me to flounder helplessly until the slides were arrested with the alpenstock or feet. The act of descending my several hundred gouged steps, which I had purposely made far apart to conserve energy, was an art in itself. Mistakes counted in this game. Once out of my steps, my slippery shoes would have been helpless to stop a slide. Such a slide down over a thousand feet of rough ice would certainly have been the initiation fee to the devil's none-too-exclusive club. The wind attained its greatest velocity, mighty gusts met me head on, and a fine sleet peppered me without mercy. So fierce was this wind that I could not bear to hold my face directly against it. (I decided right then and there to own a parka.)

"At timberline darkness set in, necessitating a slow, stumbling four miles down to Government Camp. Finally, 11½ hours after leaving, I wearily dragged in. My unusually long absence had caused some worry among my friends and well-wishers. After a belated supper, I sank into bed with a great deal of satisfaction. Of course, at 11 P.M. I had to roll out again in order to be ready for work at midnight at the crusher."

It's bad enough to think of Gary attacking Hood without an ice ax, but it boggles the mind to catch him parkaless. Gary's notes record how his thirty-second climb saw him better equipped. When I started climbing with him, he had an ice ax, rucksack, parka, and crampons, but he never had much and never seemed to care.

I don't know what arrangement he had with Charley Hill. When I substituted for Gary in the ski shop, Charley paid me room, board, and a dollar a day. Whatever wage Gary drew, he was conscientious about being on the job on time, and at the end of our climbs would excuse himself at Crater Rock or Illumination Saddle and run all the way down to make shift. Gary often said he never had a real job until he went to work for Stanolind Oil. Even then he didn't use his steady wages to buy equipment.

Gary's record-keeping bordered on the pathological. Among his notes I found names of 467 mountain climbs, with a page titled "Failures after Direct Assaults." On this page was a list of fourteen climbs and the dates on which he made up seven of the "failures." From June 18, 1933, to October 10, 1934, he climbed Hood sixty-seven times, mostly directly from Government Camp. On July 29, 1934, he left Government Camp, crossed the summit, descended to Cloud Cap Inn, reascended to the summit, then dropped back to Government Camp. He ascended 12,900 feet, descended 12,900 feet, and covered twenty-three miles in eleven hours and sixteen minutes.

Anyone writing a history of Mount Hood will probably come across Gary's climbing record in a newspaper clipping of July 13, 1936. I found among Gary's journals this penciled note to Paul Calicotte, well-known if controversial 1930s climber:

Paul, I still have a few tricks up my sleeve. I have never done near my best on this mountain. This next time I won't carry any ice ax, which is heavy, nor wear boots; even my socks will be trimmed down. No packsack, cap, glasses, shirt, or anything. Also, you or Hubert will be on the summit to hand me the book and pencil, a bit of refreshment, and *my* ice ax. When I get down the west side of Crater Rock, I'll drop it, and one of you follow me down and be sure and pick it up. You fellows on top can also take the time of my arrival, because I won't be carrying any watch. I'm going to start across the road and finish there too.

His concerns were to minimize weight, have his ice ax for safety in descending the Crater Glacier, have an official timer (Charley Hill) at Government Camp, have witnesses and helpers on top, and have a true start across the road to guarantee against crowding the starting line. His time:

> Government Camp to summit of Mount Hood—2 hours, 36 minutes
> Resting on top—3 minutes
> Summit of Mount Hood to Government Camp—49.5 minutes
> Round trip—3 hours, 28.5 minutes

This record is so astounding that I could hardly believe it then, and it seems especially superhuman now.

Gary was my hero and mentor. Our friendship included sharing one spoon to stir our sardine and strawberry-jam mix in our one Beebe Company cup (now called a Sierra Club cup), and dating sisters in the valley, but there were conspicuous gaps in the meshing of our personalities. For example, I looked askance at Gary's interest in barroom brawling. The same competitive drive that compelled my friend to practice express-train speeds on the mountain taught him to look at every big bruiser full of beer and truculence as a personal challenge. Of the three hostels in Government Camp, Hill's Place, normally little more than a sandwich shop for tourists bound for central Oregon, became the town saloon at times. Crowds of restless holiday-makers, looking for something less homelike than the quiet atmosphere of the Battle Axe Inn or Rafferty's, swarmed into Charley Hill's brightly lit oasis on winter Saturday nights. Workers from the state highway maintenance station used Hill's Place to replace Portland's cultural entertainment. As Gary's manifold duties also included being bartender-bouncer, bare-knuckle fights came to be almost a hobby for him.

For one of my retiring nature, it was impossible to understand any of this. He reminds me of Norman Clyde, whose dark side was guns. They both used to bore me with explanations of how they were protected from attack by their reputations with guns or fists.

A game like Gary's had its wins and losses. In one full fray in the middle of Government Camp's Main Street, the sure-footed mountaineer slipped on the ice, and his opponent jumped on his leg and broke it. I replaced Gary running the ski shop for a couple of months.

Gary would probably protest my listing fighting as his hobby. Unlike Norman, he was gregarious and friendly, though, like Norman, he shouldered a dangerous chip. Mountaineering was Gary's full-time religion. He worked hard, long hours to provide access to his temple. His nonclimbing, nonworking time he filled with writing mountain journals, composing poetry and fiction, drawing with pen and ink, painting with oil, sketching, photography, and sculpture. He also liked to run marathons and work out with weights. Weightlifting he did with stones substituting for barbells. During the spring after his leg injury, his body-building degenerated into a daily performance with boulders across the street from the leg-breaker's house. It intimidated his adversary, Gary liked to think. His former opponent asked to be transferred to another station.

If engines of love and power drive mankind, surely the bearings would burn to a frazzle without the oil of laughter. Gary spent much of his prodigious energy on jokes, practical and impractical. While he began to gripe about the monotony of the four-mile trail approach to timberline, he once walked far above timberline carrying a good-sized fir tree to plant at a record height.

It's interesting to speculate about whether Gary would have slowed down or become more conservative with age. As far as I know, he left bar-brawling in Oregon. In some ways he was settling down even before I did. Motoring toward Montana one summer morning, I noticed Gary begin to fidget. We hadn't overlooked any historical monuments that needed checking, hadn't passed any cliffs that needed climbing, and it couldn't have been impatience at our speed, for the Buick fairly flew. "Damn it, Smoke," Gary exploded, "I've got a good steady job now, good regular habits. I don't care if you miss breakfast on that day-and-night sleeper truck of yours, but I eat at six, twelve, and six, and don't you forget it!"

Gary suffered from extreme moodiness. His 1952 solo Sierra trip was almost destroyed by depression after he found a recently crashed airplane with charred bodies still in it. He had told me of the wreck after the trip, but not in such harrowing detail as his diary does.

I only recently completed wading through Gary's 155 typewritten pages crammed with musings about glacial geology, exact dialogues of inconsequential conversations with campers he met, hold-by-hold encyclopedias of rock pitches, and even prose charts of the inside of his head. Judging by the parenthetical explanations, the pages were not written for himself only, but they still were embarrassing. He traces, without trying to save face, an almost total demoralization after viewing the results of the airplane tragedy—a collapse reflected in an unreasonable fear of the loneliness of the dark nights. He wrote:

> Many years before, I had a similar experience. In 1934 I was asked by the Forest Service to aid in the recovery of a man's body from the crater of Mount Hood. Without any trace of fear, I could descend into those vapor-filled depths, where five or six men had tried and failed, and get the body. A full week later, when asked to climb the mountain on a foggy-night search, my approach to that hole of death was marked by a very real fear. My relief was great when the climbers were found, and I could retreat from the dark. This evidence of primordial fear in my makeup left me thoughtful and humble, for I then knew that my courage had at least one gap in it. In the intervening years I had come to believe the cardboard in my armor had changed to leather. Now I was not so sure.

He never mentioned this fear to me. Certainly he displayed bravery on the descent into the crater (for which he paid in later years from the effects of the gas). He showed incredible bravery on many occasions; it is difficult to believe that the man who made the first ascent of Hood's Cathedral Spire could ever feel fear. (I went along on his second ascent, well protected by his belay. His first ascent of the eerie spire, 700 feet down the north cliff of Hood, was alone and cramponless, protected only by an alpenstock.)

Near the end of his 155-page journal, Gary tells of reading in the summit register on the Sierra's Mount Russell a description of a climber's body being found at the base of Russell's northern cliff: "It surprised me considerably that the low-angled, northern slopes had produced a tragedy, for I had surveyed these slopes with care the day before. In some inexplicable manner the poor fellow fell to his death nevertheless. It is not too difficult to get killed, although us lucky ones blunder along for quite a while." In Gary's case "quite a while" lasted less than a year and a half more.

When Gary was killed, I wired many friends. Among the replies came condolences from a 1930s Hood climber, Bill Hackett. Our revived friendship led to climbs in Colorado (where he tried to talk me into accepting the Army title "Civilian Technical Advisor to the Mountain and Cold Weather Command") and to expeditions in Alaska, which in turn led me to people and places on the far side of the world. What ripples in all directions across the pool of the world the rock of one man may make.

Gary put it this way:

All men are adventurous in their own particular way. Each of us found in boyhood a keen desire to wander to the town's far ends or across green pastures to the tree-lined rivers in the distance. Many of us knew a desire, which some even went so far as to realize, to climb through the beckoning doors of a freight train while it pulled away for distant points. Christopher Columbus himself, as a boy, watched the sailing ships start out to sea from the wharves of Genoa. Later, as an adventurous man, his discoveries altered the history of the world.

Now adventures, as delineated by men of the world or of letters, are more than often wont to place a cloak of infallibility on the shoulders of the principals. Indeed, there seems no manner in which they may fail. However, let us not be deceived, my friends. The habit of humanity to employ these ventures in mythology as a star, at which to aim enthusiastic sights, often leads to a sad case of undershooting and heartache. Entirely flesh-and-blood creatures, the most of us are susceptible to error-making; the surest foot may slip, the sharpest eye may dim from fatigue, the keenest brain may tire. All of these are emphatically not foolproof, and they all go to make up the funny temperamental thing which is a human being.

If that wire in Utah had not been electrified, Gary would have dropped lightly to the ground, alive. He would have spread ripples, who knows how important, through our corner of the galaxy.

Trekking and Trucking

Trekking and trucking seem related only by alliteration. In my case history, they're tied by chronological succession. Trucking provided time for mountain guiding and expeditionary climbing, at which I earned a modest reputation. Shortly after I retired from guiding trucks, an adventure travel company hired me to lead an Alaskan expedition and to direct their climbing school. When I learned they also trekked in glamorous Nepal, I asked for assignment there.

I'll introduce trekking by telling of a stormy day and of a calm morning, which may explain why I came to like treks better than trucks.

We call a yearly December trek "Manaslu" to capitalize on the name of that famous Nepalese mountain, though the real destination is the sacred lake Mim'pokhari, far above timberline on the slopes of Manaslu's neighbor, Mount Himalchuli. On this trip we reached the frozen lake just at twilight, with time to pay a quick visit to the small religious monument on its shore.

Morning brought a blizzard driving powder snow into the tent. After a brief breakfast, I left the Sherpas to a difficult breaking of camp and started out with the passengers to blindly feel a route down through a foot of fresh snow. The road, used only by Garung sheepherders in summer and occasional hunters in autumn, runs across dry grass slopes and rock ledges. In general, we follow a great ridge from Himalchuli, keeping below its crest and weaving into gullies and out over cragged ribs. A glacier flows in a canyon below us, though we can't see it.

We could see little on this particular morning and nothing of the road beneath its white blanket. Although I searched for the route and plowed snow, I soon outdistanced the passengers. The dried and flattened grass under floury snow made slippery footing. I worried about my followers, but wanted to check a section of the road where, coming up, we had fixed a rope to aid porters on a steep diagonal pitch above a considerable cliff. The wind was a deep-throated cello, striking a responsive chord in me. I remembered Gary writing of a time we were caught in a storm in the Rockies: "Smoke and I always knew a strange happiness in storms." Indeed, it is still true for me.

I probably wandered off the road several times in the storm but found it often enough to arrive at the place of the fixed line. I was on top of a spur that ran down from a rocky peak. Now, great mushrooms of snow billowed over the ledges we had used for climbing. Swirling flakes hid the precipice.

I eased down a few feet, clearing off footholds and handholds with the ax, but it did not take any rockclimbing wizardry to conclude that this was no place to descend unprotected. I set down my pack, weighty with spare clothes for the odd mitten-dropper, and snatched out my light emergency rope. With it for a handline, I was able to go to the bottom of the pitch and clear the ledges. They had whitened again by the time I returned for the bulky load, but at least I knew the location of the holds. Rather than rig a rappel, I made the second descent unprotected. The swirling gloom of cliff edge did not bother me now, with most of the snow burden shoved over the side. The passengers did not catch up, even after all this maneuvering. I crawled into a slot beneath an overhang, safe from four-foot-long icicle daggers, which crashed from the cliffs above into the furry, whirling white below. While I was munching a handful of crackers—*zoom* . . . *splat*—down came the end of a climbing line hurled from above. The lead Sherpas had arrived. I tied off the lower end, and soon passengers and porters swarmed around me; it was time to move on.

I chugged up through even deeper snow to the next crest, but then was happy to fall in behind the Sirdar (the commander of a Sherpa team), his chief of staff, and the cook. They did one whale of a job finding the way and breaking trail, especially since only the cook had been this way before. Of course, we had all traveled over the route a few days earlier, but the cook had made another trip in a previous year. So had I. That's why I thought I was so smart and at one point yelled to pass the word ahead for the Sirdar to stop. "You are going too high," I declared in my most authoritative tone. He looked puzzled, faintly uneasy, but whether this stemmed from doubt of his route-finding ability or curiosity as to what possessed me, I could not tell, for just then a cairn materialized beside us out of the snowy mist.

Passengers were scattered for over a mile along the way, several of them stumbling a good deal in the snowy rocks. I was too. We stopped a long time at a second cliff, which had a trail along and down it. It was so snowed up that Pemba Thondub had to scrape the whole trail with his ax before daring to let the porters, with their big loads, go down unprotected by a line, there being no place to anchor one. We waited long enough to get cold and impatient. Finally, well after noon, we found a rock that offered wind shelter while we ate a quick lunch. The people grumbled when I allowed only ten minutes. We needed all the marching time we could get if we were to beat the darkness. There was no time to rest.

We slogged, bulldozed, clung, tiptoed, and worried our way up yet another slippery spur. Somewhere on the way down, with only six inches of snow but more precipitating, one of the Sherpas asked me to catch up with the Sirdar for some kind of conference. The clouds parted enough to allow a half-mile of visibility. I caught sight of his group ahead. What a race to overtake him! The slightly downhill traverse made breathing easy, but I puffed from trying to dodge porters, passengers, and Sherpas without knocking rocks on them or skidding off the hill myself. How those small Sherpa women could skip across three-inch ledges with their towering loads without slipping to their doom I'll never know. They often stumble on level ground.

On catching the head of the line, I found the Sirdar and his aides waiting for me to decide whether to take a long traverse up and over a high crest and down to our base camp or to drop a thousand feet down to timber. There was only a little daylight left.

"The Tamaungs want to go on. We no food for Sahibs. We use lantern."

It took me only a second to think this through. We'd already double-staged this snowy march because we needed firewood and a decent bivouac for the tentless Tamaung porters. The grove below would meet both requirements. I reckoned I drew my pay for this kind of decision and gave the order to descend. The first four Sherpas dropped immediately down in a long swooshing glissade. The snow, only four inches deep, overlaid a steep but cliffless slope of thin, frozen scree.

Within an hour we were all down in the first copse of trees, thawing out by a roaring fire. It turned out we had plenty to eat if the Sahibs could stand a soup made of sardines. They relished it. So ended one of the great days in the mountains.

As we walked into the deep canyon at the bottom of Himalchuli and across the corrugated Nepal landscape toward our trip's end, I tried to analyze why I enjoyed that day so much, why it seemed destined to loom in my memory.

There was little challenge, and challenge is not that important to me. Certainly there was no scenery, no summit. If I believed in reincarnation, I would say my happiest past lives must have been spent romping below fringes of the great Pleistocene ice sheets.

Maybe my love of cold, wind, and exercise is encapsulated in genes from remote ancestors who enjoyed guiding the band down through snowy wastes to life-sheltering trees.

The December Nepal trek leader seldom wakes to a blizzard; I will now describe a more typical morning on this same trip.

Every morning I went up to the Sherpas' camp to see if they were awake. The kitchen boys almost always were. ("Kitchen boy" is now a Sherpa word and applies to either gender, so that we sometimes have a female kitchen boy.)

This morning seemed to be a good time for language practice. Among the few phrases in my Sherpa notebook is one asking, "Is there enough firewood?" Since I knew supplies in this camp were a little short, I thought it would be apropos, and greeted the first little kitchen boy with something like, "*Te shing lang ke da?*" After not too many repetitions, he looked at the pile and answered me.

The kitchen crew numbered four, graduated in size and perquisites, and the last to get up was the cook himself. After all the pots were on, the second cook checked them, peering into the steaming bubbles with his flashlight in his mouth (the lanterns being drained and packed for carrying). The next chore was to wake the first cook. This was easy. He was only six feet away, sleeping with the big baskets of groceries, the rest of the pots and pans, the condiments and spices, the flour board for rolling out *chupatties*, the egg beater and lime squeezer, the blankets and rugs, the rucksacks, the medicine chest, the oxygen bottle, its regulator and mask, the drying clothes, six ice axes, and a few odds and ends that would be packed and rolling in twenty minutes. Now the kitchen boy gently nudged Ang Tsering awake. He uttered one short muffled "Uhn-h," and then loud and clear, "*Te shing lang ke da?*" The littlest kitchen boy, before answering, looked at me and laughed. I've won! I'm a Sherpa-speaking linguist.

The words of the head cook's next questions escaped me, but I caught the substance of them easily because the kitchen boy's head swiveled to each pot as he was asked about the tea water, the porridge water, and the washing water. "Washing wata" is also a

Sherpa word now, said almost as we say it. By now the second cook had started his rounds with Sherpa tea. He saw me standing in the gloom and served me first, but, knowing well the real line of the hierarchy, quickly headed for the Sirdar's tent. Here four cups stood in a line; four hands shot out for their handles. The Sirdar's was first, because his cup is filled first. Then the second cook went to the other tents; somehow he located all the sleeping crew in the still-dark morning and checked under a bush or pulled back a tarp to fill a cup with steaming, sweet, milk tea.

I was becoming more and more fond of this beverage and took my ritual second cup before drifting away from the fire to watch the paling sky and see what old star friends were about. Capella had just dropped below the peak, but Menkalinam and El Nath were burning bright; on the other side, Arcturus still showed yellow fire, but Spica was dim.

About this time I noticed that I was not alone; the shadowy figure gazing eastward I knew to be Halsey Davis. Halsey is also an early riser. We exchanged good mornings and silently watched the first pinks brighten the high snows. Halsey was seventy-one, which made him even older than I and a good twenty years above the average age of the group. He is a business executive from Maine, still working, a strong walker, very quiet; he exudes competence and has a bearing so dignified that the other trekkers addressed him as "Mr. Davis." I tried to kid them out of such formality by calling him "Sir Davis," but it didn't work. Halsey's small talk, when he gets around to it, is never more than a couple of phrases, and this morning he asked, "What was your profession before guiding?"

Two or three people on each trip ask me this, and his reaction to my reply was typical, if restrained. He thought it strange, and I could sense through his tactful and laconic comment the faintest disapproval. The stereotyped image of a truck driver is a boor: rude, uneducated, and uncouth. Since we leaders of mountain trips in foreign lands strive to create and maintain the illusion that we are sword-waving generals in the field and suave diplomats in the city, my passengers want to know what a truck driver is doing there. Could there be any plausible connection between truck herding and mountain guiding?

TRUCK DRIVER

Most choices at the crossroads of life are made under weak starlight with a feeble lantern that illuminates poorly the farther stretches of the trail. The mountain urge was initially nurtured by my father, who bent a frail five-year-old twig by coaxing me along a certain crumbly rock ridge.

I naturally drifted into a life on the road. Jobs weren't easy to get in the bottom of the Depression; one of few I had involved hauling flax on a farm truck. Some years later I found myself working in the U.S. Vanadium Mine lab, and it was this job that finally flung me into the cab of a diesel rig for a career lasting over a quarter of a century. Nothing wrong with the lab; it was grandly situated in California under some of the most marvelous mountains in the world, and I enjoyed the title of "chemical analyst." This job theoretically capitalized on some college chemistry, but a short-order cook's experience would have sufficed.

Probably aggravated by jogging, an old cannery-hand-truck injury to my feet began to bother me. The pacing back and forth on the unyielding linoleum behind the line of filter funnels made my poor metatarsals cry out. Besides, I could look out the window and watch the big truck-and-trailers load up for their long hauls to Utah. The open road sounded romantic; I could picture myself riding the endless swells of the desert ranges of Nevada. Like a ship's captain, I would stretch my eyes to the distant golden horizon and be going some place.

The actual experience was not quite what I had imagined, but I discovered something of the fascination, the rhythm of wheels and engine, that grips a driver and glues him into the seat for a lifetime.

By definition, the driver is confined to the cab. It is a strange mixture of freedom and bondage, like flying in a straitjacket. He locks himself into a machine which allows little relaxation. The road permits only inches of deviation and seldom fails to punish split-second lapses in attention. The driver finds himself slave to schedules, clocks, and meters. He is circumscribed by orders, engine revolutions, and laws: state, federal, county, company, and union. A recorder automatically divulges a vast range of information. The load must arrive. The distance, weight, time, and conditions are all precisely known. It is physically impossible to vary the routine significantly. Not only is it difficult to goof off; it can be fatal. But still the driver feels free.

It may be the mere fact that the boss is not looking over his shoulder. The driver's freedom, or feeling of freedom, comes from his belief that within the imposed limits he may do the job as he sees fit. This leaves a tightrope so narrow as to be invisible to the non-driver, but to the man totally enmeshed in the occupation, it is a chance to develop rapport with an engine, to stroke the gear levers ever more surely toward that smooth performance to which his ears, his tachometer, and his very guts can vibrate. The driver controls many thousands of dollars' worth of sophisticated machinery, with the help or hindrance of an unseen corps of busybodies: a dispatcher in a distant station, a mechanic or engineer in another state, a highway cop, a cowboy who races to prevent his cow from turning at the fence line and plunging across the road, or a faceless customer who ordered twenty tons of top-heavy thingdobbles to be delivered Tuesday. The driver is the one who ultimately determines how smoothly the interlocking mess is orchestrated from the sounding seat of his throne.

I have felt it myself a thousand times. I leave the coffee shop and walk slowly out to the 60-foot-by-13½-foot-by-8-foot-by-82,000-pound mass standing motionless along the road. Weary, eyes only a little better from the coffee drug, legs cramped, seat heavy, I look over the long rig automatically, bump the tires, check for leaking oil and grease, feel an axle—then climb into the cab, fire up, ease out, and accelerate. That's it, accelerate. No, it's not really acceleration but the rush of feeling of well-being, of rightness of place and occupation. There's a momentary relief from fatigue, even when the load is heavy, the road steep, and acceleration can only be read on instruments. It is power under control—like a horse, camel, sailboat—the movement of all that weight under the intelligent direction of the captain. It is never analyzed but always there. Whatever it is, it grabs boys out of high school and keeps them on the road till they die. Their bellies fold over their belt buckles. They have difficulty climbing into the cab. Unless they live long enough for a pension, they finish their life at the wheel.

Tachograph charts interpreted by a skilled reader with a special magnifying device reveal many details of the trip. Some mechanics can psychoanalyze a driver by the feel of the oil from his dip stick. Computers know how much wear the individual driver puts on each particular part. But he doesn't need all this feedback. He knows what kind of a job he is doing, and, since he becomes part of the machinery, he knows it in his bones and muscles. It is a solid feeling. He need not back up to the pay window.

Truck driving is hard. The hours can be unbelievably long, the fatigue and eyestrain something that no one can imagine who has not experienced it. The driver suffers cold, heat, danger, and loneliness. Occupational hazards include heart failure and home failure.

It narrows a man's interests. Watch a bunch of overweight truck drivers slouching in the parking lot to continue a cafe conversation before climbing into their rigs and pulling out on their lonely runs. Their eyes are on their trucks, or the next man's. The talk is of engines, roads, engines, dispatchers, wages, engines, transmissions, engines—over and over. If you were to mention a name in the news headlines, maybe with the exception of the President, a common remark would be, "Who does he drive for?" Such astounding single-mindedness requires a power as strong as the engines the drivers control, as big as the rigs they master. When another truck goes barking by, all heads swivel and conversation halts for a second, while each brain inarticulately monitors the rap of the stack; then the talk resumes without a sign of interruption.

The drivers' faces reflect their occupation in some way that I cannot explain. One cold winter night, I pulled up at a café in Mina, a wide spot on a chilly, empty road through western Nevada. I was just warming my hands on the coffee cup when I caught a glimpse through the window of the marker lights of a rig sliding to a stop. About every other stool was occupied. Miners, I supposed—there were no other trucks around. They were dressed in the ubiquitous black Frisco jeans, but so was I. The door opened, and a middle-aged man in a heavy coat and black overall pants entered. He looked quickly down the counter and sat next to me. "I've got a sick old HB pulling a thirty-five-foot sled with most of the weight on the drivers, but only a single screw. Do you think I'll have to hang the iron on the pass?" Now, what clue enabled him to single me out as one of his fellow "knights of the road"?

My trekking friends, unable to see through the veneer of urbanity, are surprised to discover the identity of my preguiding profession. I don't bother to explain the manifold advantages— good wages, steady work, and long vacations—that I found in driving.

Hauling propane, a cold-weather job, allowed whole summers in the mountains. I found it possible to tie up only a portion of my mind with instruments, gears, roads, and loads—leaving the bulk of a feeble brain to deal with the logistics of those mountain trips. If the next expedition's food requirements needed calculation, I could assign off-duty brain cells a section of my 600-mile work bench. I delighted in employing this truck-free segment of gray matter in bouts of philosophizing or in the hobby of mental arithmetic. Poetry seemed particularly suited to the acoustics of a truck cab, as singing is suited to the shower, and many a black Nevada night passed pleasantly while I listened to myself recite verses as the truck roared along. I memorized a list of my favorites, including the whole of the *Rubaiyat*, letter perfect. Captains of industry pay fancy fees to be hidden in a secret resort, guaranteed against disturbance, so that they can think in quiet. I earned a wage for using ten percent of my mind while having the free-wheeling use of the other ninety percent. I wouldn't have traded with a king.

On treks I rarely dip into the heavy, unwritten book of trucking stories. My passengers are amply entertained otherwise. I never tell them of the time that—never mind. In twenty-five years of galloping up and down and around the western states through all sorts of conditions of wheels and weather, one gathers a long collection of adventures.

In the case of Halsey Davis's puzzlement, I satisfied it with what I take to be polite New England-style grunts and let it go at that.

Alaska and the Yukon

MOUNT MCKINLEY—HIGH

When Jerry Goodwin asked me to tell him about Alaska, I had nothing to say. He deals in mountain books and has no doubt read every exciting expedition tale published about the North. I had no records or rescues to talk about, but he kept probing. He asked about Mount Logan in the Yukon, and Mount St. Elias on the Alaska-Yukon border. I gave him a brief outline of my climbs there. Then he asked the trigger question: "Have you ever been up Mount McKinley?"

"Yes," I confessed, "three times, but there's nothing much to tell." It was midafternoon in a small coffee shop in Berkeley; after Jerry bribed me with another cup of coffee, I dredged up tidbits from the trips of 1958, 1961, and 1971. My "nothing to say" kept us occupied until supper.

Dave Dingman organized the '58 trip with his Teton buddies Jake Breitenbach and Dave Dornan. Young Ross Kennedy was an apprentice guide on Rainier. Bill Hackett brought his experience as a three-time McKinley veteran. Perhaps Hackett invited me because I'm at home in snowstorms.

My wife, Vi, met me on the ski hill waving a letter from Bill. "You go," she said. It seemed a good opportunity. Propane hauling would slack off in June, and the expedition price was right. Of Major William D. Hackett's formal letter, I remember only the phrase: ". . . thirty days, thirty-five dollars, phone immediately. . . ."

Bill told me over the phone to bring my largest crampons because we'd be furnished special boots. Otherwise, I had only to grab an ice ax, stuff some wool clothes in the duffle bag that I lashed to my Yukon packboard, meet Jake Breitenbach in Seattle, and drive north with him in a brand-new Dodge furnished and fueled by Chrysler.

When I called Jake, he said the Chrysler deal fell through, but a friend had given him a second-hand Buick for the nineteen-dollar license fee. Jake picked me up on his second pass by the Seattle Greyhound Station. He didn't expect an older man, he explained. Let's see, 1958, only forty-three years old. That's okay, I saw Jake slow down the first time but figured a guy that young couldn't be Breitenbach.

So soon after spring breakup, the Alcan Highway bounced our shaggy sedan unmercifully. We drove night and day, took turns napping in the back seat, and rattled in to Anchorage in less than four days.

Once all the members had assembled in Anchorage, expedition solidarity evaporated. A group portrait vividly shows the two political parties and the outsider. Four stand in donated red thermal sweaters, one in Army uniform, and one in a red and brown plaid wool shirt. Red shirts Dingman, Dornan, Breitenbach, and Kennedy on one side, khaki shirt Hackett on the other. Smoke's plaid shirt indicates he's in the middle. Red shirts organized the trip and deserved a loud voice in its conduct, even though proximity to the big mountain bewildered them. Khaki shirt knew the mountain score but couldn't read the simplest social chart. Red-party policy consisted of standing around and wringing hands. Khaki party pouted in the bar.

I busied myself with last minute chores, the better to avoid route-selection meetings. A sudden surge of the Muldrow Glacier and the cancellation of an Army helicopter lift made the originally scheduled Northeast Ridge impractical. The others settled for a thing called the Southeast Spur of the Southeast Ridge. Mine would have been the lone vote for an easy road.

Last second skidding into the schedule is common to expeditions, whether they start in Munich, Tokyo, Kathmandu, or Bishop. We had a date with bush pilot Don Sheldon to fly to the Ruth Glacier and needed to board a train at eight in the morning. The freighter bearing our food and gear sat in the mud one-half mile from shore. "No problem," the dock master assured us. "High tide's in the morning; at five the ship will be here."

When I went to bed at midnight, the junior members still crouched over roaring primus stoves, fitting their crampons to our experimental Army Korean boots. At five A.M. we stood on the dock staring at our ship. It lay at dockside, its deck covered with stacks of huge containers strapped down with inch-thick cables. Through great luck we found our container accessible, its door unlocked, and the space between the partially opened door and cables barely navigable by our thinnest man, Jake. Our freight was even on top. Jake tossed the packages to me, I threw them to the dock, and the others loaded them onto a rented truck. Our timing turned out so close that, after we loaded the baggage car and returned the truck, the last of us boarded the train as it was moving.

The sudden transition from Talkeetna to the mountainside by air is only a little less mind-jarring than the reverse journey. When the engine sound fades and the thin speck of the Super Cub vanishes down the canyon, the world contracts to white silence.

The silence didn't last. My memory of that steep-sided gorge between Mount Huntington and the Moose's Tooth centers on the roar of avalanche and the howl of wind.

The younger members outraged Hackett, with his by-the-numbers camping efficiency, by cramponing across the plastic dinner plates, but they compensated by leading the pitches and fixing ropes for us that followed. Our crevassed route was steep from the start. Even on the first relay we needed pitons. Twice the leader fell from the topmost footstep and unzipped a line of pitons, to be held by the last one. Finally Dornan and Dingman topped out on the knife-edged Southeast Spur but declared further progress impossible. I heaved a sigh of relief, for I dreaded climbing that exposed pitch even protected by a belay from above. The retreat began.

Somewhere on the way down the steep slope I heard, "Hey, Smoke!"

I looked up through the gently falling snow. "That's strange," I thought, "Dingman's alone."

His calm voice continued, "We've got a little trouble up here. Dornan's in the crevasse!"

No big deal; Jake and I climbed back up and helped Dingman fish him out. I've heard many crevasse-associated sounds here and there in the mountains—including my own call of the Yukon, "I'm *in*, Jack!"—but I best remember Dingman's cool, matter-of-fact, "We've got a little trouble. . . ."

Down on the Ruth Glacier, Sheldon swooped to a landing. He'd been flying a TV cameraman around and around our drop site at 16,000 feet. Sheldon, guessing what had happened, searched for us. We pounced on him. "Take us around to where we *can* climb this bloody mountain."

I hadn't taken that many mountain flights. Everywhere I looked the clouds had rocks in them. I saw Sheldon scrunched down in his seat, apparently doing something desperate to save us. Scary! I figured I should see what he was doing, even if it was to be my last experience. I loosened my seat belt and reared up to look in the front. Sheldon was leaning over sideways, using the reflecting glass of his instrument panel as he combed his hair.

The year 1958 was still relatively early in McKinley climbing history. Sheldon set us down on the Kahiltna Glacier well below the present landing site. We had a long way to go with the week's food we had left. Fortunately few storms slowed us. Windy Corner blasted us with a day's delay, for which we used a snow house built by a party ahead of us. Here again Hackett got on the case of our "dilettantes," taunting them with their lack of knowledge of the North. Maybe they didn't know a snow house from an outhouse, but they proved their climbing skills again by carving a day-long blue-ice staircase up the Buttress Wall. We had no time to go on to a safer place, and balanced our tents precariously on the crest of the West Buttress. At 17,000 feet, we found Ed Cooper's party preparing to give up and go down. Forced back by weather on one summit bid, they were nearly out of food. We shared our thinning supplies, and some of their members accompanied us to the summit the next day.

The summit day took forever because the fast trip from camp at the landing site denied us time to acclimatize. I was dragging when I came upon Jake lying in the snow at 19,500 feet. Suddenly I perked up: at least I wasn't the pooped-out last. "Come on, Jake, don't give up, we started from Seattle together, and we'll finish together." We reached the summit okay, but without enthusiasm.

(I never saw Jake again after we parted in Anchorage. Every time I walk to Everest, I duck out of the traffic below Tengboche and follow the ridge to where he's buried under a little pile of stones. A serac fell on him in the Khumbu Icefall on the 1963 American Everest Expedition.)

The descent went rapidly. We chose a different route down the steep part between 16,000 and 15,000 feet. I found it easy enough but was upset by something red in the snow of the bergschrund. Jam? Ed Cooper's party descending below us had jam! And I was so hungry. It wasn't jam; it was blood. Marty Mushkin had been beaned by a rock, and when I reached them at 14,000 feet, Dave Dingman, a doctor, had just finished sewing him up.

I remember only one more incident from the descent. I happened to be tied in the middle of the rope. Bill Hackett passed over a crevasse bridge all right, but I crashed through and flipped Ross Kennedy into a somersault. He came down on his Trapper Nelson packboard and disintegrated it.

Cooper's party followed us to our landing camp, because they'd lost a tent and couldn't build snow houses with the mushy snow of the lower glacier. This worked out fine for me. When arguments started about whether Dingman had priority as leader or Hackett had become de facto leader, I could sneak off to the other camp, where my frowns would not betray my professed neutrality. Besides, I needed my facial muscles for eating. Ed Cooper was not completely out of food. They had hot cakes! With syrup!

Cooper's party also enjoyed semi-official military support through one of their members, locally based Air Force Sergeant Robert Elliott. A monster Air Force plane flew over to check on them. Since their landing camp was three miles across the glacier, under Mount Crosson, that was the only place the plane searched. Each time they circled over us, we fired rows of smoke bombs, shot off pink star shells, and jumped up and down and screamed, but they always banked a broad wing in the way, and all eyes aboard scanned the far side of the glacier. Eventually they wised up and chugged down-canyon, where they could reach Sheldon on their radio. He figured out the problem and redirected them. Back they came again and wiggled a huge wing at us.

That evening a big, banana-shaped, twenty-passenger chopper clattered into camp. In those timid days they thought it daring to fly as high as 7,000 feet with a short crew and one passenger. Major Hackett and Lieutenant Mushkin rushed up to the cockpit. "I have orders to pick up only Sergeant Elliott," the pilot said. They flew him away, leaving the rest of us to go one at a time in Sheldon's Piper Cub. (Bob Elliott's luck ran out two years later. Since he was the only person in Alaska at the time who knew McKinley, he was asked to fly as observer in Bill Stevenson's plane to look for a party in trouble. They "went in" at 17,000 feet.)

Even the flight home contained drama. (Neither Jake nor I trusted the nineteen-dollar Buick to make another 3,000 miles.) The Pacific Northern pilot circled to give us a good view of an island split in half a few hours earlier by an earthquake. We also took a bird's-eye look at a mountain in Lituya Bay whose forest had been instantly leveled to bedrock by a giant wave. When the earthquake shook forty million cubic yards of rock off a steep mountain and into Gilbert Inlet, the resulting wave surged up the opposite wall of the inlet and washed out trees to a height of 1,720 feet above the sea—eight times the height of any known *tsunami* breaking on an ocean shore. We found out later that five people died, at least one boat sank, and all Lituya Bay's tidal animals were killed. But, just as a nail sticking up through a boot sole may seem sharper than any amount of shrapnel in a distant war, we paid more attention to the left inboard engine of our DC-6 when it caught fire.

The 1961 McKinley expedition had a hand-picked crew of good friends. We used my pickup to pull a freight trailer. I overhauled it myself and installed new tires. My wife, Vi, son Bobby, and nephew Jim Blanchard went along to keep me company on the long road north, now familiar from a 1959 Mount Logan expedition with Nort Benner, Jules Eichorn, and Dick Kauffman. No route arguments this time: I ran the trip like a dictator, partly to make sure we climbed an easy road.

The longest storm of the trip weathered us in at Talkeetna with Riccardo Cassin's group from Lecco, Italy. "You don't have to speak Eye-talian," Don Sheldon said. "Just shout at them." That might work; maybe someone hearing the racket would rush up to interpret. But in a two-place Piper Cub—can you imagine the chaos when two such high-strung characters as Sheldon and Cassin shouted and gestured in the airplane cab? It didn't surprise me that the world-renowned climber and the world-champion bush pilot couldn't communicate while airplaning around a McKinley cirque. When they returned, I put in my two cents' worth about where they should place the landing camp in order to climb what is now called the Cassin Ridge. Neither Sheldon nor Cassin considered my advice worth even one cent.

One of the leader's perks is flying in first. It's good to be alone on the mountain, but hunger interrupted my meditation. I bit into a salami and broke off a gold tooth, exposing the nerve. Just then Sheldon flew in with the second man. I flew out.

Sheldon, typically, felt he had to zoom down so I could see at eye level a crevasse bridge that had broken under him on takeoff two weeks before and damaged his ski-wheels. (I knew about the damage, having spent part of our weathered-in days helping him repair the landing gear.) At Talkeetna we changed to a Cessna to speed me to Palmer. The dentist's fee was five bucks, the air fare to and from the mountain, 250 dollars.

Somehow Don got the idea I liked to prospect. On the way back in to the mountain, he weaved around the Kichatna Spires and buzzed quartz ledges at arm's length. "That close enough, Smoke? Hang on, I'll go 'round again!" In the thirteen times I flew with Sheldon, I never convinced him that I cared more for my life than for gold. (Sheldon stories are countless; a guy wrote a book about him but only scratched the surface.)

Our reunited party was caught in a big storm in Kahiltna Pass, but this gave us time to acclimatize. It also induced boredom and even depression in some members. Jack Henry lived in a blue tent next door to Dick Kauffman, Monty Alford, and I. One day during a lull in the storm, Jack knocked at the door of our gold-colored tent to ask if he could come in and share the good cheer. After he'd crawled through the tunnel door, he pleaded his case this way: "Smoke, I paid my share of the expenses, I carry my share of the weight, I do every chore you assign me. Can't we switch tents from time to time? I hear laughter from the gold tent all the time. I'm going crazy in mine. The only time Don Claunch talks is to recite the latest blood-pressure readings on his sphygmomanometer. Charlie Saylor hasn't spoken all day except to mutter, 'Has anybody seen my cup?' "

One day I told my crew, "There are about three good loads left down at the dump. Let's make it easy—you five go down and bring them up, and we three will explore forward." Our route went well, and, coming down with empty packs late in the day, we found no one back yet from the hauling party. I went down the road a little way to see if I could spot someone coming up. Yes, here they come now over a swell in the glacier. Jack, first, just passes by me growling, "You son of a bitch!"

"Jack, Jack, please, I'm sorry. I miscalculated. Let me carry some of your load." Jack was obviously overloaded and had given fifteen pounds to Monty. But to me? I was part of the problem. Pride is a strong emotion, and many people prefer crawling before giving up too much of it. It finally took an impassioned speech to win the game: "Jack, at this very spot in '58, Jake Breitenbach took part of my load for me. Now I want to pay him back. Someday you can pay me back through someone else."

Crevasse problems are routine on a big mountain. We take special care to find exactly where the odd climber-gobbler hides near camp. Monty, digging for firm snow for the water bucket, broke into a crevasse that ran right under the cook tent. I was tightening up the cords one snow-drifting day and fell into a crevasse between tent wall and tent guyline.

None of us will ever forget the storm on the ridge. Monty, who works outdoors year round in the Yukon and was our cold-and-storm veteran, said that if it had been a bit colder or the wind a bit stronger, we might have produced the kind of story people look for on mountain-book shelves. Jules Eichorn and Bruce Meyer, standing close together watching their 120-foot rope blown horizontally, judged the storm rough enough. At our 17,000-foot camp we dug straight down into the hard ice with the picks of our axes to make a hole for protection.

After only one day the weather allowed a try for the summit. I aimed straight up this time, avoiding the long traverse to Denali Pass. A few minutes from camp we came upon a crashed airplane almost completely buried in a year's accumulation of snow. Only a bit of the fuselage showed. As we stepped over the roof window some of our party said they could see two faces inside. I did not look down. My friend Bob Elliott was in there.

The slope became steep, with soft snow to stomp. Above, I needed to swing the ice ax a bit. The higher we went, the better I felt. It turned out to be one of the most enjoyable of all my mountain days. To stand strong and happy on the apex of the continent in mild weather with perfect visibility has to be a rare privilege.

In late spring of 1971, Allen Steck called from Oakland to ask if I would lead a commercial group up McKinley. I was shocked by his timing. I had started to plan my last big expedition in September and spent most of the winter bagging and weighing food and fussing over gear. "That's okay," Allen said. "Randy Renner up in Anchorage will be your assistant leader; he's packing everything. All you have to do is show up." How could I miss? No organization or packing worries. I had only to guide on the mountain and get paid for it.

The best-laid plans of mice and men, of course, often go agley. Randy flunked his physical. Who could I find at such short notice? I called my friend Warren Harding—he could sometimes get away in a few days. I couldn't remember what his subarctic experience was, but I'd heard he'd taken about as long as a McKinley ascent climbing some mountain with a Spanish name in Yosemite Valley. He was writing a book, so I enlisted Nort Benner's son Bob, who had climbed to 18,500 feet.

Allen gave me a check for 600 bucks to give to Randy as part payment for the packing he'd done. Bob Benner and I landed in Anchorage a couple of days ahead of the passengers, looked up Randy Renner, and handed him the check. "No," said Randy, "the company doesn't owe me anything, because I've not done anything."

My spouse would never trust me to shop for eggs, milk, and bread without a grocery list. Bob and I, with invaluable help from local guide Ray Genet, bought the bulk of the food for nine men for thirty days by strolling down the grocery store aisles and eyeballing the shelves, without a scrap of paperwork! And we got away with it, too. Of course, we had to lie a lot. "Oh yes, sir, we always have this kind of menu on the mountain."

The climb went off as nice as pie. No storm delayed our flying in. We missed out on the long temper-shortening sort of storm which hindered the 1961 evacuation.

We did have one fly in the pie, though. It happened this way. Early in the morning of the second day I was laying out the thirty-meter nylon lines in the snow when one of our group buttonholed me just out of earshot of the other passengers: "Smoke, I want to talk to you." The classic request, it always means trouble. "Is this the way we have to climb the mountain? Do we go on carrying loads like this?"

I tried to explain that we really needed all those piles of food and supplies—simple arithmetic dictated such slavery. We were on a three-relay program, though the relays would decrease to two, and then to the sweat of hauling everything at once. These figures promised hard work.

"I'm sick," he announced.

He wasn't sick at all. Or suddenly sick from realizing the labor involved in climbing a big mountain. Luckily we were low enough on the mountain to ship him out. I asked my assistant leader, Bob Benner, to take a rope and another climber and ease him down to landing camp, where we had a big radio. Our line-of-sight radio wouldn't reach Sheldon.

As it happened, weather, overwork, thin evening air, or something else kept Don Sheldon from coming that day. "I'll be in first thing in the morning," he assured us.

"Come in at Camp One, we'll stomp a strip," Bob requested.

"If the man's sick, you can't go up. I'll pick him off from landing camp at dawn."

"We've got to go up; we didn't bring tent or sleeping bags."

"Dig a hole. I'll be in at dawn."

"Okay, we'll be at Camp One. We'll make a strip 800 feet by 40 feet." Bob banged down the receiver.

The sick man came all the way back up without protest but winged out with Sheldon when the plane set down at dawn on our fine new-made strip at Camp One. The office has not heard from the defector to this day.

Such loads can be murder. On that trip we borrowed Ray Genet's system of loading the company freight—food mostly—into plastic garbage cans, which slide slickly into a backpack. We load the cans to sixty-six pounds, to which is added the personal gear that has to make a round-trip on each relay. Sometimes we get by with a total weight a bit over sixty, and sometimes these cruel crunchers scale a hundred. I hesitate to write such a figure, as pack weights are controversial. You can rarely trust weight figures quoted by friends and never those of a stranger.

Kahiltna Pass must be a cloud swamp. The longest storm caught us there, where a Japanese base-camp tender was terribly worried about his overdue people above. This time we carried a powerful radio. Climbing up to a crest, we got Fairbanks line-of-sight and relayed a message to Sheldon. On the first good day he flew over, spotted the Japanese party returning okay, and dropped word weighted with a package of ice cream.

We had another storm at 15,000 feet. I remember bounding from my tent at midnight to fix another tent's center pole, which broke in the snow blast.

But things went so well, there's little to remember. We got everyone to the top. Again I felt strong as a bull. We had good summit weather. Maybe we kept going for more than twenty-four hours on the summit "day," but that was mostly spent getting one wobbly-legger down. My memory contains no climbing details— only beautiful twilight colors that lasted all night. What a joy it is to climb down.

I can't remember any landing-camp wait. That's unusual. My next picture is of the big victory dinner at Anchorage with everyone clapping me on the back.

Allen Steck is not a ready back-clapper. He did give me several verbal pats, though, and asked me how I pulled the climb off so smoothly. "I'm charmed," I bragged, and made a mental note not to press my luck by volunteering for another climb.

As glorious as the summit may be, it's a punctuation point on a month-long mountain. Bone's and muscle's memory of the long strain toward the summit will more likely urge the climber to return on another expedition to the same destination. It's the snow and cold, the struggle with storm. The proposition that McKinley climbers return in order to suffer is hard to articulate—perhaps even harder than explaining how to combat monotony on a snow slog.

Of course I'd like to climb McKinley again. I used to think if I could go around again, I'd like a second life as a musician or mathematician. But it wouldn't be such a shabby life to live as a full-time

McKinley guide and just tromp up and down that wonderful
snowy mountain over and over. A couple of times, flying the great-
circle route in a 747 to Japan and looking down on the white en-
chantment of Alaska-Yukon glaciers, I've had to tighten my seat
belt to keep from bailing out on the snows.

MOUNT MCKINLEY—LOW

"All out and into the river!"

Like a foghorn of doom, the cruel leader's command echoed
through the tents of our little group camped in fog-shrouded
spruce trees on the banks of the Bull River. Dreams suddenly shat-
tered; there would be no drifting from sleep to wakefulness in that
euphoric state that sometimes precedes a summer morning. Instead, everyone scrambled to get into damp clothes and roll up
drippy tents before plunging into icy water.

For me this was a moment of truth. I'd worried about this deep
river. When our tallest man eventually got a line across to the only
tree on the far bank, I guessed I could guide our group through the
rest of the rivers, along the glaciers, and over Anderson Pass—
across the Alaska Range not far east of Mount McKinley. Despite
the obstacles we might encounter on the week's walk along the
gravel bars of the glacial Chulitna River and across tundra, alder
jungle, swirling water, and uncertain snow bridges, we should not
have to reappear at Colorado Station on the Alaska Railroad with
defeat in our faces and our tails between our legs.

The others left geographical concerns to the leader. As soon as
everyone emerged safely on the far bank, they scurried for firewood for breakfast. Soon a thin wisp of smoke was curling up from
the soaking wet wood of the nearest spruce grove.

The personnel on this 1968 trip included the captain, who had
dreamed up this walk as a bonus extension for a few members of
Jules Eichorn's Sierra Club Kenai Canoe Trip.

The first mate was my wife, Su, whom I had married in 1966.
She had listened to so many of my Alaska stories that she came to
see what truth (if any) might be in them.

Joanne French (now Barnes) came as cook, a duty she'd performed to perfection on the canoe trip.

Pat Armstrong, an old friend from my home town, might be the only tourist ever to enter Alaska without trousers. He bicycled from the States in his shorts so fast that he beat his long wool pants that were coming by slow freight.

Tall Tom Blackburn we used for sounding the depth of water crossings such as the Bull River. He could hardly wait to use his new ice ax. One day on the glacier he announced with pride and satisfaction, "I cut a step—in my knee!"

John Skinner is a retired merchant sailor. We pretended that his knowledge of cargo on ocean ships suited him to carry loads across rivers. We weighted him unmercifully. He pretended not to notice as long as the chocolate was distributed early and often.

Bill Bechtell made nearly all the fires and cared not whether his fuel was dry tinder or wet mush. He enjoyed walking the narrow boulder shores or ledges when we frequently got "banked," so we used his red beard as a beacon on those awesome occasions when the river swerved across its half-mile-wide gravel bed to pound furiously on its bank.

Bill Hewlett, Jr., we called Billy, but the diminutive hardly fit his locomotive build. We didn't let all this power go to waste, but piled a tower on his packframe.

The idea for this trip hit me some years before during a visit to Wonder Lake, on the north side of the range. We had stopped our car at a lookout point on a bold bluff. Mount McKinley, as usual, hid in clouds. We could see, though, up the tumbled moraine of the Muldrow Glacier and up the beckoning green tundra across the shiny threads of the braided Thorofare River. I smelled a good walk here and slipped it into a bulging card file of future trips I carry in my head. Then I more or less forgot it until Jules Eichorn asked me to be his assistant leader on a Sierra Club trip in July, 1968 and to lead some of the members on an extra trip afterwards.

Belmore Browne apparently used Anderson Pass to gain the northern side of the Alaska Range after his long journey from Seward to attempt McKinley in 1912. Ginny Woods and Celia

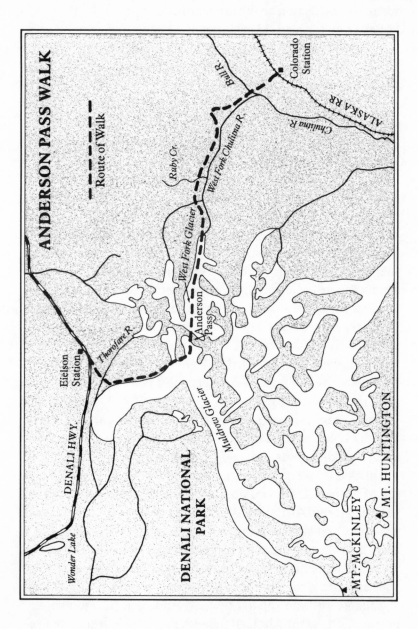

ANDERSON PASS WALK

Route of Walk

DENALI NATIONAL
PARK

Wonder Lake

DENALI HWY.

Eielson
Station

Thorofare R.

Muldrow Glacier

West Fork Glacier

Anderson
Pass

Ruby Cr.

West Fork Chulitna R.

Bull R.

Chulitna R.

ALASKA RR

Colorado
Station

MT. McKINLEY

MT. HUNTINGTON

Hunter, who ran Camp Denali and knew this area as well as anyone, had been to the pass from the north but not over it. Denali National Park Ranger George Perkins made the trip from Eilson Station over the pass to the rail in 1967. I could find no other information; if others had been over the pass, they left no record. We needed no guide map, but we did want to be assured the trip would go without undue hardship. On the basis of what little we could find out, Jules decided to let me lead a small party from the railroad at Colorado, up the West Fork of the Chulitna River and the glacier of the same name, over Anderson Pass, and down along the Muldrow Glacier to Eilson Station on the Wonder Lake road (now known as Denali Highway).

So we eight debarked from the Alaska Railroad's blue and yellow cars at Colorado Station on a partly cloudy afternoon. When the train pulled out of sight up the converging tracks in the distance, we were left standing in the stillness of the immense Alaskan landscape. A few minutes before, all was swaying movement and noise; now the clickety-clack of rail joints was replaced by the hum of insects.

After a few minutes of distributing loads, we set off for a week's walk in the wilderness. The trek started with a walk down a narrow, deserted dirt road. In a few minutes someone in front sang out, "There's the Middle Fork and it's got a bridge!" I was not particularly surprised to find everyone gathered at the brink of the deeply flowing Middle Fork of the Chulitna, staring in disbelief at the remains of a fine bridge. Its near section had not been able to withstand winter's ice and was now a tumbled mess downstream.

A single cable connected the central span across deep water to the near shore. Dropping my pack, I balanced out on the cable and some sticks that were caught on it. It was perhaps the only display of bravery and resolution I managed to muster during the trip. We were only a quarter-mile from the railroad tracks, and it would never do for the leader to sound retreat while "Charge!" still echoed in the ears of the faithful followers. Luckily we found enough driftwood planks and logs to jerrybuild a pontoon bridge, which the current pressed against the swaying cable. It looked awfully far down through the bubbling deep as I tottered my load across the scary passageway. We all made it, however. After a secret sigh from the brave leader, we stomped along the road with a cloud of mosquitoes around each walker's head.

The next river was the Bull. It also had a bridge, but only a section of it stood, in the center. Our watches said six in the evening, so we slithered down the bank to make camp. After dinner we walked back and forth in the mist on the river's edge, put up marker rocks, and tried to gauge the depth. We even took preliminary wades into its cold current.

The next morning, as I have related, we made it across. Bill Bechtell's fire warmed our outsides and Joanne's breakfast our insides. We took up the trip with renewed vigor, in spite of a steady drizzle that had set in for the day. We regained the old mining road we had left the day before. This provided sure footing, indeed almost a carpet for the feet. Our feet shuffled unhindered in the center of the road, though we could not see them. Thick alders, growing from both sides of the road, interlaced in the middle and parted only with nose-wrenching and eyeball-gouging.

The smooth path for our feet seduced us into following the road above treeline and away from our course. A view from a tundra hill showed we should have to battle off-road alders to regain the river. We sat down for a soggy lunch under a solitary spruce that wept on our cookies and chocolate. On the way back down to the river, the thick, tough, wet, slippery alders clung to the top of our packs, clutched at sleeping bags, tore at tents, twisted our feet, and repeatedly wrestled us to the ground. (After the trip, when we described "Alder Day" to old north-country hand Monty Alford in Whitehorse, he leaped up from the table with an exaggerated cry, "Don't talk to me of alders; I've been there. Stop it! I'll go out of my mind!")

All troubles end. We found spruces. We found beautiful bear trails leading easily down to a sand bar and a delightful camp where fire and soup and comfort set us right again.

If the second day merited the title of "The Great Alder Exercise," then surely the next day should be called "The Day in the River." We did some stump-jumping, some brush beating, and even a bit of strolling on open bars with tiny streams to leap, but we spent most of the day in the Chulitna. The stream kept "banking" us, and we had to get into the water to wade around a point or over to an island. It never got over thigh-deep, but even knee-deep water pushed us dangerously. John got knocked down and was dragged past us by the rush of the current.

On one narrow island, I failed to look up from my rope coiling to see where my companions had waded. I chose a place too deep and swift. When I reached the bank, I heard someone say, "Did you see the fear in Smoke's face?" That was not fear, that was imagination. I could picture myself swishing down the Chulitna, splashing into the Susitna, and surfing out into Cook Inlet in a cloud of spray. Were there any straws to grasp off Anchorage?

I worried unnecessarily about Ruby Creek and the North Fork of the Chulitna. We crossed both easily and found a campsite on the river bank even nicer than the previous one. We pitched our tents in a small meadow among spruces. Kindling sticks and driftwood fuel were plentiful, and we had soft grass mattresses. I'd like to add a tinkling brook of champagnelike mountain water or a cool spring for drinking, but I must tell it as it was. We dipped our liquid from a roaring rivulet of the branched Chulitna so heavy with gray glacial silt that the pudding would not jell.

We could find no other complaint about this green Eden, though, and wondered how much longer the pressure of mankind's insatiable greed would allow wilderness like this to exist. We were acutely aware that the park boundary excluded much of the magnificent country south of the Alaska Range. Even if the teeming billions control their numbers, could anyone keep them from conquering every corner of the planet? In the words of Ambrose Bierce, "Mankind has multiplied with such rapidity as to infest the entire habitable earth and Canada."

Our fourth day of tramping toward Anderson Pass was pre-

labeled "The Glacier Day" in the hope we'd get there. River troubles began again a few minutes out of camp. We were banked again
and again. We all grew so weary of cold water that we preferred to
cling to now-helpful alders and kick our toes into thin dirt under
wet grass in order to climb up and around the river-battered cliffs.
The last time we deserted the river, we needed a rappel to return.
More narrow beaches, more wading; then in the distance we spotted the glacier.

The snout of the glacier showed only a little dirty black ice. The
surface was covered with slate, which made for easy walking. No
slippery bare ice and only a few small crevasses crossed our course.
Our glacier did exhibit one creek, or small river, which was incised
about fifteen feet and flowed with a satisfying roar. We did not have
to cross it, and a mile or so up we found it just the right size for a
camp water supply.

We pitched our tents on a snowfield but located the kitchen on
a bare rock moraine in order to have tables and chairs. From a
boulder observatory we reveled in long views down the canyon of
our route. There were some fine peaks and glaciers up-canyon.
(Belmore Browne used one of these tributary glaciers in 1912,
when he slid down to the main glacier on his way toward Anderson
Pass.) A cool breeze from the pass played along the white slopes,
and diners that night took their places at our rock table attired in
gloves and parkas to wait for soup from the stove.

We climbed over the pass the next day with embarrassing ease.
When I advertised the trip back on the Kenai, I painted a steeper
picture. I spoke of bergschrunds, seracs, walls, and pitches with
belays and stepcutting. When we got there it turned out to be
nothing more than an easy stroll up a hill the angle of a ski slope.
A cloud helped with a cool, thick mist, which erased the perspective, so we could imagine great cliffs beneath our feet. Indeed, one
of the photos shows the leader disappearing into cloudy steepness
up a snow slope.

The way down also proved easy, though a little steeper. The
clouds parted long enough to reveal the striped rock-and-ice

ridges of the Muldrow Glacier. We lunched and photographed flowers on the moraine of a small tributary glacier.

We had just gotten under way again, when we threw off our packs to better aim our cameras at a noble big caribou. We had seen some strays (not the great herds we hoped for) in the distance, but this fellow stood quite close and watched us. I heard him mumble, "Ah, large featherless bipeds. I must observe them." What a pose! We couldn't have done better in a zoo. But the caribou decided these strange animals, whose pack-shaped humps came off and who sprouted large glistening third eyes, were not to be trusted. Off he galloped for a quieter browse behind protecting hills.

The Muldrow's surface was a nightmare; alongside was a sweet dream of a bench with soft and scented grass occasionally sprinkled with flowers. Problems were minimal: some small stream maneuvers, some steps to be cut in a snowbank that disputed the way, and a steep climb up a grass-tufted hillside to get around the swerve of a watercourse. Increasing sunshine and warmth, the downhill grade, and the beauty of the surroundings made it the pleasantest of marches. One side stream bothered us enough that we crossed with linked arms. Even so, its swift force knocked Bill down. Joanne said the cold threatened to break her legs off.

Not long after, Joanne's flippant complaint seemed almost a premonition. Water once more forced us into a high detour. When we reached the side-glacier river again, Joanne missed a four-foot jump and crumpled on the gravel with a twisted ankle. Fortunately it was not sprained; she managed to hobble well enough to cross the gravel bar to a grassy bench campsite on a moraine of the live glacier.

All evening, in the long lovely Alaskan twilight, we watched the clouds lift, surge, and dissipate westward, until the unbelievable huge bulk of Mount McKinley shone out in fully exposed majesty. To crown this view with perfection, the immense dome turned pink with rosy alpenglow from the final rays of the sun.

In the morning the gleaming white mass still stood over our

camp. It seemed to follow us as we moved off down the roaring side stream along the glacier. The sun brought high spirits, but we took every excuse to idle. Hurrying would end the trip too soon, and we felt as if we could walk on through the glorious Alaskan wilderness forever. We stopped for an hour-and-a-half lunch on an island in the river, for a recital of Robert Service, and even, so help me, for a swim in a pool of surprisingly warm water on the surface of the glacier itself. Moraine and vegetation covered everything, but on the bottom of the pool our feet rubbed on bare ice.

I worried about the half-mile-wide Thorofare River. It turned out to be finely braided and shallow, with a slow current. We easily crossed it and climbed up a steep bluff to the highway at Eilson Lookout Station.

As Joanne took a picture of Su and me in a clasped-hand salute to the mountain, clouds clobbered the scene with rain—a fitting end to an Alaskan walk. It would have been almost disappointingly irregular for sunshine to have lasted longer. While we had seen less than a dozen caribou of the thousands I had promised, we still had lived a most happy and satisfying week while walking through the waters of the Anderson Pass route across the Alaska Range.

MOUNT LOGAN

Logan is the highest mountain in Canada, reputed to be the bulkiest in the world. I only climbed that monster mountain once, about twenty-five years ago. It had been a dream since I heard about it as a schoolboy, shortly after the first ascent. I filed it away with the North and South poles as something I would attain when I grew up. Growing up involved bumping against the hard logistics of financing my way even as far as Mount Hood. The dream dimmed.

Bill Hackett's out-of-the-blue invitation to climb Mount McKinley for thirty-five dollars and its successful—despite a cost overrun—conclusion, fired me with ambition. I'd scarcely reached home when I wrote Hackett proposing we go after Logan the following year. He later claimed it was his idea, but I don't remember seeing him in the reference room of the Portland Library in the 1920s. Perhaps my letter arrived as he had a simultaneous brainstorm.

Many times in these pages I pussyfoot around about my notes, or lack of them, and quote some only to prove how vague and fuzzy-minded I am. This time I've only to drop a postcard to William D. Hackett in Portland to get a blow-by-blow account of every ounce of freight moved from Camp Five to Camp Six, and every other detail, by return mail.

One stormbound day on Logan, I overheard someone ask Bill if he'd climbed a certain mountain. "Yes," he replied instantly, "I climbed the Northeast Ridge on 30 July 1947 with Captain Earl B. Smith and Technical Sergeant Oscar P. Nielsen in seven hours and thirty-one minutes."

My mind works more like that of our fellow Logan climber Clarence LeBell, who said: "Yes, I think I climbed Mount Adams on my Northwest tour. I went with the climbing club of Seattle. Or Portland. That's the one with the beautiful reflecting lake. It's in Oregon, isn't it?" (It is in Washington.)

No, I'll not ask Hackett for his report. I doubt if anyone cares about the statistics of Logan's fourth ascent. I'll write without reference to any notes, accurate or fuzzy, and see what memory makes of a mountain that has lurked in my head for fifty years.

I trained for Logan's snows by wading up the sand hills leading to the Buttermilk pinnacles, west of Bishop. My then-regular climbing partner, Harold Klieforth, went along, and I put to him the vital question of whether Logan would ever solidify out of my childhood dreams. "Borrow the money," advised wise Klieforth. "You can pay it back, and you'll never regret it." I never regretted it, but I never forgot laboring the next winter to pay it back either.

Four of us (Jules Eichorn, Nort Benner, Dick Kauffman, and I) saw no flaw in the scheme of hauling the supplies up the long road from California in a two-wheeled trailer behind Nort's car.

We would meet the other three members (Bill Hackett, Dave Bohn, and Clarence LeBell) in Chitina, Alaska, and go the rest of the way by chartered planes.

At the Canadian border immigration inspectors were shocked at our careless stretching of their rule about importing food. To protect the interests of their countrymen's grocery stores, they permitted only two days of food for each person entering Canada. Two times four equals eight, but we had 280 man-days of food aboard! After two hours spent haggling, I smartened up enough to produce from our files a manifest of our food supplies, which showed much of the bulk of our food to be from the U.S. Army for testing on the mountain. This meant little to the officers, but they were able to find in the long list one lone can of biscuit mix from the Canadian Army. That did it. Our papers were stamped "NATO Supplies," and we passed through.

The next interruption occurred at a wayside tavern before we turned onto the long dirt road to Chitina. A congenial bartender, a fit consultant on mountain logistics, I thought, suggested a last-minute consideration: "Why don't you take the speeder?"

What a marvelous idea! I knew of the abandoned railroad that passed through Chitina and May Creek on the way to the copper mines. It seemed plausible that the rail could have been reincarnated. (This is called Olympia Beer Optimism.) I pictured our members with their gear on a little flatcar behind a gasoline-powered speeder buzzing through the black spruce and tundra without the complication of airplane logistics.

It was clearly the duty of the assistant leader to alert Major Hackett, so that he could cancel the plane contracts from Chitina to May Creek. Frantic phone calls didn't reach him at Fort Richardson. He was expected momentarily. I called at the next place and the next. The last attempt to phone created a big argument between the assistant leader, with his grand design of saving time and money by riding the rails, and his companions, who grumbled of the exhaustion of the nonstop multiday drive and sought only to reach Chitina and sleep.

My first act on arrival at Chitina was to sprint to the river to check on the railroad bridge, where I hoped to find a maintenance station complete with speeder. The remains of the bridge, one lone pier, stood drunkenly in midriver with a single rusted rail jutting up like a criticizing finger.

My friends kindly let me forget this faux pas over the ensuing twenty years. In correspondence preparing for our trip to Everest a couple of years ago, I wrote a postscript to Dick Kauffman: "If anything happens to the Kathmandu-Lukla flight, we can simply take the speeder."

A note bounced back from Dick: "Ah, yes, the speeder. Well do I remember the speeder! What a splendid sight, with Major Hackett silhouetted against the Yukon sky, epaulets gleaming, as he barked incisive orders from the command post, while work-hogs Blanchard, Eichorn, Benner, and Kauffman pumped like mad to keep the Major's date with destiny!"

We found two more members, Clarence LeBell and Dave Bohn, waiting for us in the quaint old town of Chitina, and when Hackett joined us the next morning, it was time to fly in to the mountain.

My notebook (I always have one, whatever its faults) listed two rival airplane companies. Probably their names were listed under *M* for Machines, Flying. My friends kidded me a great deal about the organization of my notebook. Although I haven't seen this notebook since the trip (maybe it didn't make it back), I do perfectly remember one entry. Listed under *O*, it read: "Olympia Beer is dispensed in Chitina by Niel Finnesen." We said good-bye to Mr. Finnesen and bundled our baggage down to the air strip. The plan was to utilize the services of both bush pilots and ride their two-passenger Piper Family Cruisers to May Creek, where Don Sheldon would relay us in to the mountain one at a time with his ski-wheel Cub. I remember saying: "Hey, Nort, let's you and I go with that one. He looks like a safe flyer." Of which more anon.

Howard Knudsen got us safely to May Creek, making only a slight detour to show us what he said were the remains of a skeleton of a man on top of a conical forested hill. I remember seeing a flash of white in the all-enveloping green as we roared by, and I've never forgotten his explanation: "Probably a prospector who climbed the hill seeking wind to get rid of mosquitoes, but they killed him anyway."

May Creek turned out to be a strip and a log cabin with a powder box nailed to it for mail for the mines at McCarthy. When Sheldon came in he acted more frantic than usual and explained that the CAA inspector was around and we must get airborne before he caught us with such a terrible overload. It was an overload all right. I had a tiny peephole on each side through which to see some of the grandest glacial scenery on the planet. Luckily I could also free one arm to reach cartons of milk Sheldon passed back to me. I hate milk and would never have thought of drinking the vile stuff, but he assured me that it would cure my sickness gotten from imbibing too much gasoline. Damn, that Sheldon is the most persuasive guy I've ever been around. Next time I'll let the pilot start his own siphon.

Of the long trudge up the mountain I retain only the vaguest memories of relay slavery and storm-racked tents. We really appreciated Hackett's Logan-model Woods tents, because we had recently heard of a mountaineer who had suffocated from snow buildup on a pup tent. It was comforting to be able to lie there and look up at the seven-foot peak and realize that we had plenty of air before we had to dig out again.

Somewhere around 17,000 feet, a couple of minor calamities provided lasting memories. Jules Eichorn fell victim to a bad strep throat, and Bill Hackett somehow carried all the stoves over the pass onto the plateau. This meant sick and weary members had to travel an unnecessary distance for shelter. The resultant quarrel was bitter and loud. Dave Bohn accused Bill of risking the safety of the party from misguided machismo, and Bill countered by accusing his party of being undermotivated. The next year the two principal disputants locked arms and marched off to K2 together, so I guess they were able to call it a normal anoxia problem.

For Jules's safety Dr. Nort Benner went down to a lower altitude with him. Dick Kauffman, Clarence LeBell, and Dave Bohn brought up more supplies, while Bill and I slogged across to the far edge of the plateau and climbed a bump on its edge. Bill made much of the fact that we had just accomplished a first ascent of the "North Peak of Mount Logan," but our heroism was a result of flailing around in a snowstorm trying to figure out where we were.

When we learned a minimum geography, the five of us boosted a camp high up an endless slope to where we hoped a day would see us to the summit. We all started out the next morning, but Hackett and I soon outran the others. We found out later they reached the same snowy summit some hours behind us.

The scene on that cloud-bound pinnacle is still etched in my mind. Bill shouted with happiness, "We did it again, Smoke!" Just then a hole in the cloud momentarily revealed a higher piece of rock very far away. "Uh, did you see that, Smoke?"

"Yes, but I'm willing to ignore it if you will."

"You know we can't do that."

Yes, I knew it. Fortunately I wasn't roped to a companion less resolute than myself. We set off.

Crossing and recrossing the deep gap separating the two summits was a big job. It was a fitting final examination for mountaineers involved with a lifetime mountain. Not only did we have to lose and regain the devil knows how much altitude, but we had to do it twice, because the way home lay back over the West Summit. And we did it with conditions icy enough to require step-cutting in poor visibility against a strong wind. In spite of, or maybe because of, these conditions, it remains the one day of the whole expedition burned into my memory. I remember the small crevasse I fell into, the clouds blowing and snowing on us, the tremor of the ax shaft as I sliced steps, the crunch of the crampons as I footed into the steps; most of all I remember the spot of sun that showed us the final steepening rise to the satisfactorily small summit, and, glory of glories, a hole in the cloud permitting a view of the Pacific Ocean! If ever a summit deserved a loud "*lik pa de lo*" (an esoteric Sherpa remark cried out when entering new villages, and lately, with the encouragement of trekkers, used also for crossing passes and reaching peaks), this one deserved such solemn and special recognition. With one voice we shouted, "Let's get the hell out of here!"

We had to shout because the wind continued to rise. Although we carried no instruments, it was obvious that the higher wind speed had chased the wind-chill factor right off the end of the card. For years I've described that weather to credulous audiences as "thirty below with a thirty-knot wind." I may have colored it a little. Anyway, color us blue, especially on the long up-go over the West Summit, on whose interminable slopes I got winded if I followed Bill fast enough to keep warm, and my poor toes, frozen in 1955, numbed if I slowed in my steps. Bill seemed to feel neither altitude nor cold, but when he realized how long and late the day had become, and how very far back to camp it was, he turned to me with just a hint of fear in his voice and said, "I've never been this far out on the hook before!"

Somehow we found the camp long after the others had assumed we'd settled for a frozen bivouac. Good old dependable Dick, hearing us shucking our crampons, got out of bed and cooked us some soup. Through the years since, I've often had the luck to be a guest of the Kauffmans at their home in Hillsborough. Dick's wife, Ellie, sets an excellent table, but never has she served anything so satisfying as Dick's Logan soup.

Only one detail of the descent remains with me. We encountered some hefty crevasses near landing camp, and, instead of enjoying them as I usually do, I became irritable with my ropemate. Maybe the stresses had caught up, for Hackett seemed to refuse to slow down to my pace. Once I stopped him and explained, "You son of a bitch, I've told you over and over I can't go that fast; the next time you speed up I'm going to yank you off your feet." I did, too. I planted my ax at his next speed-up and flipped him off his snowshoes into the soft snow.

At landing camp we were weathered in for nine days. When Don Sheldon finally came, he said it looked like a good day for landing at the base of Mount St. Elias. We'd almost forgotten St. Elias. The expedition was to be a two-mountain effort, but we'd blown nine days' food in idleness, and much of our good fellowship in orneriness. We were out of time and out of sorts, and when Hackett asked me to go with him to St. Elias as a member of a two-man team, I turned him down.

The next thing Sheldon said set us back more: "Did you hear about Howard?"

"What do you mean? We've been on this cussed mountain for a month. How could we hear any gossip?"

"Howard went in. Oh, he survived okay. Totaled the plane. He lit in a spruce tree; he was flying next day."

Sheldon never had time for small talk. "What's that garbage down-glacier?"

"Don't worry about that, Don. That's just a little cloud that's been hanging around all morning."

"It looks bad. Something's coming in. Let me have the first and second men; we'll fly them out together. Something's coming in."

Jules had drawn the short straw, but he wasn't quite ready yet, so I, being second, jumped in, and Jules climbed onto my lap. Down the glacier we roared, but we didn't seem to be lifting. I knew we had to lift off before we came to a flock of crevasses. I could see one ski, but the strain of watching it clamped to the snow was too much, so I steeled myself and gazed fixedly at the back of Jules's neck. "Now," I said to myself, and took a cautious look over the side. Still the ski slid along as if glued to the snow. Suddenly Sheldon stopped the plane and shouted for Jules to bail out. "But I'm first man," Jules protested.

"Doesn't matter. I'll get you all today. Get out. Get out!" Sheldon yelled.

Jules tumbled out and off we flew. It was another grand ride, and the grandest part about it was that while zooming down on the May Creek field we saw the once-a-week DC-3 loading there. I wouldn't have to wait for Howard Knudsen but could be in Chitina almost instantly. Don buzzed the big plane to alert them, then set me down alongside. The first thing I saw was a sight more beautiful to me than any rock or serac on the mountain. A well-dressed stewardess stood in the door. While it is true that in this imperfect world many of us endure the deprivations of single living, only prisoners, sailors, and mountaineers are locked away from even the sight of the other half of the human race. (Last January Peter Hackett walked through my house gazing fondly at his toothbrush and said, "I carried this thing and used it almost every day on that blasted Everest. It was the only thing I had to remind me there was another sex in the world.")

Sheldon got all the others out that day, and some of them talk about their flight yet. Like all subarctic bush pilots, Don was too busy to sleep in summer season. It was common for a sudden lurch of the plane to alert his passenger to shake Don awake from his latest doze. His nodding habits are still good for stories which, of course, now translate "lurch" as "thousand-foot dive."

Meanwhile Howard Knudsen drove me from the Chitina strip and told me the story of his crash. On his return home from the next flight after he dropped off Nort and me, his aileron cable parted and whirled his plane in a disintegrating fall. Howard was ejected into a tree and came crashing down from limb to limb. He was unconscious for twenty-four hours. He woke up, hobbled down to a lake, shot a fish, opened up his emergency rations, and signaled the search planes with his omnidirectional sun-reflecting tinfoil wrapper. A wheel plane dipped its wings and brought back a float plane to fly him out. Later they went in with a chopper, but the only things salvageable were the wheels.

"How come the aileron cable parted, Howard?"

"Sabotage!"

Just then he stopped the car, jumped out, and parted the brush to reveal a float plane. His wife slid over in the driver's seat to take me on to Chitina town while Howard prepared to take off.

"Aren't you afraid to let Howard go flying off like that?"

"No. We know who did it. He won't try again right away."

Since far-northern villages seemed to harbor such excitement,

Nort and Jules and I decided to tour as many of them as we could reach by car on the way home. Dick said he'd already seen a couple of thousand miles of spruce trees on the way north and had to get back to his business. Nort is fond of repeating the story of our farewell with Dick and may have touched it up a bit. According to Nort, I walked up the ramp to the plane at Anchorage with Dick and handed him a going-away present, which Dick accepted with a tear in his eye. Closing his hand on it, he tottered into the plane overcome with emotion, which may have subsided when he found his old buddy had slipped him a moose turd. Dick was a good sport about it though; he had it varnished and mounted on a tie clip to wear at Logan reunions.

I've seen Logan from sea level at Yakutat and many times from airliners, and its great size never fails to impress me and to make me recall the time we struggled to its summit. The cold monster that most epitomizes mountain majesty is labeled Mount Logan.

MOUNT ST. ELIAS

"I think Blanchard is crazy," Bradford Washburn said to Dick Kauffman. Nothing unusual in the famous mountaineer's agreement with a standard judgment. The particular aberration he complained about, though, is worthy of discussion.

Wanting my second McKinley expedition to strive for moral respectability by eschewing machine approach, I had pestered Washburn for information on walking in to the mountain from Talkeetna. My companions, however, would not even discuss adding a month to the trip to indulge in such shenanigans. I stuffed the idea deep in my brain, where it fermented through several other airborne expeditions.

It's true we walked into the Katmai, Chilkat, and Wrangell mountains rather than flying onto their sides, but my dogma dictated an approach to a really cloud-scraping peak from sea level. I still needed to go after Mount St. Elias. I was part of a 1964 expedition that had used an air landing on the glacier between Logan and St. Elias. Our plan then was to cross over the summit of Mount Newton and join the Duke of Abruzzi's route up St. Elias at Russell Col, but we reached only Newton's summit. So, in 1965, it was my goal to walk from the sea to the top of the tallest coastal mountain on earth.

I had no intention of wetting my toes in the ocean, as Seton Carr did in 1886, or I. C. Russell in 1891. It seemed legitimate to use an airplane to avoid the risk of landing from a boat in the surf, as long as the airplane transported us no farther than the beach under the mountain.

I estimated we'd need forty days to walk from the sea near Icy Bay, solve the difficulties, outwait the storms, reach the summit, and return. Right away I ran into problems recruiting people with that much time off. I settled for four who, with forty days, could await the airdrop and start to relay supplies up the mountain and four short-term men, who would come in later and join us. It sounded logical at the time.

I personally packed the mound of food. I weighed and measured minutely, and carefully layered the cellophane bags into cardboard barrels for the airdrop.

No ski-wheel planes this time. No cheating by leaping the lower difficulties. This time we'd fly across the bay, land on the beach, and attack our mountain, as though we had crawled out of the water like our remotest ancestors.

First we had to transfer from a four-motored airplane to a single-engine flying machine at Yakutat. Yakutat reminds me of one of the most fascinating stories in exploration, and I must digress to tell it.

Mount Logan was seen in 1891 by Israel C. Russell from what is now called Russell Col, at 14,500 feet on the slopes of Mount St. Elias. "I expected to see a comparatively low, forested country, stretching away to the north," he wrote. "What met my astonished gaze was a vast snow-covered region . . . broken by jagged and angular mountain peaks." He should not have been astonished. Weather permitting, Mount Logan can be seen from the coast at

Yakutat and from far out in the ocean. Vitus Bering saw Mount Logan a few days after he sailed into Controller Bay on St. Elias Day in 1741. The Indians have been watching Mount Logan from the sea for centuries.

Read what happened to Blanchard on a 1964 visit to Yakutat. His companions asked him to point out Logan. "Don't be silly, Logan was discovered from Russell Col. Uh, wait a minute. I saw the sea from the summit of Logan. Oh, there it is!"

The subject of mountain visibility, often attacked by the termites of ignorance, ambition, and prevarication, is complicated in Yakutat by clouds. Anyone who has waited out weather anywhere in coastal Alaska may be excused for imagining that Mount Logan may simply have hidden in clouds for 150 years. But Logan can be missed by the careless viewer in clear weather. Perspective and the curvature of the earth sink the giant peak low amongst a ring of closer white mountains.

So we landed at the very bottom of Mount St. Elias hard by the sea. And marched up the broad glaciers, up the tributaries, down across the Tyndall Glacier (my proudest glacier-crossing feat), and up to the ridge we'd selected for our drop site. And here came the plane on the first fair day. So fair and calm he almost handed us our freight. All the barrels and all the fuel came in perfectly. On the last pass a familiar face leaned out and grinned at us. Assistant leader Hackett dropped a note. "We've learned the route, we'll join you in a few days, no sweat, Bill."

We spent part of the week ferrying loads up a steep shale cliff. I guess it was fairly difficult. The only thing I can remember now is that when we first reached the top on reconnaissance, Roy knelt in the snow.

"What are you doing?"

"I'm thanking Jesus for getting us here."

Now I don't remember whether his fundamentalism had burred me that early on, but I do remember whirling on him and saying rather sharply, "Thank *me*, *I* got you here."

We had plenty of time to divide into liberal and conservative teams. After we got all the food and gear to the top of the wall, a great storm locked us in the tent. For the first two days wind-blast and tent-flap cancelled conversation. We whiled away the next nine days playing chess and arguing. Bob jumped on Roy's side so that democrats would not dominate. When Dave asked for a book from the tent library, Roy checked the title first. Apparently he thought hand contact with Nabokov's *Lolita* would contaminate; he pushed that one across the tent floor with his foot.

All storms end. A beautiful day lured us out to lurch upward with the first loads through deep avalanching snow to 10,500 feet. No sign of our four members below. The storm should not have stopped them down there. The next days were fair, and we knew there'd be an airplane to observe and drop a note. No plane. Our powerful binoculars revealed no sign of a trail in the snows.

"It's like we are two expeditions. They've all the power they need to take care of themselves. We are high on the mountain. Weather stable. Route visible. No problems. We've no doctor, but we have first-aid supplies. Let's go for it." So went Bob Swift's argument.

I objected. "Wait a minute. My son, Bob, was originally a member of that group. He couldn't get enough time off to come. Had he come—I'd descend. Those four men below are as related to me as my son. We go down."

Down, down, down. We trudged step by slow step down the Libby Glacier to the beach. At the first place where we could get off the snow, we tromped our hated snowshoes right through a field of moraine boulders to where a little open patch of sand gave us room for dancing and willows for fire. It was time for a ceremony.

Bob, Dave, and I soon had a bonfire hungrily devouring our wood-and-web contraptions, while our fourth member, Roy, always the frowning conservative, sulked with his snowshoes clutched to his breast. We had been four weeks outvoting Roy, though, and stirred the crackling parfleche with glee. Maddened by the flames, we took to leaping and shouting and vowing loudly never again to use such an ugly tool to contaminate the holy snow.

We jumped the crevasses, slashed through the brush, waded the creeks, and reached the sea in five days. There we found a note explaining that our valiant and hardy followers had suffered soaked sleeping bags and down clothes, and had given up and returned to Seattle! None of us had the heart to retrace our steps up the mountain.

The pilot had told us there were many oil-prospecting choppers buzzing around and that it would be fairly simple to flag one down and get a message to Yakutat. "Or," he said, "you can simply walk down to the seal camp as I did once. The Indians have a radio there." We set off down the beach on one of the most memorable coast strolls I've ever taken. Huge Kodiak grizzly tracks among stranded icebergs! After some miles, a broad, raging, ice-choked river cut off further marching.

We sent a message out by chopper, and finally a plane came for us. We flew over the river with the seal camp visible in the distance. The pilot said, "Oh, I forgot, I must have landed on this side of the river that time I walked to the seal camp." Of course. This geographic revision perfectly illustrates the rationale behind the expedition's plan. We wanted to avoid the geographical alienation of the airborne.

Flying may not keep you aware of every nuance of the terrain below, but sometimes flying can be good for tree watching. Fog lay so low over the Malaspina coast that we flew the ninety miles to Yakutat between wave top and tree top! At Yakutat Bay the pilot zoomed high so he could glide beyond the icy waters in case of engine failure. At the far shore, though, he came down below the fog again and shot through a slot in the trees made by a road. Five miles farther we broke out of the trees at thirty feet of elevation and set down on the field. A chopper pilot who observed our startling arrival exclaimed, "I didn't think your plane's wings would fit between those trees."

"I didn't either the first time I tried it."

One more reference to expeditionary personal relations. One of us proposed we repair to the airport bar to syrup our nerves. Roy refused. But they have soft drinks. No. Now, although Dave had often muttered and I had said many rude and sarcastic things about Roy, Bob had never, in a whole month, uttered a disparaging word. He turned on his stool and said to me, "Smoke, I'm going to say this once, and I'm never going to say it again. Don't you ever ask me to go anywhere with that son of a bitch again."

Climbing the tallest coastal mountain in the world directly from the seashore is a vast project. We started from the ocean and got halfway up. You could say we did a half-vast job.

Pacific Northwest

SOMETIMES it takes awhile for expeditions to gel. My Oregon and Washington coast walks took about forty years.

In grade school I read an article in the *Oregon Motorist* about a honeymooning couple who walked the length of the Oregon coast. This smoldered in my mind, underneath more glamorous ambitions that were stirred by constant reading of the geography book. In 1979 I finally completed the last of the three trips that in toto took me along the entire coast of Washington and Oregon.

I initially fell under the spell of the Great Seagull at age four, when my parents first rented a house at Seaside, Oregon, for the summer. Dad put us on the majestic stern-wheeler *Georgiana*, and we steamed down the Columbia and then took the train from Astoria. He commuted on weekends to take us beach walking. The family later switched allegiance to Oceanside, near Tillamook, where my father introduced me to sea-stack climbing. Six summers at the Boy Scout camp near Sand Lake Bay served to stir in the salt, sand, and sharp, moist air.

The idea of a long coast walk got buried so deeply I nearly forgot about it. But I always liked the sea and strolled, ever so briefly, on

Alaskan and Hawaiian beaches, on the west coast of the Pacific (Japan) and the east coast of the Atlantic (Europe), on both sides of the Mediterranean, and any other seashore my travels took me near.

I backed into my first long coast walk in 1962, when a forest fire shut down an Oregon Cascade mountain walk. I spent the remaining two weeks of vacation walking the northern Oregon coast and thought again of the *Oregon Motorist* article. I started from the Columbia River jetty and pounded down the Clatsop Spit at a terrible pace. I wanted to go as far as possible, but speeding on hard sands at low tide punished my metatarsals so badly that I soon slowed to a reasonable stride.

The next year, 1963, I sent for USGS maps and bound them into a bulky book. I was determined to walk from Canada to California. I had only two weeks walking time, but it turned out to be enough to complete a walk from Neah Bay to Ilwaco—the whole Washington coast.

The summer of 1969 gave me another chance at coast walking. I decided to start in the mountains at Stevenson, Washington, follow the mountains to the South Sister, and then aim for the coast to pick up where I'd left off in 1962.

The ideal order for walking the sea border of the Pacific Northwest is not northern Oregon coast, Washington coast, and then a Z-shaped course through western Oregon. But that is the way it turned out. Let me take things in chronological order.

OREGON'S TILLAMOOK SHORES, 1962

Only about half the length and a quarter of the time of coast walking was spent on sand. Mountains met the sea often enough to ensure that the walker was much engaged in forest forcing, brush beating, rockclimbing, surf wading, and even, if he was not careful, swimming. Swimming is not my long suit. I took care to avoid walking the water-level course at the bottom of Tillamook Head, which I remembered from childhood seaside days carried the ominous epithet "Deathtrap Cliff." While I was wondering why the trail had not widened in forty years, it disappeared altogether in a tangle of down timber. Oregon loggers call such a Douglas fir maze a blowdown. The local Indians say "whimstik." To me it was a bowl of spaghetti at a picnic, and I was the ant trying to crawl through it. Eventually I threaded my way out and picked up the trail again in a fairyland of moss and flowers that carpeted the forest floor under naturally pruned Sitka spruces.

The fair day suddenly fogged, demonstrating the dramatic change possible in Oregon weather. Great round drops plopped down from the huge ancient trees as I reached the far end of the cape. Fog below obscured all sight of the ocean, but the surf was loud in my ears as I cautiously peered over the vertical sides of the head into uprushing vapors. The boom of breakers and an eerie foghorn recalled stories of the lighthouse on Tillamook Rock. Stones of several tons were once bowled across the base of the island lighthouse ninety feet above the sea. The roof has been smashed in by a great rock flung well above its 135-foot head, and, in 1902, the keeper reported that solid water poured on the roof from 200 feet above mean sea level. Oregon has hundreds of ocean-continent battlegrounds in its 400-mile meeting with the sea. I looked forward to seeing many of them on my short, spontaneous walk.

I squished through, around, over, and under the rotten logs, and selected a small bivouac site hard by a cliff that dropped into the unseen fogbound ocean. A really fine way to begin my walk!

Much of the coast has undergone a deplorable trashing from civilization in the last four decades. Fortunately, some patches of near-wilderness still survive. The paved highway that now goes beyond Cannon Beach and follows the coastline all the way to California often isolates some undevelopable cliff when it seeks an easy route inland.

The name Hug Point, my Dad told me, commemorates a bit of trickery. Strangers, not to be outdone by the rustic locals, would try to motor beyond the road's end at Cannon Beach. Naturally, they'd pick low tide and hug the cape to avoid driving in water. At this the locals could laugh. Firm sand lay under six inches of water; quicksand hugged the point to trap city smart-alecks.

Fortunately there are only a limited number of places where cars can reach the beach. In those unhappy places it is not uncommon to see a stuck car salting into the sand. On one accessible beach near Lincoln City, I watched the frantic owner and his friends attempting to save a car caught in soft sand and threatened by the tide. I felt that he had driven into my church and that the punishment fit the crime.

At some places the walker travels inland from the highway to find peace and quiet. Where it crosses Neahkanie Mountain, the highway follows a shelf blasted on the seacliff side, but a man on foot can turn in behind the rock mountain and follow the massive hoofprints of elk through the silent forest. This way he tops the mountain high above the road on a rocky crest, with a far view down the coast. The Indians thought Neahkanie Mountain a spooky place and peopled it with gods. A Spanish ship wrecked in the surf at the base of the mountains; for decades beeswax from its cargo washed up on the Nehalem beaches. Rumors of treasure washed over the mountains and into the Portland newspapers.

I like to read about the coast and panned some nuggets from the small-town newspapers along the way. My notebook records a story illustrating the zeal of the Nehalem town fire department. A fisherman in a skiff steered his flaming outboard to the riverside dock to seek help in saving his ship. The volunteer fire department turned out in such numbers and with such elan that, jumping from the dock into the skiff, they succeeded in putting out the fire by sinking the boat under the weight of their enthusiasm.

I coasted along northern Oregon, "the land of trees, cheese, and ocean breeze," and enjoyed every ingredient of a walker's gourmet menu. Always the ocean roared at my right. Ever the land varied on my left. I reveled in the infinite variety of sand, the mirror sheen of tidal flats, the flick of wiry grass against sun-tanned legs, the wave-chased sprints around some jutting sea stack, the drifting fog. Mountain capes and water crossings provided challenge. The possibility of frequently resupplying made packing easy.

My rucksack load was elementary. As Basho says in *The Narrow Road to the Deep North*, "I threw away quite a number of things, for I believed in traveling light. There were certain things, however, I had to carry on my back—such as a raincoat, an overcoat, an inkstand, a brush, writing paper, medicine, a lunch basket— and these constituted quite a load for me. I walked along with faltering steps, giving such power as I could to my trembling knees." So I confined my load to a poncho (a crude device, suitable neither as a traveling raincloak nor as a tent, it shredded to rags as it whirled around my neck in a strong south rain squall), a minuscule pot for boiling ramen on a tiny flame of driftwood sticks between round stones, a coat for the chill of a dawn fog and long pants for same, an old and frayed sleeping bag of matted down, a small library of nature works for education, a paperback of poetry for fun, and the indispensable bread, cheese, and wine. This gear did not trouble my knees, as Basho's gear did; far from faltering, my steps were springy most of the long days. I was able to spend a comfortable night scrunched in some nest of spruce above the booming waters.

Although the seacoast offers limitless study, and although my rucksack contained the Field Book of This and That and the Gospel according to Edward Ricketts—*Between Pacific Tides*—the student in me was always a truant. I studied mainly the larger mammals that are ever present on the beach. Something about the cool strand seems to stretch the walker in people. I spoke to all who would hold still.

I caught up with a trio of nuns who were mildly amused by my comment that I had neither the feet nor the faith of my hero Hillaire Belloc. Do you remember his walk to Rome?

I found an elderly lady who directed me to the beach by a spruce and salmonberry-thorn shortcut. "It's rough, avoid the cliff, follow the elk tracks. You can probably make it. I can." She came around by car to make sure.

A real-estate agent stood by a "For Sale" sign in front of a house. A good sort, really. I tricked him into showing me the house so that I could escape by the side door and thus avoid a detour around some private property. Well, I *am* mildly interested in settling on the coast. Damn them, they built right on cliff edge, and the way around was by hard asphalt streets.

The two wood choppers I never saw. I only heard them in the forest after I had literally fallen onto a one-way dirt road from a sky of dense hemlock that camouflaged my course. The road ran perpendicular to the coast, and I needed to know which way to go to find its bend to the south. "Stand where we can see you," they advised. How could they tell which way I faced? They never could. That particular part of Oregon was so full of trees, leaves, and bushes that, although we carried on a conversation in normal voice, we were each invisible to the other.

I judged even wordless encounters interesting. An old lady who was wheelbarrowing firewood around her house tried to answer my wave with her right hand. The wheelbarrow tipped dangerously. The left did not work either, so she set the barrow down and waved with both hands.

Old lady? Yes, something about the Oregon coast seems to preserve people. The next woman I spoke to was very old. Buckets of rain poured down as I sloshed to a halt at an antique shop. She had been cleaning house and was caught by the sudden shower. I rummaged through a pile of used paperbacks soaking up water in the yard, and chose one that appealed. *Philosopher's Holiday* by Irwin Edman had "5¢" penciled on its cover. The price was right, but she wouldn't let me pay.

"That's okay," I pleaded, "I'll dry it out and 'twill be as good as new."

No, she would not sell damaged merchandise, but she would give it to me. I still wanted to buy something because she was a nice old lady. "Oh, I've always wanted to walk along the coast and if I was young like you—but I suppose being eighty-one, I'll put it off till too late now."

I told her of my sister-in-law who collected antiques, and asked
about the brass lamp. She would quote me no price and refused to
sell it to me. "If your sister-in-law knows antiques, she really
wouldn't want any of this junk I have." We spent the rest of the
visit over coffee, talking of beach walking.

It was still raining when I clumped across the old wooden bridge
at Pacific City. My eye caught a sign advertising a lumber yard and
"Books—New and Used—Bought and Sold." Ever the biblio-
phile, I hastened off the bridge and entered the store. The book
stock resolved into one moth-eaten rack of paperbacks. *The
Thirty-Nine Steps*, a murder mystery for ten cents, was the best I
could do. The lumber yard turned out to be a textbook illustration
of serendipity. Needing shelter and a bath, I took my problem to
the proprietor. The old woman, probably an Oregon-preserved
seventy, assured me that neither Pacific City nor neighboring
Woods contained hotels or motels. She summoned her assistant
(Oregon lumber yards in that rainy climate are fully enclosed)
with a robust yell and asked for housing help. Her assistant was
also a woman, sixtyish, bib-overalled, hip-booted; she allowed as
how Mrs. Gray in the grocery might have a room to rent. Arrangements were made over the phone. At one point the proprietor
rocked back on her broken-wheeled swivel chair, the better to take
a long look at me before counseling the unseen Mrs. Gray, "Yes,
he seems like a nice young man."

Mr. Gray took me upstairs above the grocery to the third floor.
The second floor had two bathrooms. One was reserved for the
permanent renters of the other room, and he hoped I'd use the
spare bath. Rent would be three bucks. Even in 1962 I could not
quarrel with that price. True, the furnishings were a little spartan:
single cot with one blanket and no sheets, one straight-backed
wooden chair, twelve buckets of assorted agates and shells. I had
to violate the agreement on the bath, though. My tub was one-
eighth full of sand. I sneaked into the other bathroom and used my
pliers to turn on the water when the faucet handle fell off.

Inflation and tourist rip-off had not yet hit the Oregon coast.

Bed-and-board bargains were matched by the reasonable price of boating. When I arrived on the shore of Netarts Bay, also in pouring rain, I was invited into the house of a boatman. A stripling of sixty-five, he had once done some walking near the Three Sisters Peaks and fed me a sumptuous meal in return for tales of mountain climbing. He would have had me stay overnight, but it was only two o'clock, so I asked for a ride across the bay. To do this he had to fetch the gasoline, a pair of oars, life jackets, a funnel, and a filter from a boat house above high-tide line. Next he had to transfer all this to a small boat and row out to where the larger boat tugged at its anchor. Transferring from one boat to the other was dangerous enough to require a belly crawl in the bouncing chop. Then he had to fire up the outboard of the bigger boat and drive in to shore to pick me up. Naturally, most of these maneuvers would have to be reversed on his return journey. The fee for this service was fifty cents!

Many of the small anecdotes relating to people along the coast have faded from the rotting canvas of my memory, but one I should detail. I found myself forced inland by some bay or headland and then beelined back toward the sound of the "old roarer," as I personified the ocean. While shortcutting across a golf course, my flashing legs attracted the attention of a middle-aged golfing woman similarly clad in shorts. She hailed me with, "I see you like to walk. I also like to walk."

It seemed unlikely. She was large and a bit heavy. But I fell in with it and confessed, "I like to climb mountains too."

"Well, then, you must know Billy Hackett!"

Yes, I did know Billy Hackett. Bill Hackett, the brash high school youth, whose black mustache quivered in the rear view mirror as he wrestled with the other half of our double date in the back seat. Major William D. Hackett, special advisor to the Army Quartermaster on mountain and cold-weather equipment. Hackett of McKinley, Aconcagua, Kenya, and K2, Herzog's companion on Mont Blanc. My climbing partner of the instant belay when Naydene screamed backward off the wall of the South Chamber

Route. The harsh, military, inhuman demon of the fight with Dave Bohn at Camp Five. The friend of the solemn handshake of solidarity as we stood in wind and cold on the summit of Logan. The veteran of so many mountain escapades that touched my own ventures at so many points. Yes, I knew him.

Why should this golfer on the coast of Oregon assume that my love for climbing would automatically include an acquaintance with Billy Hackett? Could his swollen ego convince a golfing woman that he was a hero known to all? No, but his mother could. The golfer lived across the street from Bill's doting ma, who spent her widowed years at Taft, just down the beach a bit.

Near the end of the walk, while bivouacked in sand dunes some distance from a small town, I had an encounter with a four-legged mammal. I'd awakened at dawn, but before I could open my eyes, I felt something wrong. Then I saw the underside of a large animal standing directly over me! Just then the big boxer licked me full in the face. It took a second to collect my thoughts and realize that I was not going to be eaten. Now how do you suppose that dog sensed that I harbored a boxer just like her, along with a litter of pups, at home in Bishop?

Time ran out. I had to return to the trucks. I drove a stake into the sand of Neptune Beach at Cape Perpetua and swore to return.

Tillamook is the common name for the north coastal region, its Indian tribe, biggest bay, and principal city. I have read that the first settler, Joe Champion, who lived in a hollow spruce tree in 1851, corrupted the native name from Killamook. Ever since, I've thought of this area as the "cool Killamook country." When this oceanshore dance culminated in the walking of the entire two-state seaside, I retitled the north Oregon slide show "The Killamook Cakewalk."

WASHINGTON COAST, 1963

The original plan for the 1963 walk included three couples: Vi and me, Jack and Dottie Henry, Bill and Hildagard Hackett. Since both Jack and Bill had been with me in the Yukon and Alaska and both lived in the Northwest, they were natural choices. Somehow our schedules did not match, and Bill Hackett and Dottie Henry had to drop out. Hildagard had only recently married the famous mountaineer and still ranked as a tenderfoot. Her only beach experience had been on the French Riviera, and she had never carried her own rucksack. "Don't worry about it," we told her, "we've a special easy-carrying rucksack for you called a Kelty."

I will skip over the annoyance of the split pistons in the brand-new car fifty miles out of Port Angeles and ignore other routine matters. Imagine the four of us launched on our expedition, straggling along the beach, packboards groaning with supplies for a week, including stoves and half-gallon glass jugs of wine.

The northern coast of Washington is full of rocks, tide pools, cliffs, headlands, and all the good things. Incursions inland were fraught with ferns, logs, trees, brush, swamps, streams, and assorted hazards that made us feel like four Stanleys in the Congo.

Jack and I forged ahead of our companions, rounded a bend, and stumbled upon a cove crowded with three bears dining on a beached whale. The three crashed a few feet into the forest and clambered up separate trees where they could observe both the whale and the new menu.

I looked at Goldilocks, and he looked at me and asked, "Do you want that whale, Smoke?"

"No, Jack, let's leave it for the bears and get out of here."

I don't remember how the women got past this hazard, but I am sure they arrived safely in camp that evening, where we holed up very late in the day on a tent-sized patch of sand under a cliff. Sometime after supper Vi managed to unrelax us with her theory that, since we had only ten feet of leeway between us and the cliff, since the tide was coming in, since the full moon promised higher than usual water, and since the recent Chilean earthquake had produced *tsunamis*, we stood an excellent chance of drowning in our sleeping bags. We decided to sit up by the fire until the midnight turn of the tide, the better to make a break for safety by springing for handholds on the cliff if the ocean attacked us. Five minutes before midnight, the fire went out as if someone had thrown the switch, and indeed old Neptune had. In the twelve-inch space between wet fire logs and oceanside tent peg, the tide turned. An hour later we were sound asleep.

The next night the tent blew down. It was the start of a four-day storm that wetted and chilled us and dampened our Riviera member's spirit to the nadir. At each moan Jack and I once more propounded the official expedition motto: "It doesn't make any difference."

I guess it came near to making the difference between life and death. As Jack told it to me later, he thought Hildagard came close to getting zapped by hypothermia. The two of them were a mile or more ahead when they came to the spit across from LaPush. They were soaked to the skin in wind and cold, and Jack thought the situation dangerous enough to wave in a passing Coast Guard cutter. Vi and I struck a bargain with an Indian to help him pull herring out of his net in return for a ride, and we arrived via dugout canoe to join Jack and Hildagard in the squishy, clothes-dripping, mold-smelling, wood-stove-heated shelter of a motel cabin in downtown LaPush.

The girls had had enough and deserted us to retrieve the car by bus. Jack pushed on with me for a couple of days. I remember a delightful change from gloomy, wet spruce forest to sunlit hemlock dales, some skittery rockclimbing around a point, and a rather disgraceful pathfinding faux pas. Somewhere in a mist-wrapped vale of the Hoh rain forest, we whooped with joy at finding the key to a current confusion.

"Look, Jack," I crowed, "there are tracks; we're on the right way!"

"Yeah," said Jack studiously. "Uh, say, Smoke, let's just try those tracks for size."

I can't remember now whether we approached those exact-fitting marks from left or right, but it must have had something to do with fog and the Coreolis effect. I swear that we had long since disposed of the alcohol.

Jack's wife, Dottie, later joined me for a day, and then the whole gang deserted, leaving me to a solo venture on to the Columbia River. Southern Washington is not nearly so wild or interesting as the Olympic strip, but my trip had its moments. One of the lesser wildernesses is contained in the Quinault Indian Reservation. I was able to get permission to cross this outpost of Native America through a letter of introduction to the assistant chief, whose wife oncce belonged to the Mazama Club. She gave me valuable assistance in directions: "This black forest tunnel is the trail to our clam beach; you'll have to crawl quite a ways, and then you'll come to a set of steps we cut down the sandstone cliff. If my husband were home he could tell you the names to call out when you come to the shore of the Quinault to get a ride across to Taholah."

I emerged on all fours, descended the footholds, waded around a couple of points, and escaped from a jungle onto the deserted north bank of the Quinault, opposite the Indian town of Taholah. There wasn't a hope of shouting that distance, with or without names. In a little more than an hour, a rowboat came with two small Indian lads.

"Hello, boys, what are you doing?"

"Looking for you!"

Some sharp eye had seen me standing on the beach, and, reckoning anyone appearing on the lonely shore needed a ride, had dispatched the boys to ferry me. Taking care to wait till we were nearly across, I asked the captain if I could row. I hadn't propelled a vessel that way in twenty years—it should be fun. It wasn't. While we swept frighteningly seaward, I grabbed one oar in both hands and strained to the job; we bumped a salmon-net pole and luckily lurched onto the shore. After I had paid off the crew, they oared upstream as if powered by Evinrude, with the faintest of smiles on their stoic faces. All the small nuisances seemed to resolve themselves at the last minute on my saunter southward.

At Point Grenville I wasted so much time looking for the bottle that Juan Bodega y Quadra and Don Bruno Heceta had left as evidence of their claim to Washington that I was nearly caught by the tide. I hurled my own bottled note into the sea. I felt no betrayal of my Sierra Club anti-litter oath because, along with my penciled "Help, I'm trapped beneath unclimbable precipices!", I added figures on latitude, longitude, date, time, and tide. The Hydrographic Office likes to know these things and would never class my empty claret container as trash. I wasted almost too much time and had to hurry at an unseemly pace with many a fearful glance at water and cliff, whistling like Ulysses sailing between Scylla and Charybdis.

Approaching Gray's Harbor, one of the major water-crossing problems, I ran into a monstrous resort complex abuilding in a waste of sand dunes. Upon inquiry I was told to get on down to the new boat dock because the daily ship to Westport left at two. Since it was then one, I naturally asked how I could be expected to go five miles in one hour.

"Take a taxi."

"But I'm walking."

"Yes, take a taxi."

As you can see, this chitchat could just as well have been carried on in Urdu. I arrived at the boat dock somewhat late, my land speed being less than five miles per hour. Here I found a great ship, but alas it was fast ashore. In fact, the dang thing was a hotel! A hole had been cleverly cut in the side. I tripped out to the entrance on a plank walk and rooted out a room clerk who listened more sympathetically to my problem. He was more than sympathetic, he was miraculous. He must have had a direct pipeline to the Great Seagull, because he produced a thirty-foot ship that was on the point of sailing for the boatyard in Westport and would take me immediately and for nothing. The fly in this gravy clamored for attention as soon as we got beyond swimming-back distance. The captain was having engine trouble. That was what necessitated the quick trip to the boatyard sans passengers and crew except for his twelve-year-old son. Sonny steered fine on the crest while papa worked head-down in the aft engine hatch, but in the troughs it was obvious even to a landlubber that the kid couldn't keep her bows-on. The old man kept rushing from wheelhouse to engine room, while I cowered in the cabin dodging my pack, which flew across the room with each sea.

Just as Mark Twain's mother said: "One who is born to be hanged is safe in water." Again I escaped the clutches of fate.

Willapa Bay was anticlimactic after such a show of the power of the sea, but it took me awhile to sort out a ride. For a time I thought I had the Coast Guard talked into hauling me, but when they radioed inland for authorization, their superior answered, "Negative!"

Back in the waterfront café, I told my sad tale to anyone who would listen. It is eighty miles around this body of water. Eighty miles more than I felt like walking. I began to notice that a salty type down at one end of the bar had been surreptitiously surveying me all this time, and at length he sidled up and said, "I'll take you. Sail with the tide at dawn. Cost you ten bucks."

"Okay, I'll be here." I could be laconic too.

Next morning I stood beside the stocking-capped, pea-coated oysterman as he chugged through a pea souper. "All my life in Tokeland. Good place. Tried Seattle once. Too hot and dusty."

His lifetime in the gray mists of Willapa Bay paid off, and by some kind of magic he found the other shore and put me down where I could again proceed on dry land.

In lower Ilwaco I asked a riverside idler, "If you had started walking from Neah Bay and intended to walk all the way to Oregon, would you consider this far enough?"

"The Oregon boundary is right out there in the middle of the river. All the way, huh?"

WESTERN OREGON WALK, 1969

Su and I abbreviated the title of this trip to "WOW," which may hint at an explanation to the six-year gap in my coast ramblings. Changing mates puts the walker off stride.

Without Su, I could never have completed the coast walking in such style. She provided the logistics that enabled me to ease through mountains and valleys on a long detour to reach Cape Perpetua, where I continued my seashore stroll. Oregon's many backwoods roads made resupply simple. While waiting for me to come walking into their forest-lake camps, the children paddled their folding canoe, safely moored to Su's reading chair.

Logically, I should have started again at the mouth of the Columbia or even (I had the time this year) at Neah Bay. However, the mountains sang louder than the sea. I started at Stevenson, Washington, just across the Columbia River from Cascade Locks, where so many of my adolescent adventures began. This old base camp, which had served for exploring Mount Defiance, Benson Plateau, Greenleaf Peak, Wooly Horn Ridge, Wahtum Lake, and Mount Hood, made a fitting launch pad for re-acquaintance with western Oregon.

Herman Creek used to be the popular route up into the hills, but I chose Eagle Creek so that Su and her children, Lorelle and Glen, could walk two miles up with me and enjoy some of this spectacular canyon. Modern civilization has treated the trail lightly, only adding a guardrail or two and a couple of new bridges. A campsite we used to like because an old fire scar let sunlight through to berry bushes had been reseeded. Now a fair Douglas fir forest shades the campground. Fifty years can make a big difference.

Notebooks! Is there no way to keep them from tailing off into half-legible abbreviations with three-quarters of the pages blank? My now-and-then notebook describes the day up Eagle Creek and over the ridge to Lost Lake this way: "wrong trl, fog, bk to trl again, rain, Su's camp Lost Lk 2105." This number signifies nine P.M., dark. Sounds like I got lost on the way to Lost Lake. Fog and rain, often disagreeable at the time, have a way of falling out of the memory. I'm surprised now how often this kind of weather drifted or spattered into the notes.

My nephew Jim Blanchard met me for the Hood climb. Jim had also been with me in Alaska, and thereby hangs a tale. On the way north in '61, Vi, Bobby, and I stopped at my brother's house in

Portland. On a sudden impulse, I asked my brother, Bob, if his son could go along with us to wait in Talkeetna while I climbed McKinley. Absolutely not! Jim was a scholar; great things lay ahead of him; mountain climbers would ruin him; he'd turn into a bum like his uncle. But such an opportunity: a free vacation in Alaska, maybe his last chance for adventure. The two boys got on well. I'd get them a job, keep them away from the mountaineers (those no-account doctors, music professors, chemical plant managers). I won. I took Jim along, kept him away from the above-mentioned ne'er-do-wells, and got the boys jobs working for Don Sheldon on his new hangar. My brother lost. Jim came back, dropped out, and tuned in to the mountains. Twenty years into an extraordinary mountain career, he's highly respected, happy. I think Jim won too.

The notes on the Hood climb indicate snow firm, crevasse bridge weak, clouds puffy, wind light, Columbia River visible. Most important, they comment: "Summit warm in sun, stay two hours eating and talking." Of nearly a hundred Hoods, this one sounds as successful as any, for everyone knows that a chief concern in climbing is to keep the adrenalin levels low.

Between the big volcanoes the Oregon Cascades exhibit little relief. Roads snake everywhere. Monstrous powerline slashes scar ugly avenues straight through once-beautiful forests. Logging on the lower slopes has forced the Forest Service to relocate much of the old Skyline Trail. This makes for better scenery than the 1930s route, although multiple-use forest pollution often creeps so close to the crest that frequent signs read: "Roadhead one mile." Su found that ideal campgrounds on placid lakes made perfect playpens for the kiddies. I particularly enjoyed the brush-free wandering in open ponderosa forests east of the crest. I typically became too carefree a time or two and had to search for the trail.

Joanne French (Joanne French Toast, the kiddies called her) joined me for Mount Jefferson. Another old Alaska buddy, Jack Henry, brought two of his friends, so we totaled five climbers camped under Oregon's second peak. I suggested climbing the

East Face and descending by the North Face, as Hubert and I had, but got shouted down. Jack proclaimed himself captain, the route preselected, and no argument permissible. I probably couldn't have remembered our 1936 route anyhow, but I did think one A.M. an uncivilized starting time. It turned out the southeast route needs that much time to spiral around the mountain and avoid all difficulties.

As we ate lunch on the narrow summit in calm weather, I couldn't help thinking about another Mount Jefferson lunch I read about. I think about it every time I climb or walk a narrow crest in wind. I want you to do the same. According to the newspaper article, two brothers sat at lunch atop Mount Jefferson's pinnacle. One man turned to offer the other a peanut butter sandwich. His brother was gone. Blown over the cliff.

The descent I remember for some fun glissading around easy crevasses. I also remember the bell. We'd overtaken a Mazama party with one member carrying a small bell attached to his pack.

The second time I ever saw a bell on a pack, I ripped it from the rucksack of a passenger on one of my Nepal trips. He said he always carried it to alleviate the silence of the hills! I can scarcely think of any greater sacrilege. Like the victim of a coughing fit in a symphony, these sick people should be firmly escorted out the door of our mountain hall. It may be one more instance of my being out of step. Now I find Eiko Company, rot their souls, making mountain-cap badges in Japan complete with bells.

Hong Kong Chinese undoubtedly carry off the noise pollution prize. Exuberant teen-agers sallying forth on school holiday grate the auditory nerves with high-pitched nine-toned Cantonese giggling, but when the freedom of the hills urges them to turn up the volume on their suitcase radios—enough said. If you see bands of youngsters bounding off the ferry bearing bundles of wicked-looking oversized barbecue forks, pick another path. The custom is for a party of thirty hikers to carry five large radios tuned to five different loud stations. I wish to retract my snarl at the bell bearer that day on Mount Jefferson. When I'm vacationing at school's-out time in Hong Kong, I'd be happy to meet, on a New Territories trail, a whole herd of Mazama Clubbers fully fitted with pack bells.

I first climbed Three-Fingered Jack the year I turned twenty-one. Somehow it's grown steeper, a common habit of mountains. Luckily I had a good crew to help me. Sylvia Kershaw joined Joanne to walk a week with me. Sylvia looks the part of a rugged mountaineer, with her stub pipe clenched tight under her alpine hat. Since she stands less than five feet tall, she is, as they say, short on one end. Legendary John Salathé trusted her climbing. When she was in fine form he let her lead and, trusting his belay and her skill, she put in no protection. At the completion of the pitch she was startled to hear John's voice at her heel. "Dot vas a goot lead, Sylbia," he congratulated her, having followed her up without bothering to belay.

Sylvia not only marched through the Japan Alps with me, she bought a ticket for Glen and Lorelle also. The kids scampered to the head of the line every day, while I had to search the rear for Sylvia. "Damn it, Smoke, you know me better than that; don't you wait around for me. You know I'm always slow, but I'll get there eventually." She almost didn't. We found her hobbling toward Nishi-dake with a bent ankle that later turned out to be a hairline fracture.

Joanne also came to Japan. I suggested as strongly as I could that, for the unusually rough course we chose in 1981, she equip herself at least with a walking stick. "When you can climb as well as I, you need no aid for balance," she said, and proved it.

I brag of the prowess of my friends to explain how I got up Three-Fingered Jack. The notebook is no help, saying only (filling in the abbreviations): "rope-up, slings, chimney, top, rappel down, lunch, other rappel." I remember "The Jack" as the peak with the flying ants on top.

I'm going to quote once more from that so-called notebook and then give it the old heave-ho. It's not only near useless; it has begun to tattle on me. The entry headed "Lava Lake Camp" shows unusually bad handwriting. The squiggles look like mine all right, but they're large and angular. The last sentences read: "They've all gone. My cup is empty. I sit here alone with the pine trees, the lake, a few clouds, and two hummingbirds, trying to review my first nineteen days on the trip and plot my course in the Sisters Mountains. I love Su, Lorelle, Glen, Joanne, and Sylvia. And while I'm at it, I must say I love all the rest of the animals on the planet, including my country's official enemies in Vietnam." Shocking! I've almost forgotten that wine used to be a standard provision on my mountain trips.

Mountain records sometimes jar recollections of affairs outside of our special world. The entry I found in the summit register book on the North Sister echoed my sentiments. Some climber said he spent the night on that rather small rocky point "in order to watch the full moon once more before man sets his cruddy foot on it."

Outdoor people often frown at technological breakthroughs that others acclaim. I remember trekking in Nepal when members talked about the moon landings. Bertram Gale Dick, a trekker from "darkest Utah," defended the moon efforts this way: "Rich and powerful nations will spend their resources on projects mischievous or frivolous, so . . ."

The Three Sisters are such fine mountains. Long ago we used to sneer at them as peaks for the underprivileged who didn't live in Portland near Mount Hood. It was sour grapes. We couldn't afford to go anywhere else. I had forgotten how much wilderness surrounds these volcanoes. I'm glad I remember the view down the steep East Face of the Middle Sister, because Jim Blanchard called me yesterday bubbling about how he'd skied wide open down it. His father should be proud of him now.

I enjoyed the South Sister most. So many old memories hung around it. One summiteer testifies in the register book: "This is the finest view in the world or anyway that I have sean." I have "sean" many, and I say it must rank among the world's best. (Of course, grading mountain views, if one were to undertake such a

foolish exercise, would depend greatly on subjective feelings.)
Eastward, an airplanelike perspective of central Oregon disclosed
towns where I'd once lived. The long north-south file of volcanoes
gleamed with friends from Rainier to Shasta. Westward, I recognized Mary's Peak (1936, East Face) and my route to the coast. To
the southeast, the lake-dotted pine forest hid a ranch where I went
to work as a real teamster, driving hay-hauling horses, when I ran
out of money on a Depression-era Skyline Trail trip. Best of all,
almost directly underneath the summit of the South Sister, in
Devil's Lake Campground, Su, Glen, and Lorelle waited to spend
a day off with me.

The Cascade Range, where I left it, plunges satisfactorily down
to the Willamette Valley. On my cross-California walk, I was dis-
appointed by the way the Sierra tapers so gradually into the flat-
lands. Oregon offered a decently steep transition from mountain
ridge to valley floor. I've often wondered why I missed Eugene. It
couldn't have been because it's too big; my favorite city is Tokyo!
I suppose that, as a beeline from the South Sister to Cape Perpetua
passes north of Eugene, I decided a visit to that interesting city
would have pounded my feet on too much highway pavement.
Junction City, though, is *not* my favorite.

I've always liked the Oregon Coast Range, although it's the least
alpine of any mountain chain I've ever had anything to do with. In
the Boy Scouts we used to ride horses over Mount Hebo, sometimes visiting funky farms so far back in the brush that they had
no road access at all. Freight—disassembled hay-field machinery
and canned goods inbound, mink fur and chittum bark out-
bound—traveled entirely by packtrain via narrow trail and frequent river fords. Until the CCC road construction in the 1930s,
some towns in southwestern Oregon could not be reached by
wheeled vehicles.

At Cape Perpetua the Coast Range drops directly into the sea. I
balanced my bivouac on a ridge-crest elk trail aimed at the ocean.
Four elk, bounding seaward at dawn, slammed on the brakes and
skidded to a surprised stop only inches from me. I also was sur-

prised. Just beyond the Devil's Churn at Neptune Beach, I found a reasonable facsimile of the stake I'd driven in 1962. The writing on the paper fluttering from a cleft in its top read: "We've gone for a walk on the sand. Su and kids."

There is no way I could have done justice to all the glories of the southern Oregon coast in less than a century. Some day I must return with full mountain gear to explore some quarter-mile-long beaches I bypassed. It would take a rappel descent and a piton-assisted climb up the opposite wall. Cliffs, dunes, bays, rivers, forested mountains, grass-covered mountains—the south coast parades all the manifold environments of the continent's edge.

Two scenes are still bright in my mind's eye. Shortly after a 3:00 A.M. start, necessary to catch a boat across the Umpqua, I walked among high sand dunes in pitch darkness. Suddenly a star gleamed almost underfoot! The pinpoint light, reflected in a small pond, kept me from blundering into the water. Fighting the toughest brush battle of my life on Seven Devil Mountain, I'd become almost used to being suspended far from earth on slender swaying branches as I bulldozed my way near a cliff. Once the lacing under me thinned, so I glanced down to judge my height above the ground and saw the sea!

One morning, I woke in wind-swept bivouac on a grassy cliff, with the somewhat sad realization that the trip would soon end. I had only a day's walk left. To make sure that there would be no shortchanging at the end, I walked a few miles into California, until I came to the Smith River. To ensure that I really reached the river, I waded right out into the middle, clothes and all. The fifty-one days and approximately 600 miles of the Western Oregon Walk was finished, and my feet had finally touched all of the Pacific shore of the Northwest.

7

Bishop

S U

Cleaning out the files the other day, I ran across a seed that ultimately grew into the partnership between Su and me. It was a postscript to a letter from my old expeditionary friend Jack Henry. His wife, Dottie, wrote: "Jack forgot to mention in his letter a newcomer to Bishop, who is an acquaintance from our rockclimbing section of the Sierra Club. It's Su Ahlstrom at 336 Hanby Avenue. She's the widow of Myron Ahlstrom and has two small children. Perhaps you could say hello for us sometime." Yeah, sometime. I couldn't be bothered right then. I was too busy hauling propane and acting as company dispatcher. I threw the note on a pile of unpaid bills and forgot about it.

Two days later I got lonesome and looked up the note to see if the address was easily found. Three-thirty-six Hanby was a block away. It turned out to be an old house I'd once lived in myself, and there was a pigtailed woman in the front yard raking the leaves around a small disaster area of kiddie garbage and two dirty-faced toddlers. I stopped and jabbered a bit, suggesting she ought to drop around to the local Sierra Club meeting. "It's at the high school. You can find it. It's a small town."

I took one lonesome rumble down the road and was back cautioning, "I'd better show you the way to the high school; it's pretty hard to find." Soon I was courting her by bringing around chunks of stove wood. We would sit stiff with cold, side by side on the creaky old settee, primly looking at mountain picture books before the lukewarm stove. My home was warm and comfortable and filled with books and music, but I needed company. More and more I'd walk the block down Willow Street, with fuel from my fireplace stores under my arm, to call on the widow Ahlstrom. At about this time I finished composing the following highway verse:

> All down the road
> My heart's a load
> My skull's a gong
> Keeps clanging how long
> How long, how long
> Till I'm there with you
> Oh Susie Susie Susie Q.

I gave her number to drivers who needed to find me for dispatch orders. The predawn alarm bell still awakened me on Willow, though. After all, I was committed to my plans for five months of foreign mountains.

Su, her mother, and the kids gave me a bon voyage party in the Buttermilk pinnacles, near Bishop. Over hamburgers and beer, Su argued, "I think you are spending too much time on the big island and not devoting enough time to Maui."

"If you're so all-fired informed on Hawaiian geography, why don't you come with me?"

"You haven't invited me."

"Well, I'm inviting you now."

"You're leaving for San Francisco tomorrow. I haven't a ticket or reservations."

"That's your problem. There are telephones."

"What about expenses?"

"We'll camp out. Let's go back to my house and rummage around in that old expedition food I brought back from Alaska."

We found ten days' worth of freeze-dried groceries. We divided it in half for the purposes of luggage weight, and I was off in the morning, with no time to help Su with logistics.

All expeditions must exit from the City—so many good friends in the Bay Area. Reminds me of Basho's: "I was invited to parties on a boat, at my friends' houses, or even at my own hermitage. I became used to the pomp and splendour of feasting, unawares, and I almost fell victim to the illusion that a man of importance was going on a journey."

Su was still on stand-by when they called the plane. She just made it, seated in another section.

"Su! Here we are in Honolulu. Wasn't the champagne wonderful?"

"They don't serve it in economy class."

It was a great trip. We tromped up and down a lot of loose volcanic cinders, oohed and aahed through some fairly fierce jungles, made all kinds of bumbles and blunders, muddled up some mountains, and talked a blue streak all the way down the leafy trails.

Loneliness was no problem for me while sorting out mountaineering maneuvers from Japan to Europe. But when my old climbing partner Dick Kauffman met me for a month's climbing in the Alps, I was soon to see the light. Dick had brought Ellie Grambergu (later to become Mrs. Kauffman) along to help with our milder walks, and, although she was absent with leave when Dick and I lunched atop Mont Blanc and may have missed battles on Somethingspitz and Whatsitshorn, she always showed a light in the window when we returned valleyward.

I began to think of the pigtailed companion I walked with in Hawaii. I phoned Su from Washington, D.C., asking her to meet me in Seattle. And proposed marriage to her as we sat on the summit of Mount Hood.

THE FOOL'S NEEDLE

"I thought you said you'd been up this peak before?"

This is about the most embarrassing question a guide has to parry. "Well," I say, "that was a long time ago. I've forgotten the route; it must be around here somewhere."

I rationalize, to myself, that the *plasmodium falciparum* malaria, contracted in Kenya in 1973, snapped the brain-cell neuron connections that I'd wired to remember handholds. Besides, the Sierra Nevada fault block still actively tilts. I'm getting stupider, the mountains are getting steeper, and I've only to go out climbing to prove it.

Regardless of what may or may not have happened to my brain, there are many peaks near Bishop I will not forget. One of the peaks whose routes I can remember with perfect clarity is our local Aiguille du Fou.

Thinking of it reminds me of an old mountain-walking companion, Bill Fettkether, whom I found in the local camera shop. Bill was one of the pokiest walkers ever. His mountain expertise was complicated by a total lack of athletic ability, a high regard for comfort, and a body adapted to cushions. On top of all this, he liked to travel with a large view camera. The result of these defects caused some late stumbling down dark canyons, lit sometimes by moon, sometimes by stars, many times with homemade tin-can lanterns, fancy imported folding candle lights, flashlights without number (often without function at critical moments), and, on one memorable descent of our Aiguille du Fou, by the flickering, faithless light of a book of paper matches.

My writing about these things must offer clues to the undiscovered country of my character. I enjoyed climbing McKinley and Moran and Logan and Lamjura and Mount Fuji and Mont Blanc and K2 and Everest (some of these are imaginary feats), and I enjoyed traveling with Sir So-and-So. But I also like to climb Mount No-Name with a Fettkether, who though creaky on crevasse crossings is a delightful fellow withal and turned out to be a fine downhill skier. Perhaps I am more able to identify with the underdog barking quietly in the lowest echelons of climbing heroes or standing mutely in some sagebrush outback. Another strange turn to this climber's brain is my preference for repeating the same peak or route or experience over and over. I told my wife that this trait keeps me monogamous. Told all of them—mostly it works.

The more I review my career in the local mountains, the stranger it seems. Without conscious planning, I seem to have concentrated on a quite limited area. This is brought to my forebrain occasionally when people ask me for information on Mount Farback or Well-Known-but-off-Blanchard's-Track Peak, and I realize with a start that I've never climbed it. The Palisades have been the main theater of my mountain activities during my years in Bishop and even when my Sierra expeditions originated in Government Camp, Oregon. My routes above Big Pine must be almost as varied as those of all-time champion Palisade Mountain explorers Norman Clyde and Don Jensen. Most of the trips above Bishop that did not sag into the lower and oh-so-accessible Buttermilk ended up in Piute Canyon or Pine Creek Canyon, and most of these trips attacked the cliffs of my own Aiguille du Fou, or Gunsight Peak, or the larger and lesser pinnacles on Scheelite Cliffs, or Wheeler Wall. Here there are named, nicknamed, and unnamed peaks, pinnacles, cliffs, and ledges that have known my boots in every season and with such frequency that I can actually find my way about.

The Aiguille du Fou is a name I hung on a granite spire of Piute Canyon, after a famous peak in France, because the name translates to "Fool's Needle." I never got any closer to the original Fool's Needle in France than the Aiguille du Midi, but I've managed to clamber up its namesake so many times I haven't fingers and toes to count them.

Why don't you come along with Bill Fettkether, my son Bob, and me? Bob's been up this route regularly since he was six, so we have two pathfinders. We start up the Piute Pass Trail with a pleasant half-hour stroll through cool and beautiful forest. This forest, incidentally, harbors six red-fir trees that leaked south out of their normal range. The route then crosses a stream and chugs up a hill of birch and willow that holds no man-trail, but shelters all sorts of other animals. We follow a deer trail alongside springs and through hidden mini-meadows with flowers—altogether a most delightful short ramble.

Before we reach the cliff, *roches moutonées* (ice-rounded bedrocks) stop us so we can inspect them for glacier grooves and chatter marks. In early season, a patch of snow justifies carrying that favorite instrument, the ice ax. The whole thing turns into an alpine outing if we can cut a couple of steps, or a hundred, up some steepening snow tongue and swing the ax around on the descent to tripod a swishing glissade.

Now we mount a ledge. It measures a foot in width, but, if you happen to be a photographer like Fettkether, with a black-cloth monster-tripodded view camera, Bob and I will uncoil our 120-foot nylon line and tie you in. It is possible to fall off, and on the next pitch or two this possibility is sobering to contemplate.

The route in general goes up a sharp rib, which twists into a wild spire of red granite. Then a calm little perch of quartz. Next a shaggy cliff of clothes-tearing crystals, leading, after one squeezes up a short chimney, back to a three-inch-wide ridge crest, just before the crazy edge springs up in a scary green pinnacle with a clutter of large and loose head-knocking debris lying about its sloping top.

Next comes a dark red crest, which combines the right-sized holds with narrowness to provide a charge but not a fright. And here is lunch ledge, one of the finest. The eye sweeps down over multicolored cliffs to green meadows and past the scarlet Piute Crags to the dim and dusty valley ten thousand feet below. It is an old, traditional lunch spot, where Bob and I serve the nuts and cheese, French bread and white wine (red we save for the summit).

Now we move up a couple of hundred feet of dull talus blocks to help the digestion, and then we come to dessert. Dessert is a great tilted slab and acrobatics—a swing out around the newly sharpened edge, where a three-inch ledge hangs over a thousand feet of air. Great for pictures but not difficult, nothing a novice can't do on this whole climb. But the new climber is never sure it will not be hard.

Then a six-inch ledge, not so exposed, goes around a corner that leans over a couloir a hundred feet below. Although wider, this ledge lacks handholds, and a waist-high bulge midway along makes sucking in the gut essential.

Now the gully has come up to our level. We stretch across it and mount a small rib. Rib sides begin to drop rapidly and leave us perched on a pulpit facing a mantel maneuver. Take-off foot steps are quite adequate, but one can't help glancing left and right and wondering whether, if the manteling doesn't quite succeed, the return to the landing will feel secure. These considerations weaken the resolve in the knee springs, and usually it takes a second try to sort out spring, hand and arm placements, balance, and nerve.

Above the mantel we must recross the gully by an even more acrobatic maneuver. Indeed, things are "cresting up" now. I invented this crude term when I noticed Sierran ridges doing rude things to me near their crests. Some law of geology or mountain perversity must decree that the rockclimber often be surprised by enormous blocks inhabiting the crest. In this case we find them surmountable by strenuous stemming across a chimney.

What a door-opening experience to emerge on the ridge top, with the southern horizon suddenly extended from inches to miles! On the three-foot-wide top, flat and safe as a tennis court, we need not hang on. "Look, ma, no hands." There, look at those peaks, the blue lakes below; and there, over that jumble of craggy knobs, that stack of square blocks jostling up against the western blue is the summit!

Ridge running is always delightful. Even though the route may be known, the way is not obvious. Towers and notches, hidden bypasses, magically revealed key ledges, passages to left and right, ups and downs and round-abouts, make a wonderful winding rock road, ever fresh. All too soon we spring across a last gap and begin a tussle with the last chimney. It ejects us squirming, scratched, and breathless onto the top of the second highest of a great pile of Brobdingnagian stones.

Off with the rucksacks, out with the feast; there will be time enough to reach the ultimate summit later. *Our* summit rock is eight feet square and flat enough to remind us of a queen-sized bed, when we're surfeited with the good groceries. It won't be the first time we've pillowed on rucksacks and watched the soft summer clouds until cumuli become dreams.

This pinnacle is made of flawless, clean-cut giant's play blocks, supposing he had hands that could palm an elephant. Fortunately for us the blocks have been left tumbled, so that there is always a man-sized reach between them. By standing on tiptoe we can just curl our fingers over the edge of the true summit block and pull up to where we can stab an elbow over. Then a quick grab across the foot-wide top to secure the other edge. This will bring us up, but it is not easy, and we never stand if the faintest wind blows.

Summits are grand almost by definition. They have some kind of magic in them no matter how they may be constructed. They vary from the gently rounded and easily attained to the fierce, frightful, and hardly won. They can be trashed with an ugly radar station, as on Kowloon Peak, motored to by the millions, as Mount Diablo is, swarmed over by train-borne trippers, as Mount Snowden is, but they all retain some of the same magnetic attraction that is a main feature of the never-visited-except-by-me summit of Mount I'll-Never-Tell. If there is an ideal summit, it must be that of the Fool's Needle, California. Although I have four times seen snowfall in August (I've been there many Augusts), it is always pleasant. Midsummer snow in the Sierra may call for earflaps and gloves, but the sun will soon show, and a peanut butter picnic is always possible.

The down-go is double-honed perfection—an ideal mix of all that is best in peak disengagement. We are treated to a pleasant series of easy reverse mantels (what a joy to climb down) on the blocky continuation of the ridge to the west; a pair of wild half-inch ledges that scare us onto an apparent diving board poised over an abrupt drop to a blue lake far below; a Z-shaped double rappel from a rather rickety anchor, where we might install a new sling through the rusty soft-iron piton to keep the adrenalin levels manageable; an easy talus chute, where some leftover snow might waft us down in ski-like glissade. This brings us down to a canyon whose string of glacial-bench lakes set among alpine meadows, timberline trees, and flower-banked laughing streams must have been designed as a preview of paradise. This canyon is much higher than the one on our beginning side of the peak, so we must pay for our rapid transition from rugged crags to springy grass by walking a long forest trail. If threading our way through dark trees requires candle-lantern light (not unlikely), then we must watch for the odd patch of ice on the trail. There may be a bit of splashing and thrashing to find a bridge across the larger stream fifty yards from the car, but it only serves to punctuate a great day in the hills.

Pity the poor peak-bagger who, by the nature of his obsession, cannot return over and over to an unknown, unsung, but near-perfect Fool's Needle.

BUTTERMILKING

"Hey, Smoke, got time to go Buttermilking?"

He should know me better than that. I've always got time to go Buttermilking. That's our coined verb for climbing in the local rocks. Please don't call it practice climbing. This is the real thing, even if it's walking. (We sometimes go Buttermilking to study flowers or to meditate.) And it's not bouldering; that's another sport. For forty years Buttermilking has been as essential a part of my life as any other ingredient.

No one knows the origin of the name *Buttermilk*. We borrowed it from the USGS, who splashed it across a large swath of the Sierra slope on one of their maps. Climbing locals restrict its use to a particular parade of small peaks.

The rock course evolved over a long time. I first climbed the Big Slab Pinnacle by the vertical four-sided chimney at its back, the one I now call the Aboriginal Chimney, in 1942. For many years, I corkscrewed into the great rock maze from all directions. The twistings and turnings of the holes, hollows, chimneys, and prongs of this vast jumble curl so complexly that even today I am the only one who can follow the exact pattern of all the routes. Bobby has been with me on more scramblings there than anyone, but he has always climbed as follower and has not yet learned the course. People who have spent a couple of years of winter weekends there still lose the way.

Obviously this is a source of pride to me, because mountaineering is an extension of my love of geography and exploring. The Buttermilk, though, taught me an appreciation of the grace of rockclimbing. Surprisingly, it seems to be this new skill that has gained this clumsy guide his local fame. Most people don't realize how easy it is to look good on moves done hundreds of times.

For decades I've taken out almost every person who has come visiting here. One beauty of the Buttermilk is that we can get there, climb, and return in just one hour. Or take the whole day. To go through the whole course takes from six to eight hours. Few people have the stamina and hand skin to complete the course in any amount of time; fewer yet can do it in record time. Climbing for records is stupid, anyway. It means no leisurely discussions on a sun-loved ledge, no time for trying a pitch over and over to smooth a technique, no chance to watch an owl mother's flight lesson, no ear for coyote music. (On Su's first arrival at the second highest summit, she asked, "Why do you call this one Coyote Singing Summit?" Believe it or not, on cue with that stage direction, an obliging chorus proved the name appropriate.) It is good when one or six show up with time and determination to make a deliberately slow tour through all twelve pinnacles on the course.

Better yet is a big picnic, which Su used to refer to as a "Buttermilk Bash." This means a general circus for all, sans program. A large but not atypical one gathered its population from Bishop locals, Allen Steck and colleagues from the Mountain Travel Company, and Yvon Chouinard and his crew from the Great Pacific Iron Works. The count was fifty-one, which may have included some dogs and most certainly included babes in arms. Maybe even George Miller's children's milk goats. That's okay. That is the special feature of Buttermilk ambience: the possibility of assembling in rock-inspired communion all categories of outdoor people, from the most sedentary of picnickers (nonambulatory, even) to the most acrobatic of overhanging boulderers.

Picnic Valley, twenty minutes by easy trail from the new sand-pit parking lot just ten miles from 387 Willow Street, is as spectacular as any site in cragdom. It is not really a valley, just a picnic-wide sagebrush-and-boulder-strewn space between the frowning brow of the bold Big Owl Pinnacle, the overhanging wall of South Mount Klieforth, and the sheer cliffs of Big Slab Pinnacle. Here nonclimbers can laze in sight of friends who are clinging to walls and peaks on every side. The haul from the car is short enough that nonclimbing types can be persuaded to pack in the food and water and wine, so that climbers arriving over the Skin Diver, Henry's Hill, and other narrow, airy places can balance unburdened.

Because the usual course crosses twice through this valley, people committed to different routes can mix at lunch. Groups may use this recess to rearrange. Here are some granite gropers eager for chimney wrestling; here, kids bound for Mount Klieforth on a tight rope; there, upper-echelon athletes dangling from an overhang. When such madness was popular, two young guides streaked a mixed climbing party that was belaying its way up the Slab. Bobby topped the streakers by traversing the complicated route over the summit, down the rough backside chimney, and around by Patterson's Night Route and the Belly Tester Crevice—fully clothed but barefooted!

Regarding climbing costumes, I tell visitors freshly arrived from the city, "We used to say, 'Put on your old clothes, we're going to the Buttermilk.' But now we say, 'Wear your best suit. If your technique is correct, you won't hurt it!' " This latest advice recognizes the skills we acquired at keeping ourselves out from the rock and climbing using only feet and hands. Beginners tend to grovel in chimneys, which is detrimental to clothing. Buttermilk rock is rough, round, and relatively holdless. It requires different gymnastics than the high-mountain rocks and allows us habitués to look good.

It is hard to say who will look good on those shaggy round bulges or tight scratch cracks. I must hasten to add an important message: the Buttermilk Course has always been just for fun. We have but one rule: don't fall off. Confucius say: "He who fall from Buttermilk rock loses face (very scratchy granite)." The credit to be gained from completing the course or reaching the summit of any of the twelve major pinnacles? As Bodhidharma answered the Emperor Wu of Liang to his inquiry on the merit of religious works: "None whatever!"

Still, if part of the fun is perfecting one's grace and balance, then surely it is legitimate to observe and appreciate one's companions' efforts as well. The peculiar nature of that strange rock leads to many a surprise. Sometimes mountaineers of wide experience and great reputation come around and find the rock so unlike the clean-cut edges of the heights that they struggle embarrassingly. Among the hundreds of nonclimbers trying the rocks with me, there have been some surprises too.

A couple from one of my African trips showed up, and the woman was anxious to get back into rockclimbing. She had kletterschuhe and knew how to use them. Her man, though, wore shiny, brass-buckled, leather-soled fashion boots. Impossible footgear: the uppers would be ruined by gouging crystals, and the soles could skid a man to ruin. He was told to wait at the bottom of the Porcupine Pinnacle, but he got so excited watching us, he came anyway. He climbed perfectly safely and with consummate skill.

The "Ring-tailed Cat Man" was a guest lecturer at the Palisade School of Mountaineering. A shy, gangling, stringy, black-stubble-bearded, frizzy-headed speaker, who scuffed his toes in the dirt, stared at the ground, and mumbled inaudibly about high-altitude squirrel habitats, Derham Giulani is most comfortable with a high-camp audience held in the glow of his nocturnally bloodshot eyes. (He earned his nickname by staying up nights observing ring-tailed cats.) One climbing team of two clients, who hunkered by a small fire at Camp Robin Hood for a two-hour nature lesson, rated the encyclopedic animal lore, detailed with red-eyed intensity, the highlight of their entire week at the school. They were startled the next day (it's happened more than once) to catch sight of the loose-jointed cat man flapping by with his untied tennies and butterfly net right up through the course they were attacking roped, belayed, and protected. Yes, the Ring-tailed Cat Man also floats up knee-gouging Buttermilk cracks with perfect unconcern.

My old friend Bob Swift once showed up with a friend who looked over each pitch very carefully and then climbed with ballet beauty. From the top of the short chimney above Sharp's Scenic Stroll, I threw down a rope for the stranger's protection on that airy promenade. He tied on without a word and came up with his usual aplomb.

When Swift got a chance, he inquired critically, "My God, Smoke, do you know who you tossed the line to?"

"I didn't catch the last name," I lied. "Chuck somebody."

"That's Chuck Pratt, perhaps the third-best rockclimber in all the world!"

He's a gentleman. The famous Stroll is a little nerve-tingling, but I'm sure he crossed it roped only to be polite.

One who should have worn a rope a time or two was our most spectacular climber of all. Helmut Kiene, in selecting a high-school exchange program from his native Germany, chose Bishop. A few locals imagine that the fame of Bishop's climbing has filtered all the way to the Alps. While this harmless conceit may be unjustified, no doubt German maps are detailed enough to show the capital of eastern California snuggling up to the Sierra Nevada.

Whether this inspired his choice I don't know, but Helmut came here for his senior year of high school. Within minutes he was out on the rocks, where with his natural balance and grace, he fit perfectly into Buttermilking. Skinny enough to rise up the narrowest of chimneys as if by capillary action, he was tall enough to finger the most distant hold and strong enough to hoist himself with ease. Soon he scampered up problem pitches like Spider Man.

His unroped antics nearly did him in one day, though. It was the great day Susan Denton and Jay Jensen were married just below the cragged peaks, and with hundreds of their friends at the ceremony it was not difficult to recruit Buttermilkers. We were all fairly full of wedding champagne, but rucksacked in several magnums in case of need. We had just begun the regular descent of the Big Slab Pinnacle when the bubbly momentarily captured Helmut's toes-on-ledge brain cells and off he came. Even here at the safe stance of the typewriter table, it scares me to think about that flight over those cliffs. There is one small, round, boulder ledge between take-off point and pancaking bottom. Helmut landed there in perfect knee-sprung crouch, bowed to the crowd as if twenty-five-foot jumps were on his program, and sprang down into the vertical chimney out of sight below in perfect control.

For a quarter of a century I knew everyone I saw out there, and for half of that time the only human tracks in all those hills were mine or my chosen companions'. Even today most of the traffic aims for bouldering on Doug Robinson's Peabodies. He hung that name on them and hung up most of the routes while spending weeks exploring their problems. Over a score of Yosemite hotshots have been attracted by Doug's boulder broadcasting. It is not my thing. I put on Doug Robinson's special rockclimbing shoes once and aimed them for Grandpa, but they didn't take me up. Bobby uses mountain boots like mine and climbs routes on Grandma and Grandpa that no one can follow.

The huge boulder Doug named Grandpa is famous now—featured in a photograph illustrating a Robinson essay on clean climbing. Most people think bold Grandpa the biggest boulder around the Buttermilk area. It is second. Number one we hide by geography and benign neglect. We hid it because the only way up will require bolts, and so far we've kept bolts out of almost all our rocks. Locals laugh because the rope in the Grandpa clean-climbing photo runs through a bolt, but that's okay because all agree that Doug is certified pure, and the editor needed the picture.

If we've only an hour or the new visitors want to climb only one pinnacle, I usually head for the first peak of the course, the one we call the Porcupine. That way we can use the old parking place, below where the weekend cars park.

Just before reaching the base of Porcupine, I take my party across a few shaggy rocks and past the Christmas Card Boulder. This sorts out the group instantly. Xmas Boulder can be climbed. Super experts gluing the tip edges of their boots to footholds too narrow to balance a bean appreciate that we have a parallel course for them where they can practice such absurdities without being ostracized. The rest of us check our rubber soles, adjust to the smearing of boots on slopes, and relax our bodies for balancing. I then know who needs a rope on the first pitch and approximately how much rockclimbing instruction to give.

Lately I've been carrying a fourth-class rack, which works fine—just a few nuts for setting up anchors. I don't climb fifth-class routes any more. I've been told that my solo routes in the Scheelite Cliffs rank 5.6. Never did understand those numbers. If I like it, I class it 4.9, and if I don't I'll call it 5.7 and stay the hell off it. In the heroic words of Norman Clyde: "This can be climbed but I'm not going to do it." Yes, the rack fits in a belly-band pack and has all the anchor, prusik, and descending gadgets I need.

The Porcupine Pinnacle gives us a chance to climb cracks, faces, ledges, and chimneys. Most likely I'll give a running commentary on all the different types of jam and cling holds we use. I'll demonstrate a jump we call the Flying Squirrel, teach manteling, show how to wedge, and give an example of the lieback. Probably there will be philosophy, deep or shallow; undoubtedly there will be gossip about famous climbers. I'll criticize Royal Robbins for claiming to have invented the elbow lock in the 1950s. I hope he meant that he had progressed far enough in his climbing experience and athletic agility to rediscover what my friend Gary Leech showed me in the 1930s, when he rediscovered what A. F. Mummery had probably used early in this century in his famous crack on the Grépon, and what no doubt was used before him by old Pithecanthropus J. Erectus when he deserted his tree to try a little rock-crack problem in pursuit of dinner.

There will be many anecdotes. A lot of them I tell to illustrate something about climbing in the Buttermilk. When we thrash in the chimneys, I point out that they come in all sizes, like people. The beanpoles gripe in Charcoal Chimney, the shortlegged have trouble reaching across the wide chimney under the Breakfast Porch. The Frog Wedge is supposed to require great arm strength, but Mary Sharp and Marlene Miller squirm out of it on coordination rather than biceps. I tell how the first two guys to straddle-leg the entire Bobcat's Passage were tall, skinny Tex Mock and a sawed-off Yvon Chouinard. I may offer the rope with a story about how Bob Swift and I assured a client at the climbing school that "you can't fall out of a chimney," and she did.

If all goes well, my chatter sparks my friends into talking too, and we jabber all the way. This uses up climbing time and leaves some unclimbed pinnacles to beckon them back.

If I charted every hold, mapped every move on the course, asterisked all the alternatives, compiled a large book with the most accurate evocations of the moods of that molded granite paradise, and managed accurately to portray by character sketches the people who sometimes inhabit the Buttermilk, I would still sell it short. There is no way that I know of to pass on by paper the feeling that permeates the person who steps out of the shower with epidermis cleaned and tingling from crystal scrapes, muscles pleasantly tired, joints well-oiled, and mind and spirit glowing from a full day of Buttermilking.

EWAC

Immediately after Su moved into my house on Willow Street, we began a frenzied conversion of the garage into her pottery studio. As a fringe benefit from all that sawing and hammering, I sealed off a corner of the shop for my skis, ropes, eleven ice axes, and nine thousand artifacts of mountain equipment I'd accumulated in the last several raccoon's ages. The duplication and general proliferation exhibited by my closet collection so startled Su that she asked me if it included mountain gear for the entire club.

"What club?"

"Why, the East Willow Alpine Club." She set to work carving a wooden sign for the closet door, and the East Willow Alpine Club was born. "EAST WILLOW ALPINE CLUB—Members Only" read the beautiful sign, quite the classiest status symbol of our newly refurnished garage. I hung it over the door of my gadget closet and swore that EWAC would live. It lived.

It lived a life of its own so fruitfully complicated that I long ago lost track of its ramifications. As EWAC's form letter hints, after being the unwitting instrument of its incubation and designing the badge by which it is known in the far corners of the world, I found myself relegated to a minor position.

The post of secretary is not a high one and entitles me to no more than a nodding acquaintance with officials of the Membership Committee. I have never seen the officers of the Department of Rules, Records, and Reports, much less the august Director of Data. It is a highly complex organization, with a lofty, though possibly obscure, purpose. After working many years as secretary, I have not yet fathomed much of what goes on behind the scenes, but certain intimations give me confidence that I am connected with something big and important. Last summer I thought I heard the whir of a computer from the clubroom loft, but it turned out to be a wasp nest.

Since the management sent down word that I can use a form letter to avoid the laborious composition of each membership announcement, I have more time to listen to scuttlebutt. I have heard that a report on the grading of climbing difficulty has been turned in to top management, and a new system is to be published. The former Class 1–6 system has been abolished. The new grading will read:

1 point = 1 rump. Examples: Pike's Peak, Colorado, by the ordinary route, with rump of climber firmly fixed to mule saddle or car seat. Dollar Mountain, Idaho, by chair lift.

2 points = 2 feet. Examples: Mount Tabor, Oregon, from the south. (Rumor has it that the original Mount Tabor in Israel is the preferred example, but it must await examination by our Department of Near East Affairs.) Mount Tamalpais, California, from Muir Woods via Bootjack Camp.

3 points = 2 feet + 1 hand or ice ax. Examples: Mont Blanc, France, via the Grand Mulet Route. Grouse Mountain, California, via the Northwest Arête.

4 points = 2 feet and 2 hands. Examples: Mount Whitney, California, by the East Face, Eichorn Fresh-Air Traverse Variation. The Grand Teton, Wyoming, by the Owen-Spalding Route.

5 points = 2 feet, 2 hands, and "pegs and aids" or teeth. Examples: El Capitan, Yosemite, by the Wall of the Early Morning Light. The Big Owl Pinnacle, California, by Bob's Balcony Route.

6 points = no such thing.

Many people ask if the club is small and local. I do know the answer. At the moment we have just under 500 members in fifteen countries. I also know that the club sends expeditions to all continents, sponsors climbing school candidates, and collects for charities.

When Per Temba Sherpa confessed to the secretary, "I have many breathings for high mountain but no technicals," our club joined others in financing his training in Europe, where he acquired the technicals that took him to the summit of Everest over the West Wall.

The club has acted as agent to collect and forward donations to Sir Edmund Hillary's Himalayan Trust, which builds bridges, village water systems, and schools in Nepal; for the Sherpa Scholarship Fund, which sends deserving Sherpa children to high school in Kathmandu; and for the Himalaya Rescue Association, to help in operating their hospital and trekker's aid post at Pheriche. Currently we solicit contributions to the Tengboche Head Lama's scheme for building a hotel and *gompa* temple for Sherpas in Kathmandu.

We have received many fine letters of thanks from those awarded honorary memberships. It is always a pleasure to see members wearing their pins with pride. A story reached Bishop that a German and an Austrian in different climbing parties met on the summit of Der Watzmann and were pleased to discover that each had decorated his alpine hat with the red badge of EWAC.

We do not have a perfect record. My good friend and fellow Logan expeditioneer Dave Bohn, an ardent nonjoiner, sent back a strongly worded letter in an attempt to reject membership. His letter got lost in the round file, but I include a copy of my personal reply here to explain why I call it an *attempted* rejection.

Dear Dave,

Your last letter carried a postscript which sounded almost as if you wanted to reject our sincere good fellowship in making you an honorary member of the East Willow Alpine Club.

I am very sorry if this is really the case, because, you see, there is absolutely nothing that can be done about it.

You would be quite within your rights if you did not want to join a specific organization, although, contrary to your sweeping statement, you cannot refuse membership in all categories of organizations. For example, you belong to the organization of the human race, from which it is quite impossible to resign.

Among the heterogeneous population of the club, we have had

pickle personalities before, so I am somewhat familiar with the problem of resignations. I knew there was no way you could get out, but, because of our long friendship, I tried. I took it upon myself to communicate with the Department of Ethics and Morality to determine if it was possible for you to dissolve your relationship with us by committing ceremonial harakiri. Perhaps ritual disembowelment with an ice ax?

Alas, a reply in my in-basket this morning from a clerk in the Eschatology Section of the Office of the Vice President for Religious Affairs stated that such a dissolution would do nothing to alter the indelible records of higher authority. All EWAC members are optimistically registered for posting to St. Peter's Archives, and, due to the nature of mountaineers, seven copies of the honorary membership rolls are required to be forwarded to the Chief Recording Angel of His Satanic Majesty's Forces. Fortunately the membership lists are completely sealed and privy to no one but the secretary, the management, and a few old gossips. The executives, of course, are absolutely incorruptible. But it is highly possible that the secretary could be bribed into silence about your membership in the club.

Sympathetically yours,
Smoke Blanchard, Sec.

The walls of the climbing closet may tumble in the same earthquake that brings down the Sierra Nevada. Parkas, packs, and pitons may wither into dust, but the spirit of East Willow Alpine Club will live on.

8

Norman Clyde

THE AERIAL BURIAL

Newspaper accounts of Norman Clyde's death at age 86 said he would be buried in Tonopah. A couple of people muttered that Norman had nothing to do with that small town in Nevada. Most locals ignored the newspaper sentence, or restated a prejudice that Norman was strange anyway.

There was nothing that strange about Norman. The statement in the newspaper article had something to do with a law, since rescinded, which was evaded with the help of the authorities. Instead of Tonopah, the summit of Clyde Peak was the burial ground chosen by his friends. For a good part of a dedicated mountain life, Norman was involved with that great peak, which divides the South and Middle Forks of Big Pine Creek in the Sierra Nevada. We were then ready to select a burial party for Norman's ashes.

My son Bob's long association with Norman earned him a place on the team. Young Bob used to play games around Norman's raggedy 1926 cloth-top Chevrolet that was parked in our yard. He listened to the interminable harangues of the old man instructing me on how to hand-load for maximum muzzle velocity, on the merits of the eight-inch barrel as against the seven-inch barrel in his latest handgun, on how to tie a fly which would appeal to the big ones in the high lakes, on the "world's worst" mountain climber and how she fouled up the whole trip to Colorado by objecting to Norman's really fine mush, on how "I told them *plainly* where the route was but the old hammerhead . . . ," and other such mountain lore. The little house had only one bedroom, and Bob and the big old black dog usually slept on the davenport in the front room. Of course, that had to be given up for the few days, or weeks, when Norman was in residence. Bob and the dog cared little, though; they knew there'd be many rides up into the mountains in the pickup to go walking or climbing.

There were other houses and other dogs, and Bobby grew up, but Norman was still part of Bob's landscape. Inherited Indian taciturnity prevented Bob from babbling an analysis of the relationship, but I figured twenty years of Norman's crag-worn face and crotchety manner entitled Bob to a firm spot on the funeral team.

Jules Eichorn had been Norman's partner on many a month-long venture in the Sierra. The two enjoyed a remarkable affinity in mountain outlook, which included a thorough awareness of everything in the scene.

Jules once found half of an Indian *mano* (corn-grinding stone) on a high mountain slope, and searched on his hands and knees for two hours until he found the matching half. Jules's scratched knees and Jules's sharp eye gained the prize, but it was Norman who had put the idea of Indian artifacts in the Sierra in Jules's head in the first place.

On our Logan expedition of 1959, Jules sat beside me on the long drive north. "Stop the car!" he would yell, and leap out before Nort Benner could fully brake. As the door swung roughly against the hinges, Jules sprinted into the forest to gather some odd mushroom he had spotted with his Norman-inspired eye.

Jules was well qualified to be marshall of the memorial party.

For some decades he and Norman had been coleaders of boys' trips in the Sierra, and Jules made some rockclimbs still harum enough to be placed in the modern scarum books. He attended many Clyde classes in outdoor appreciation.

Nort Benner's invitation was legitimate, because he was best friend of the other three on the team. There was more. A long time back, while organizing a Yukon expedition, Jules phoned me: "I've got a doctor interested in going . . . he's a good athlete . . . skis . . . plays championship tennis . . . uh, I don't know if we want him—he's never been on an expedition—knows nothing of falling into a crevasse . . ."

"Do you want him?"

"Sure."

"We want him." It was Nort.

Many expeditions and many important parts of the Benner and Blanchard lives meshed since that phone call. Su and I were married in Nort's garden. There were plenty of once-removed connections with Norman.

My credentials included thirty-six years of assorted Norman contacts since the first time he showed me the tall peak that towers up-canyon from his old cabin. Also, through the inspiration of Norman, a lot of stubbornness, and dumb luck, I was the only one of the crew who was, at the moment, a professional mountaineer. This meant my back was the one accustomed to additional loads. Some of the weight in my rucksack was a paper sack of ashes: the mortal remains of Norman Clyde.

Scattering, unlike interment or consigning ashes to the Ganges at the burning ghat, can be done long after the funeral. There is time to sort out what is important for the ritual. We could have used an airplane, which would have been efficient and economical, but few really important things are done by counting minutes or money. It was important that we pick a particular peak, and important that we struggle to make its summit the scattering point.

For more than twenty-five winters, Norman daily saluted Peak 13,956 as it peered in his cabin window. It has a great ship's-prow precipice riding above its spiked spur, Peak 12,222. (Peak 13,956 designates a summit that Gary Leech, Hubert North, and I bandied about in a dim lantern-lit hut in long-ago Oregon, as we hunched over the USGS Big Pine Quadrangle map, 1912 edition. We had not seen the peak at that time, but Gary made us memorize the number. From the contour lines on the latest map, one can see that the USGS has kept this height, but goofed by transposing the numbers to 13,659.) This great mountain has now been officially designated Norman Clyde Peak.

On either side of the prow, glaciers are fed by snow blown leeward by the prevailing winds and work at chewing vertically headwalled cirques. To get above these walls, the mountaineer finds the only breach by climbing up into a rounded col between the East and North Clyde Glaciers, where the saw-edged ridge of Peak 12,222 rounds off to join the base of Clyde Peak. This is the only reasonable route onto the upper cliffs, whose slopes are only a bit less steep than the cirque walls.

The opposite, south, side of the mountain is even steeper, in violation of the general rule that erosion gentles sunny sides. (The Palisade Group's Middle Palisade and Mount Winchell also break this rule.) Besides being a steeper route, the south face requires a difficult two-day march over a glacial col. The approach we used from Big Pine Canyon to the base takes a full day. We knew that when we reached the summit we would stand on a sharp crest, with row on row of peaks spanning almost the entire Sierra Nevada in view. We judged it a fitting scatter stance.

Su, with Jules's son Peter, went along to run the base camp, which we situated in the last trees at Finger Lake, under the East Clyde Glacier. The four "officials" struck off at dawn up the steep grass slopes above the lake and up the boulders to the col. Routes have been pushed up the cliff above the East Glacier cirque; we never considered it. Hoisting our rucksack with its special burden up piton-and-bolt ladders would have been inappropriate even had our skills been up to it. We chose a series of ledges diagonaling above the North Glacier. This way turned out to be steep enough.

Although I had been up before, the steepness fooled me off the correct path. I angled too far to the right and brought us up on the crest after midday, some distance from the summit.

A guide should be especially aware of this common Sierra error; cresting too early on a peak may mean a difficult ridge run. We found nothing complicated enough to require connecting the two roped teams, though, and reached the summit without having to steel our nerves overmuch. Nort calls it "getting lost" and still kids me unmercifully about blundering off route.

There was a gentle west wind blowing over the wild craggy summit of that most spectacular mountain, as we took turns tossing handfuls of the heavy, ground-up, shell-like ashes. Su was watching with binoculars from Finger Lake, and could just make out a tiny figure on top with the arm out in a throwing motion. She said later she thought Norman would have wanted it that way.

I suppose so. I hope so. He never talked about any plans for disposal of his guns (his sister in Pennsylvania didn't realize the value of them, and apparently they fell into the wrong hands and she will get nothing), much less the more difficult subject of any funeral arrangements. He made jokes on occasion about "going to the hot place," and I guess his training for the ministry left him with rather conventional ideas of life after death. Yet, as far as I know, he never showed the slightest interest in things religious. Nor did he ever, in conversations with me, talk of philosophy or agnosticism or anything so remote from the practicalities of the outdoor life. Now and then he muttered about the latest political news. He seemed to be mildly liberal, or at least somewhat antiwar and antiaggression, but I doubt if he bothered to think of such things much.

We tossed the ashes over the Northeast Face, because that was Norman's side of the mountain. Jules reminded us that all sides of the mountain belonged to Norman. He recalled the time when he and Norman caught golden trout in the sparkling lake visible at the foot of the windward side of the peak, so we tossed a token handful into the breeze in that direction as well. We would have had to travel widely to sprinkle Norman's remains on all the mountains that belonged to him. He possessed mountains by fervently climbing and tramping through them throughout the Sierra Nevada, the Trinity Alps; the Crazy, San Juan, Gold, Columbia, Panamint, Inyo, and White Mountains; the Sierra San Pedro Martir, and probably ranges I've forgotten.

To me the Christian theories of afterlife are at least as silly, and powered by the same wishful thinking, as Buddhist reincarnation, yet I'm a firm believer in immortality. I think it so obvious as to be beyond argument. Exactly as the law of conservation of matter requires the preservation of the electrons of the body, so does the energy of the soul live on in its effects on the survivors and their survivors. Norman's physical self went up in a little smoke and down in a little wind-blown calcined bone to eventually become a temporary part of the East Clyde Glacier. His spiritual self lives on in his ideas, which some of us will treasure; in the memories his friends will keep and pass on, by mountain stories, to new generations; and in his contribution to mountain lore, which may live as long as men tromp the Sierra.

NORMAN CLYDE OF THE SIERRA

Smoke:

By all means use the "Norman Clyde letter" again if you wish. However, if you use it, I would ask that you give a short abstract (a sentence or two) on *how* it came to be written (I jabbed you on it for one year), *to whom* it was written ("Dear Dave . . ," etc.), and for *what book* (*Norman Clyde of the Sierra . . .*). Also that I edited some of your clumsy phrases, re-sorted your paragraphs, and such.

I'll be in and out of town, as far as I know, in March and April. Give a call. (You say you ". . . expect to be in the Bay for a week or more." This is a *long* time to be in the water. Watch out for hypothermia!)

Dave

Well, here goes "a sentence or two." (Dave Bohn should know me better than that.) Some years ago, when Norman used to come to our house to escape the sanitarium at Big Pine, Dave asked me to write a letter about Norman for the book of Clyde's writings, which I'd talked Dave into compiling. Did he really "jab me for a year"? I thought it was more like a couple of months, but then it seems only weeks since he wrote the February 18th letter, and now it is August. I think I am only thirty-nine years old, too.

Dave Bohn does not waste words. I can't remember how he phrased the first request, but he must have told me he was going to Alaska, so I procrastinated and had nothing written when he phoned me on his return.

"Smoke? Dave. Where is it? I want it, and I want it now."

Dave can be gruff in person; over the telephone he sounds like Jehovah. I jumped to the typewriter and pounded out something that I thought might get by. I'd put it off, hoping to be touched by some miraculous writing ability, but now I knew the wrath of Bohn, and it was too late to pine for missing talents.

Perhaps Dave went to Alaska again. (He was writing a book on Katmai.) Again he growled on the wire: "Smoke? Dave. About that Norman Clyde letter. . . ." I knew it. I'm a truck driver, not a writer. Why didn't he ask me to haul some freight for Norman? "I want you to write about three to five times more of the same stuff and send it to me instantly."

That is how I came to participate in *Norman Clyde of the Sierra Nevada: Rambles through the Range of Light—Twenty-nine Essays on the Mountains* by Norman Clyde; Foreword by Francis Farquhar and Prologue by Jules Eichorn, with a long letter from Smoke Blanchard and fifteen photographs of the old gaffer; with an explanatory Epilogue by Dave Bohn. Scrimshaw Press, 1971.

Bishop
January, 1971

Dear Dave:

By coincidence, your letter from Alaska asking me about Norman arrived the same day we went to Big Pine to see him. He is in the sanitarium there with a little flu, and on top of that his leg is acting up again, and he couldn't walk very well. He had a grocery box of books brought down from the Baker Creek cabin, and was churning through Goethe in German, with a six-inch thick dictionary, which he picked up at a rummage sale in Bishop, and a New Testament in Portuguese which he bought for Spanish but was reading anyway. On his night stand was a life of Napoleon in French, which he has already read three times.

He is just about recovered and looks very well because the hospital holds back on his potatoes and he trims down a bit. "These places like to keep a man in, to make sure he doesn't have a relapse, and they have their regulations, but I've got a lot of chores to do up there, there's wood to cut. . . ."

Nonsense. He has wood for several seasons, and the rest and relief from doing everything for himself is good for him.

We camped on a little snow-free patch of rock on the frozen lake in the Palisades during that early-season trip long ago. I can still remember my awe at the collection of gear Norman drew out of his duffle bag. The duffle bag was lashed to a six-pound Yukon packframe, which also supported a Hudson Bay axe. But the kitchen bag was the most surprising item to Hubert and me, as our meager assortment of pans scrounged from Depression cupboards was no match for Norman's six large kettles, the cups and spoons, the dishes and bowls, the salt shakers, condiments, servers and graters, and, for all I know, cookie cutters. I remember my astonishment at seeing his special stick-mop for washing dishes. He even had extra food for us! Bob Clunie would never believe this, because Norman used to drop in at that well-supplied artist's camp with great frequency and famous appetite.

The duplications in Norman's list contrasted strongly with our Boy Scout style. Boots? He carried several: ski boots, tricouninailed boots, rubber-soled boots for the rocks, camp slippers. "It's not true that I carry an anvil in my pack. Only this little piece of iron to put in the heel for replacing tricounis. That's something these go-lightly boys never think about. Some gaffer is always tearing out some nails and needing repairs. And anyway, if I want to carry a rock in my pack to keep me steady down the trail, that's my business."

A camera? Norman carried five. That's right. One 35mm loaded with Ansco and another with Eastman film, a 120 for black and white, another 120 for color, and his "throw-in-the-lake" camera, which was the spare.

A book for evening reading? Norman usually travels alone and on long trips, so he had a large library, in many languages. "They last longer—especially the Greek, as I'm usually a little rusty in that." And a pistola, or maybe several, in different types and calibers. Evenings on the trip we watched him throw chips from the woodpile out on the ice and shoot at them. If hit dead center the chip would scoot across the lake without spinning. If he hit a chip and made it twirl, he would mutter angrily.

We weighed one of those loads once. Norman showed up at my house around 1955, complaining of losing track of the days. It seemed his stick-notching was inaccurate, and he was a day late meeting Jules Eichorn and his party for a month's cache-and-carry trip. Cache and carry because Jules had already deposited food along the route, and Norman's pack contained only five pounds of edibles for emergency. Still the pack weighed ninety-two pounds. We divided it into four loads and carried it to Piute Pass to help Norman catch up with Jules. At the pass, we lashed the whole mess to the Yukon board, along with two fishing rods (eight-foot for streams, nine-foot for lakes), reels for each, and a spare reel. Away he went.

He caught up with the party but did not come out again for six weeks. When he was two weeks overdue, we began to worry, and went to Independence to check on him, but there he was coming out over Kearsarge Pass with a pack that weighed in at 106 pounds. The surplus was accounted for by pots and pans he scrounged along the way, food he purchased at Giant Forest, and a string of fish.

You asked me to write some memories of my trips with Norman, and I seem to have gotten stuck on his packs. There's lots more I could tell, as one recollection triggers another; more stories of the packs come to mind. I think many people might find his way of travel in the mountains strange, especially with today's gear, but, you see, Norman was not just visiting the mountains or passing through the peaks. He lived there!

When I first got acquainted with Norman, I thought it would be a marvelous opportunity to get all the inside dope on mountains of the Sierra Nevada, the Colorado and Wyoming Rockies, the Lewis and Livingston ranges, the Beartooths of Montana, the Selkirks, Monashees, Caribous, Purcells—just to roll these delicious names of far-off British Columbia ranges around. And now, just across the old cabin from me, was a man who had wandered through those romantic places making solo first ascents! What a gold mine of information. Not so. Not really. It's kind of like pulling teeth. One gets a little blood, and after a long effort maybe a bit of broken tooth, but the aching arm is scarcely worth it.

What bothered me most about my early basking in the limelight of a hero was that Norman seemed unconcerned with heroics. His name was a household word in Government Camp, Oregon—at least among a handful of mountain bums of the 1930s. (I was never able to call him Norm, and few people do. Last week someone addressed him so, and it seemed strange to hear it. Although he has come to my house bimonthly for two decades and is almost one of the family, he has always inspired a little too much awe and a bit of dignified aloofness. One does not carelessly nickname him; besides, he's somewhat older than I.) Oregon boys being oriented toward the northern mountains, it was the ambition of my school chums to climb Mount Robson, but Norman was matter-of-fact about the giant of the Canadian Rockies. He talked of his climbing companions and maybe the hotcakes—no hair-raising escapades at all. One day I pinned him down to naming a peak in the Sierra, selected from the short list I had climbed, to compare with noble Geikie in the Rampart Range of Canada. "Oh, it's just about as hard as Mount McAdie or a little more so, and about twenty times longer."

Not much for a man not mathematically minded to go on, yet eventually one day there he was in flesh and blood, climbing just above me. I heard him mutter and thought to myself, "I must move up close to him, for we are on a steep wall and no doubt coming to a tough place. I must listen for wisdom from the master." We were not roped and with some effort I drew near him. He was muttering, "Ah, the damned old bitch, excuse my French." How terribly prosaic and matter of fact. I thought surely he would be commenting on the dizzy space between us and the glacier below, but no.

Yes, it was often a woman. Somehow he was always involved with them: as tenant and landlady, guide and client. These two categories pertain to years of long and not always smooth negotiations with certain people who ran mountain lodges at which Norman was the snow-shoveler and watchman during long, isolated winters, and to numerous trips to the Rockies with a couple of women whom he never seemed able to teach to climb up to anything near his lowest level of tolerance. Apart from these there were only infrequent and casual contacts, but how he could fume at women who presumed to tell a bachelor how to raise petunias. Damned old busybodies!

I'm coming awfully close to saying Norman is cantankerous, and now that I think of it, that is about the best word in the dictionary for him. As far as I know, he has always accepted me and approved of my mountain habits—a very important qualification from his point of view—and he has never uttered a word of criticism against Jules Eichorn and certain others of the Sierra Club, with whom he has been on many trips, but the rest, meaning practically the whole rest of the world . . . !

Gary Leech and I were surprised to find that Norman liked to fish. In our single-minded preoccupation with cliffs and glaciers, we could not conceive of a true outdoorsman wasting his time on such a pedestrian pursuit. However, what we did not fully realize was that Norman lived his whole life in the mountains. The mountains are as broad as life, and just as life is much more than a craze for cars or booze, mountains are more than a speed record for ascending a volcano or a list of 5.9 pitches conquered. Norman spent all his time in the mountains and was as deeply into fishing as into any other aspect of life in the wild. He considered himself a fine fisherman, and indeed he was. He would not fish unless they were biting. He would lie all afternoon in the sun reading Dumas in French, gazing out across the lake to check for ripples, and when he thought there was enough breeze on the surface for fly fishing, he would be off for one circuit of the lake and would return with his limit of golden trout.

Fishing is an art and a highly scientific sport, he told us, and an adept fisherman can always catch the wily trout, but he should do so only when he needs or desires the meat, never just for sport, and never fish just to be fishing. He gave my wife and son good lessons on the tricks of fly fishing but quickly detected an unteachable pupil in me. Besides being an intractable student, I possess a mite of meanness and occasionally twitted him about getting a spinning outfit. You may well believe this subject can bring a fine show of sparks to Norman's eyes. I dared not mention bait. But Norman himself was not one hundred percent pure. He seemed to take a chuckling delight in mentioning times when he broke the law. It might have been just a week or two after season, and his bag might have been just a few over the limit, and anyway it was way back there on the other side of Mount Something-or-Other, and he was out of food—he would explain with another chuckle—and if a game warden was around, "he might have arrested me, but he'd have eaten the fish too."

Jules will have to tell you of trips in the mountains with Norman, Glen Dawson, and other climbers of the thirties. I was mostly in Oregon then; later I was here but gone on expeditions in the summer. We saw Norman mainly on his periodic one-day to three-week visits to our home in Bishop and on our trips to check up on him in Big Pine Canyon. Most of our trips then were in winter and only for a day. Part of the reason for walks in Big Pine Canyon was Norman's aversion to being caught at housekeeping failures. Two or three times in the 1930s, on trips from Oregon, I looked up Norman in wintertime and received an invitation to stay in his cluttered-up house, but I think he was apprehensive about my wife seeing him in such disarray. So he would slip out of the cabin as soon as he heard us outside and ask if we wanted to walk. Usually we would walk up the old trail to the "first falls." Naturally Norman would be carrying a rucksack containing two or three cameras, target pistols with different barrel lengths, spare film, a coat, a cup, a canteen, and a light lunch. Strapped to his waist he usually wore a .22 Colt Woodsman, and he carried one of his numerous rifles in his hand. I suppose even hand-loaded ammunition was expensive for him, so the rifle was seldom used. It would be leaned up against a convenient Jeffrey pine after an elevation gain of a few hundred feet in order for Norman to search the south canyon with binoculars or to sit and wait for the right cloud to hover around the peaks for a proper picture. Including lunch stop, a half day could easily be used up. For Norman, who no doubt made the climb to the top of the first falls almost daily, the walk was a never-ending delight. He always managed to find something interesting: a bush or a bug, or a cloud shadow on the mountainside.

In the 1950s, Norman's car was often parked in the field next to our little house. It seemed to fit Norman perfectly. The old softtop, lashed down with extra straps, the expanding-gate carrier on the running board overflowing with gear, the tonneau loaded with packs and skis and ropes and ice axes—all were a perfect match for the driver in his battered campaign hat. To see him crawl out of the succession of secondhand disasters he acquired after the old Chev never seemed right.

Many of the visits to the little house in Bishop were in springtime when Norman was, by agreement, cast out of his mountain cabin at Big Pine Creek, and the proprietors began their annual cleaning to get ready for fisherman rentals. For thirty years or so,

Norman really had no permanent year-round home, as he always had to vacate for the tourist and fishing season. This suited him, in spite of the grumbling about removing his valuable collection of shovels and ice axes, his woven-rope snowshoes, his rusty traps, more than a score of large boxes of ancient, squirrel-gnawed literary classics, boots and boot nails and hatchets and saws, three-foot and five-foot and seven-foot skis, boxes and boxes of photographs and writings, and twenty tool boxes of handguns that he sometimes brought down to be stored in the valley for greater safety. Everything else was piled in a great cache in the rocks of the mountainside. This migration was, as I have mentioned, earlier than the onset of fishing season because of the time needed to muck out the cabin for visitors from the city, so Norman often came around in blustery early spring, suffering from a cold that came from having to start his six-month summer sleeping out. He'd chug and sputter up to the house in his old clunker and announce that on account of old so-and-so, he had been forced to vacate a day or three early, and he had a cold already, and he didn't get the correct consideration for all his winter's work, and he really ought to be packing for a trip to the Rockies, and he'd rather go to the Coast Ranges of British Columbia, and he had just bought a fine new "toy," a war-surplus Italian army-issue carbine of so much horsepower with eight speeds forward and reversing fine tuner, and damnation, he had a cold and would have to go to the hospital after a few days at our house resting up. Hospital? Yes, there's a little sun-filled clearing in a grove of white . . . oops, I've almost given it away. Anyhow, in a certain canyon near Bishop is the finest hospital a man could wish for—just a couch of leaves, and a clear running stream, and soft breezes, and three weeks dozing in the sun under those great cliffs can cure most anything. It is absolutely private and free of cost.

I have just been looking over my copy of *Close-ups of the High Sierra*, a book of Norman's writings of 1928 or so. Walt Wheelock says in his brief biography of Norman that "much of the gruffness of his early years has disappeared." This was written about ten years ago, and I think there is an increasing mellowness lately in Norman's personality. A few days ago we visited him at the Big Pine Sanitarium, where he is residing temporarily, while he gets his cabin refurnished after a looting incident, which left him without lamps for reading or pans for cooking. We asked why he was not up at the old Baker Creek cabin, and Norman explained with such a sudden and loud burst that a passing nurse jumped a foot. The point is, though, that in ten seconds Norman was smiling and laughing and saying, "Well, that's the way it goes." There are always gripes, all the time I've known him. Something is always wrong. Often it is his own fault. Even the cop could see that, but he let him go. It was a good story and believable, knowing Norman. He really did leave his driver's license on a stump, and a squirrel ate it.

I hate to write all these things, in a way. I do not mean to make Norman a buffoon. He was not and is not. It is just that he is so noble that comic relief is welcome. He laughs at these anecdotes himself. Laughter is one of his notable traits. He laughs often with gusto that sparkles around the edges when he gets into a good story, even, or especially, when the joke is on himself. Yes, he is noble. My wife says, "A gentleman, a thorough and complete gentleman—honest, reliable, dependable, kind, with an old-world courtesy." His watch may have stopped and he might be marking X's on last year's calendar, so he'll be a day late, but he'll be there.

I mentioned the "hospital." Norman very rarely said anything about it. However, he used to be fond of telling everyone about his "hotels." He had hundreds. They were scattered in every corner of the Sierra. A rock ledge, a mossy bench, a hidden tarn. They were isolated, ideal campsites, selected, stocked, and used by Norman alone. They were chosen for their firewood, water supply, and access to climbing routes, but primarily for their scenic inspiration. One of the most often-used, which overlooked the North Palisade group of peaks, he called the Palace Hotel: "The view alone is worth fifty dollars!"

Norman's mountain clothes and gear always interested me, because his reputation inspired respect for the equipment that helped to get him up so many peaks, and because everything he did had a special Norman Clyde style. Most notable and identifiable was his trademark, the stiff-brimmed Stetson campaign hat that he wears on every mountain trip. Even in town, he can be spotted two blocks away by his campaign hat. He must have had a half dozen in the old cabin on Big Pine Creek one winter when I visited him there. I couldn't help laughing at the oldest. It had spent so many seasons buffeting against rocks and bowing into storms and fanning so many camp fires that the four-ridged dome had become creased and broken, and he had sewed up the top with white cotton thread, making an ornamental though ragged pyramid. Some of the hats were new and apparently used for his rare visits to the city or rarer trips to the East Coast.

Regular climbing pants were not available in this country in those days, but he manufactured serviceable knickers by cutting off long trousers and combining them with a unique gaiter. I have never seen such a gaiter elsewhere, but it guarded Norman's legs for a lifetime of climbing. He would cut off the tops of sixteen-inch boots, install and lace them on his legs, and then tie the bottoms into the tops of his regular six-inch climbing boots to make a firm seal. His selection of climbing boots followed the regular course of evolution of mountain footwear from Swiss edge nails through tricouni nails to Bramani soles. (Now generically called lug soles, these textured rubber grippers went by the name of their inventor, Victor Bramani, for many years.) Bramani soles, of course, have completely replaced nails for American mountaineers, but before their introduction into this country, Sierran climbers used smooth-soled rubber, while Northwesterners with their icy mountains more often used nails. Norman carried both. And with skis he carried a third pair to fit the bindings.

Norman's ideas on equipment were heavy but practical. I often imitated him. As late as 1953, to my partner Gary Leech's consternation, I carried two pairs of boots on an ascent of the North

Palisade. As Norman said, "For secure footing—rubber on rock, steel on ice." I was still using some of Norman's heavy gear on my first big expedition to Alaska in the 1950s. I had picked up his habit of using a duffel bag lashed to a Yukon packboard, though maybe that was the year I first saw a strange new thing called a Kelty pack. Anyway, Norman's six-pound packboard proved rugged and strong enough to survive a flub-dub crevasse mishap in which my partner's lesser packboard collapsed.

Is a mountaineer's life in town of any interest? Perhaps. Actually, there's little to report here, except that Norman is not an uncommon sight in Bishop. He comes to town in recent months quite regularly, about once a fortnight, parks his old car in front of our house and walks Main Street for "raids on the ten-cent store," visits to the secondhand store or a church rummage sale, and maybe a check-in with the sheriff's office to moan about the latest vandalism at Baker Creek Ranch. Might be he would stop in at the Forest Service office and get involved in "one of my tomfool stories about life in the mountains during the Eocene era" and, most important, a sortie to the grocery store to lay in a supply for the old cabin. This is quite a contrast to the old days on Big Pine Creek, when he sometimes came to town so seldom that he nearly lost the power of speech. Lately he comes to get some home cooking, and how he does love to talk. Walt Wheelock called him "taciturn." Does Walt really know Norman? Maybe a long time ago he was aloof, but today he is no stranger to many who recognize the slightly stooped figure, slowed but little by his eighty-six years, always crowned with the Stetson, a rucksack on his back and a sagging briefcase in his hand.

When I was talking about campaign hats, I forgot to mention Norman's other hats and caps. When a man is such a character and bears on his crown such a distinguishing advertisement for most of a whole century, it is positively startling to see that shock of unruly white hair escaping from under a stocking cap or a ski cap or a fedora. I'm only exaggerating a little if I say there might also be a fez in his pack.

Walt Wheelock mentions that Norman's first-ascent cairns are found all over the Sierra, by bold climbers who think they are first to reach a rock summit. Harold Klieforth and I came upon one in the early 1960s, with no record other than Norman's for thirty years before our arrival. I think it may be, too, that Norman did not mark all his first ascents by the customary erection of a stone monument, or even comment on the feat. In more recent years Norman has been going on Sierra Club outings as a "king of the woodpile," general storyteller and a sort of museum exhibition, being, as he says, "about nine hundred years old."

I have followed Norman on innumerable short walks and watched him build his famous green-log-fireplace campsites in many a wilderness bivouac, panted up his snowsteps, shinnied up his rock routes, and skied far back in his wake across the glacier, but I thought the time I invited him to go with me on a cattle-hauling trip across Nevada I would surely catch him off base. Hauling cattle in a truck and trailer is a hot, dusty, noisy, tiresome grind across dirt roads through endless desert wastes, but Norman sat stoically across the cab from me for the whole thirty-hour trip, in apparent enjoyment and appreciation of the scene. My proud manipulation of the rig impressed him not the least, but he had many comments on the sparse vegetation and scattered wildlife of the steppes whenever the engine noise permitted. Whoever calls him taciturn does not know our friend well or needs a thesaurus. Mostly the frequent stops—to check on the cows and the loading and unloading—reminded my companion of his time spent on cattle ranches, and a flood of memories ensued, unfortunately all lost in the fogs of my poor memory.

The other day, Doug Robinson and I went down to Big Pine to check up on Norman, where he lives in an old house at the rear of the Sanitarium grounds. He is there because he has been raided by the hoodlum kids of Big Pine and lost the very necessities of life, including his pots and pans, his kerosene pressure lamps for reading, his axes and wedges. He estimates it would cost 150 dollars to replace his stores and make the cabin liveable again, and he has been trying to save out of his county pension for a car. Of course, he should not have a car at all, because he is a hazard to himself and others. His reaction time has slowed, and one eye and one ear are not quite up to the increased speeds of modern traffic. On the other hand, here is a man who has lived more than fifty years in total independence, and now he is subjected to the insulting and degrading position of being waited on by well-meaning but impersonal nurses, who have rules and regulations and their own ideas about the proper temperature for a reading room and when lights should be on and off and whether smoking should be permitted—though they themselves smoke and foul the air with vapors medicinal and poisonous, while failing to guard him from garrulous vapidities. With a car Norman could stock his old cabin at Baker Ranch with groceries, drive to Bishop for the advantages of the big city, make that long-delayed trip to the Last Chance Range, and once again be in business for himself.

So Norman, Doug, and I drove up to the old ranch, which is only a mile from the Sanitarium. This time he did not make a pointed effort to dissuade us from entering the unkempt house by showing us the outdoor living room—a spot fifty yards from the old vine-covered three-room ranch house, where he has dragged four old davenports from the town dump and arranged them in a circle. I knew that the reason he could let me in, and even Doug, who was a stranger, was that the chaotic mess could be blamed on the looters. And indeed it was terrible. Cardboard grocery boxes full of photographs, lantern slides, drawings, magazines, writings, articles, notes, and all the paperwork a part-time professional nature writer might collect in a half century, were no longer stacked to the ceiling around the walls of the three small rooms of Mrs. Baker's old house, but now lay strewn across the floors like a cartoonist's drawing of an earthquake. I could feel through my boots the slick texture of photographic paper, which, I realized, bore images of mountainscapes, images that recorded high and dangerous adventure and a spirit of noble sportsmanship probably inconceivable to the vandals responsible for such outrage. But

I knew, from rare previous glimpses into the pack-rat decor of Norman's boar's nest, that only the worst of the disarray was caused by forces beyond Norman's control. He was never a neat man. Perhaps he wanted to be, or meant to be. I suspect his intellectual turn of mind predisposed him to a regard for order, but he was most disorderly, and, if my theory is correct, this is what made his failing really hurt. Perhaps because it would wound his fierce pride, he almost never allowed anyone to see the inside of his house.

It puzzles me, now that I think about it, that the cabins he occupied during the winters at Glacier Lodge could be so cluttered. After all, there can be only so much crap a man can lug into a one-room cabin, to mess it up with in only one winter. You remember that every summer he had to get out. Nevertheless, those cabins were a weird and wonderful display of the largest one-man Seattle Co-op mountain-equipment store I've ever seen. I think he never in his life threw out anything and was convinced that there was at least one right and proper piece of equipment for every conceivable situation that might happen to a man in the mountains, and he believed in having it ready to hand—if possible in duplicate.

Starting from the ground up but not wishing to go into extreme detail, I might call your attention to the different types of slipper one can find advertised in the Sears and Sawbuck catalogue. It is a good idea to have the slipper with just a toepiece and no heel, because they are the fastest to put on, but then they are a little cold, so later on in the winter one wants a warmer model with heels, and as the temperature really drops it is nice to have sheepskin-lined slippers, and once one could get cheap, war-surplus aviator boots with rubber soles and sheep lining, but the leather deteriorated after awhile, and the straps were generally taken off to repair snowshoe bindings. Then too, if some hungry coyote comes around asking to be shot, and it's one of those real frosty, frozen-crusted nights, then it's best to have a slipper that's quickly thrown on but still has a good, nonskid sole—maybe an old Bramani handsewn on. I still haven't got off the ground, but you get the idea.

There is a photograph of the old Glacier Lodge cabin on our bulletin board here, and it reminds me of a couple of things. The picture shows me arriving at the cabin on skis, with a hundred-pound sack of potatoes on my back. I've kept the old picture all these years because it is completely out of character, and the only time I've ever carried one hundred pounds on skis, but it was nothing out of the ordinary for Norman and was exactly how he got his supplies into the then isolated house in the little grove of Jeffreys in Big Pine. Anything that wasn't hauled in before snow time had to arrive by muscle power from wherever the snowline on the unplowed road stopped the old Chevrolet. Also, he would go down to Big Pine for his mail several times during the winter, occasionally making the entire trip on foot. I don't think he ever had a regular schedule for mail trips, because that time I visited him when he complained of almost losing his power of speech was after a five-month absence from the valley.

The cabin in the canyon was deep in a grove of big trees, but one window—the one by his bed—offered a day-and-night view of the most spectacular peak standing boldly at the head of the canyon. This beautiful mountain had long been called, by those geography freaks who have to identify every spire in the Sierra Nevada, Peak 13,956. However, for at least three decades it has been known as Clyde Peak, because Norman was the first to climb it, and because of all of Norman's first ascents, it is the one mountain that dominated his cabin and in some ways his life for a quarter century. He could watch the topmost crags turn pink from the morning sun while still in bed, and all day long he would turn and gaze at it from time to time. Its starlit snows still gleamed faintly in the clear Sierra skies when he doused the lantern at night.

Probably a startling proportion of the photographs he has taken are of this noble peak, taken either from his front window or from pine-leaf-framed viewpoints nearby. An appropriate mountain to carry Norman's name. Its elevation, just short of the nearby fourteen-thousand-foot Middle Palisade, guards it from the ravages of the multitude, and, like Norman, its visage suggests the adjectives *wild, aloof, dignified, difficult* and the phrase "prominent yet unknown."

Norman was never really what I would call a close friend. Actually, I never had a comparable relation with anybody else. He was about thirty years my senior and a man of formidable reputation to one who has made mountain climbing a chief excuse for living and who heard of Norman many years before encountering him, while still in the romantic grip of hero worship of the classic pioneers of our sport. Yet Norman was an institution we took for granted. He was always simply part of the scene. We knew he could be found up there at the cabin on Big Pine Creek or the old ranch on Baker Creek, ready to show us some new-fangled aluminum slingshot he had just bought, or to walk three thousand feet up the mountainside for a color photograph of the snow blowing off the peaks, or to make an overnight trip to that high tarn where we could get on the cliff early enough in the morning to return for trout fishing. We knew that anyway he would sooner or later be around to dig into my library and scatter everything around the living room and jam-and-butter-and-syrup-up the tablecloth and tell us of the summer high trip and how to load for a little more muzzle velocity.

Someone said once that Norman was "open-ended," meaning, I suppose, that his life was unstructured, as the current cliché has it. Not so. Not if the someone meant that Norman is the least bit unreliable or inclined in the slightest to live a loose, unscheduled life. Other people have made the same mistake in assuming that, because Norman lives an unconventional life, dresses in outmoded clothes, and seldom gets around to the barber, he has the free and easy attitudes of hippies and others in our modern, liberated subcultures. Yet how he does fume when people don't show up when they say they will! His famous temper can shoot above the flash point at even the delayed receipt of expected mail. It is true he is not that careful himself, often losing his calendar and constantly losing his watch, but, perhaps like the neatness he does not practice but still regards as appropriate, he really admires punctuality.

Punctuality and the programming of time are characteristic traits in spite of the fact that one may find him spending an entire afternoon in the outdoor parlor of his old cabin or sleeping late in the equally outdoor bedroom. Sleeping late means being in bed— on the ancient couch covered with ragged tarpaulin under a locust tree, where Norman slumbers for ten months of the year as a respite from the claustrophobia of the house—until after the summer sunrise. But you can bet he has his arising time planned, and the afternoon talk or all-morning reading session that is also part of the program.

He is perhaps as he has been described: the old-fashioned gentleman, with a little bit of Victorianism or even Puritanism unwittingly seeping from his minister's son background of many years ago. He would have to be labeled a conservative, at least in most senses of the word not immediately connected with politics. He may read and appreciate Thoreau, but it is easy for an awed young Clyde admirer to get carried away and compare him with Vinobe Bhave, the walking saint of India, when a more apt example might be Kit Carson. When he comes to our house nowadays, he may sit in the straight-backed chair by the window, with his old campaign hat on to shade his good eye from the overhead light, and read through the day and into the evening, stopping only for his three squares, a snooze, and a blast now and then at something. If a book is on the davenport, he will pick it up, and if the title reads anything like *The Awakening of Faith in the Mahayana* or *The Affluent Society* or *Modern Chess Openings*, he drops it instantly and heaves to his feet to follow the well-worn path to the section of our bookcase where his thumbprints mark *Some Problems of Pleistocene Morphology*, *Land and Land Forms*, *Life on the Arctic Slope*, and similar light classics.

One time he got hold of a book on a couple who had spent some winters in the Brooks Range of Alaska. He got a lot of mileage out of that one. For a couple of years he found a way to work anecdotes from this book—I think there was a series of books—into almost every conversation. He never could remember names, or doesn't try to, but just as he nicknames almost everyone he meets, he captioned the authors of these books the "Eat-a-Mooses." Apparently they shot a great many moose, so he lampooned them by declaring that they ate a moose a day. After explaining the nickname, he would launch into a long discussion of their particular methods of wilderness survival. About half the time he would grant a grudging approval of their techniques—and then think of something that touched one of the numerous exposed nerves in the body of gospel of how to go out and live in the woods with only a gun and a bag of salt according to Norman Clyde, and wham! Like a sonic boom he would blast us out of our complacent inattention to the dull monologue with loud and pithy profanity. But just for a few seconds, for the chuckle is always close upon the curse, and then he would be off on a theme of his own: a long-winded story of what happened in that canyon over on the other side of Mount. . . .

It seems to me, Dave, you told me over the telephone not to philosophize about Norman, or eulogize him, and that you did not want an essay on what a noble specimen he was, what a great contributor to literature on the mystique of the outdoors, what he meant to the cosmos and vice versa, and all that crap. Well, I apologize if I have sometimes gotten close to what you did not want. I know you wanted a string of anecdotes of trips with Norman in the mountains, and although I'm sure there must have been a book's worth of these had I the sense to have written them down, I just cannot think of many now. Therefore, I have tried to describe what he was like and, more particularly, because of my short memory, what he has been like recently. Also, I wanted to use my frequent and more intimate acquaintance than most people have had with Norman to try to get a bit inside him to see what kind of a man he is.

Of course, while Norman is almost garrulous on some occasions

and some subjects, he is extremely reticent when it comes to anything personal, and this is where observers go wrong in trying to
assess his character. Neither Jules—his intimate companion on a
long list of first ascents in the early thirties—nor I ever suspected
that Norman had been married, as it turned out he had. It is an
interesting comment on our relation to the man that Wheelock obtained this information simply by asking Norman. Anyhow, Norman does carry a certain reserve and obviously does not want to
discuss his private life. If one gets to prying so much as to ask his
age, he will pointedly suggest that it is none of anybody's business.
I don't really know him. Who does? Does anybody really know
anybody? Actually, Norman has been for so long a permanent fix-
ture of the landscape of our lives here that he has become like an
old uncle who is sometimes a trial and often a pride, but normally
an integral part of the scene—whose wrinkled contours of eccen-
tricity, familiarity, or inscrutability are no more to be noted or analyzed than the cragged face of the mountain outside my window.

Well, I've been dogging off quite a bit since you called a couple
of months ago, and have only the excuse that I've been down with
a bad back and a bum hip much of the time. We plan to go to Big
Pine to check on Norman again, so I'll knock this off and hope that
all this rambling garbage contains some nuggets you may be able
to use, Dave. Sure wish I had kept notes all these years. Also apologize again for so much personal stuff, but that's the only way I
could think of to write it, and anyway you are going to edit the hell
out of it, I hope.

Yours,
Smoke

9

Cross California

I'M OFTEN asked to name the best trip I've ever made. An easy answer is the most recent trip. If asked to specify the trip that seems least liable to fade in memory, the 1967 "Cross California" leaps to mind. I concocted it to celebrate my thirty years in California since the Leech-North-Blanchard climbing expedition of 1937 first brought me to the Golden State. My plan called for visiting some of the mountains of that first Sierra trip and also to walk entirely across my adopted state—sometimes observing nature in worshipful solitude and sometimes enjoying companionship in boisterous laughter. The recipe contained all the correct geographical ingredients: purple mountain majesties, fruited plains, and shining sea.

I charted my course to satisfy certain criteria. It had to start from Nevada. The 14,000-foot mountains on either side of my home valley—White Mountain Peak and the North Palisade—made natural points through which to draw a walking line. I would spend most of my allotted month-and-a-half in the Sierra. I would stay off trails and traveled ways as much as was practical. I wanted to stay east of the crest whenever possible to be able to look back on Owens Valley. The incomparable Yosemite Valley was part of our '37 itinerary, and its walls and waterfalls needed worship. I wanted to commune with both mountain and coast species of redwood trees. San Francisco, the Paris of the Pacific shore, required visiting, and I would walk along the beach to finish at Point Reyes on the Pacific Ocean. All of these objectives matured as planned, and I won't deny that ticking off goals added much to the enjoyment.

Before plunging into the task of measuring, weighing, and packing food, I drew up a schedule, which I published for friends with invitations to join me whenever possible. Rather than trying to get word out as I encountered slowdowns or shortcuts along the way, I decided to adjust my speed to the schedule, so that friends could rely on meeting me. I kept to the schedule so accurately that when I checked into the hotel I'd reserved in Berkeley near the end of the walk, the phone was ringing!

I knew all along, even as the trip took shape in my mind, that I enjoyed the ultimate secret weapon guaranteeing success. I refer to my absolutely indispensable helpmate, Su, who resupplied me at frequent intervals. The meeting places we built into the schedule were above roadheads, away from polluting cars. We chose them to be not only logistically sound but to provide a pleasantly shared rest day.

A recently acquired aversion to heavy loads influenced my equipment list. I pared everything to the bone. Climbing gear included the trusty ice ax and a light line. Crampons would have added only a pound, but I begrudged even that and looked forward to many bouts of step cutting during this year of record August snowfields. Maybe I cut a little into the bone selecting my sleeping gear, as I took only the cover to my bag and shivered myself to sleep most nights. The fly to my tent worked well for rain shelter. Kitchen gear got almost luxurious with spoon and cup, teapot, stew pot, water carrier so I could camp above streams, and even a plastic pudding shaker. There might have been the odd pair of slippers, and a paperback (*Philosophy of the Buddha*, by A. J. Bahm, a very high protein, low fat, sugarfree book), but little else not usable for fueling the body.

Su hauled me over Montgomery Pass to Dyer, Nevada, with Dave Sharp and his nine-year-old son, Ted, my companions for the five-day crossing of White Mountain. A couple of years before, Dave climbed with me in Alaska, where we nicknamed him "Big Stomper" for his ability to break trail in deep snow while pulling away from us and disappearing over the hill ahead. His great strength guaranteed young Ted's crossing the mountain, for Dave could have carried him if necessary.

Dyer, Nevada, turned out to be just a post office with a dirt road running up a slightly inclined alluvial fan a half-mile toward the mountain from the level plain. To make doubly sure we started properly, we asked an Indian woman whose cabin stood in the shadow of the great mountain for her name and permission to photograph her—everything but an affidavit that we were still in Nevada.

Between us and Bishop stood one of the chosen barriers of the walk: one of the greatest mountains in America. The immense fault block of White Mountain rises to 14,000 feet from level plains of 4,000 feet on each side. The arid range knew little glaciation during Pleistocene times, and no deep canyons were carved into its monolithic bulk. As a result it carries little water and no lakes. This "lack of points of interest" restricts the destructive two-legged animal. A fine stream flowed in this heavy-snow year, and we soon found a good campsite in cottonwoods an hour into the evening.

Highlights of the morning: a tricky stream crossing, and Dave's catching with his hands a trout, which Ted insisted he release. Melted into the memorable events of the day: mountain mahogany. "*Cercocarpus ledifolius*. Rose family. Evergreen shrub or small tree, six to twenty feet high. Flowers inconspicuous, but the silvery-feathery tails of its fruits are distinctive; leaves rigid, dark green above, slightly curled under at edges; foliage has sweet spicy fragrance on warm days. Dry, rocky slopes."* As these rocky slopes were also the temporary habitat of three climbers bound for White Mountain, the description should include the information that mountain mahogany tears shirts, knocks off hats, scratches knees, and punctures patience. Brush fights figure in all cross-country travel in Alaska, Washington, Oregon, and much of California. They scratch many an offtrail walker in the dry Sierra, but we didn't expect to do battle high on a desert mountainside.

I'm trying to reconstruct this trip from memory to see what fifteen years does to impressions. The notes, though, recall that all was not hot steep mahogany-maze. We lunched in limber and albicaulis (whitebark) pines, watching blue jays. Ted brought along comic books and small plastic toy cars to fill in these sit-down intervals. When our talk bored him, he muttered to himself, "Some people say that animals have it better than kids because they don't have to go to school, but not so, because they have to find their own food."

By late afternoon we drew up onto rounded slopes sprinkled with alpine flowers and tempting rock pinnacles. The rockclimbing ambition didn't overpower us after such a big day, and, when we saw a fair meadow below with a stream running through a mini-grove of bristlecone pines, we glissaded the snowbank into camp.

The next two days treated us to as grand a high ridge tour as we could ask for. We walked on a carpet of delicate alpine flowers, traversed a sharp rock ridge where we roped Ted for safety, and bivouacked right on top of the 14,000-foot peak. We watched a storm hurl lightning across the ranges of Nevada, and, afterwards in evening calm, the lowering sun's rays mirrored ponds and even irrigation ditches in Chalfant Valley, two vertical miles beneath us.

We were off at dawn, gloved and stocking-capped for a glissade

---

*From *Deepest Valley: A Guide to Owens Valley and its Mountain Lakes, Roadsides and Trails*, edited by Genny Schumacher Ward (San Francisco: Sierra Club, 1969).

down to meadows populated with deer and marmots, where we walked through more flowers. The spring we'd marked for evening camp came too soon, so we declared it our lunch stop instead. But we could not laze long in the perfumed grass, near two mountain sheep skulls, because we had to spend a long afternoon looking for water. It turned out to be an extra long day, which had us padding down a winding sandy wash through bristlecone pines, aspen, and finally piñon, then down, down, to eventually come upon water under a great cliff just at dark. The notes, already terse, describe no suffering from that long day but succinctly mention the caterer and the dessert: "Dave—anchovies—brandy."

The next morning we walked along the stream, munching watercress, until we could exit from the canyon and take a beeline through sagebrush flats to the Owens River bridge. After a refreshing swim, we soon reached my house having completed the first leg of the long trip.

I also chose a beeline toward the next 14,000-foot peak. I've thought a lot about that course, because from my window I can see the 7,000-foot hill of sage and rocks I climbed on the way to the high peaks. My route made no bees jealous of its straightness, but it is not every August that a man goes on foot by any course out of the hot bottom of Owens Valley up to ice-floe lakes. The notes for that twelve-hour day sum it up well: "Cows, flowers, view of Ralston Peak, meadows on top, lodgepole forest, moraines, mosquitoes."

A day later I sliced steps with my ice ax to outflank the bergschrund on the North Palisade. Norman rated this mountain the finest in the Sierra. I agree. The enormous summit boulders provide a royal throne from which to watch row on row of snow-spattered peaks march along the Sierra. The gods do not offer this grandstand to the casual stroller—tickets go only to mountaineers with proven credentials. My notes for this day wax less listlike in comparing this peak with the trip's first fourteen-thousander: "No, no, Dave. I like your White Mountain Peak, its loneliness, its aspect as an island in the vast desert, its peculiar beauty, and the feeling of airy isolation from being suspended between two deep valleys, but compared with the North Palisade? No, it cannot compare with my view now: so much snow, so many cliffs, the sun sparkling on lakes. I can even hear rushing waters far below!"

From the down-go I can still remember the taste of these tidbits: a hummingbird buzzed my bright neckerchief as I eased down foot- and handholds; a red seven-millimeter rope used as a handline can compare with a Morris chair for comfort and is more portable; snow is a variable substance, but when it is firm enough and the slope safe enough to glissade, we can class it perfect; the sound of a rock kicked onto pond ice is most musical whether or not it plays the okay-to-cross-me tune; the sound of frogs is even better.

From the high basin under the far side of the North Palisade, the John Muir Trail aims toward Yosemite, but I couldn't risk smothering in peopled forests. I determined that my course must wind among the peaks, keeping my home valley in view as much as possible.

My journal gushed with ardent phrases for the scenes and activities of each hour of the first half week. After that it crashed from a literary crest to a level list, reading like this excerpt: "false pass, pass, couloir, cut steps, unclimbed peak, lower pack, raise pack, cliff, lake, other pass, snow up, down, cold wind from south, calm now." If I cannot translate this code now, it means little. I wouldn't write everything anyway, any more than I would diagram emotions of any other love affair.

The high peaks flashed almost every jewel in the mountain vault, and I was as greedily happy as any miser. The nine-hour off-trail days kept me busy with mountaineering exercise, and I was content to sit on rock furniture arranged within arms' reach of the kitchen fire in the evening. I soon learned to patronize an infinitely varied library and read the flames till heavy eyelids forced me to bed.

The heavy snows not only gave me much step-cutting drill, but provided afternoon glissade descents. Twice I walked right across lakes still frozen in this Pleistocene mid-August. Thunderstorms frosted the cake of my delight with hail-whitened ledges. I was never lonely and often not even alone.

I was bound for the first resupply rendezvous with Su, in the Evolution group of peaks. Good Su, she was right there with groceries for the belly and good spirit for the soul. We immediately declared a holiday to enjoy our solitary lake.

The next two weeks contained a distillation of everything that is right and good about mountain traveling. As anticipated, I made my way almost entirely off-trail, cutting steps up and glissading down snowfields, and solving rock climbs on the numerous spurs I crossed. I met many mini-challenges, but nothing I couldn't readily solve with my trusty ax and light line. The days kept me fully occupied the whole of the sunlit hours, so that I spent my evenings in sedentary position. Maybe I should say sedimentary, as my pants, at least, became part of my rock seats. I wore a hole in the seat of my wool trousers from shifting on rock chairs to reach piles of firewood, the cook pots, and the groceries in my pack. Once I had selected a ledge, carried up water, built the furniture, and started the cook fire, I remained seated till bedtime.

I climbed over the top of Mount Darwin by a route new to me, which presented my favorite kind of pinnacled-ridge climbing. The names of Gary Leech, Hubert North, and Smoke Blanchard, from 1937, still graced the pages of the register book on the small summit! That made me want to come down the route we used so long ago. I found it still steep.

Midway along this wonderful section of mountains opposite Bishop, Su met me again with my son, Bobby, and his buddy Fred Slemsek (who was later killed in Vietnam). Pat Armstrong, an old Buttermilk climbing buddy, walked over a pass from his Forest Service job, with his guitar on his back, to sing for our evening campfire. When Ted and Dave Sharp joined us, we knew we had a quorum for the business of climbing Mount Humphreys in the morning.

During the second week of this phase of the trip, afternoon showers began to chase me around. They didn't stop me from climbing Bear Creek Spire, which I reached from a high camp to which I hauled firewood. Down the other side of the mountain I dropped my pack, the better to go lightly down-canyon to meet Su and her children.

This time she guided Lorelle, age 3, and Glen, age 2, up the easy trail. As you might guess, the children were practiced walkers; even so they drew many startled comments from trail hikers who didn't expect to see short legs so far into the hills. Six-foot, four-inch Bob Patterson had longer legs. He had climbed many mountains with me, and came in with Su to join me on the Mono Pass-to-Mammoth Pass stretch.

To celebrate joining the youngsters and to give them more of a holiday, we declared another day off. Before making camp, though, I had to go back up to retrieve my pack. I circled around and then came back down with the rucksack, using the route I'd originally descended past a camp occupied by a man, a woman, and six girls. They giggled, "You or another fellow just like you came by three hours ago."

"That was me," said I. "If you are the same girls, then I must be going in circles!"

The main thing I remember about the day with the children is the thunderstorm. This one didn't wet us, but it threatened so loudly and flashily, with such an excess of noise and exaggerated display of lightning in blue-black clouds just outside our camp perimeter, that we would have preferred a drenching to a scaring.

Patterson and I enjoyed many fine lightning displays on our section of the walk, but they always stayed a decent distance from us. The cross-state trip wasn't supposed to be a mountain-collecting exercise, but I seemed to stumble onto plenty in my path. I managed to find my way up Red Slate Mountain while Bob waited for me at the base.

When Joan Patterson met us at Mammoth, she did the best thing for mountaineers: she brought fresh bread and an enormous tossed green salad. Joan's car-hauled luxuries seduced us into violating our rule against camping near roadheads. As a result we were awakened in the pitch-black predawn by a troop of Boy Scouts chopping up the forest. They did me a favor, really, as I needed an unusually early start to traverse Mammoth Mountain and still meet Su on the other side early in the day. I told her I would swing by the lake and ice-ax holes in the Scouts' canoes so they would drown and campers would have the next morning quiet.

Mammoth Mountain was so sad! Volcanoes always look dreary in midsummer, stripped of winter white, with the few old drifts covered with dirty cinders. I knew all this, and I knew progress in the form of buildings and ski-lift machinery was coming to ruin the pure muscle-powered ski traverses I'd made so often; still the ugliness of construction shocked me.

Su joined me for the seven-day section to Yosemite Valley. Now, at last, she became a full-fledged member of this cross-country expedition, and could participate in moving the food bags over the hills and in cooking and consuming their contents. She got to climb her very own mountain, too. For this we selected Yosemite's highest, Mount Lyell. From the summit I pointed out White Mountain, back near the start of the trip, and showed Su approximately where San Francisco hid in the haze many days ahead.

My sometime-kept notebook has totally blank pages for most of this section, and when the pages show any pencil scratchings, they turn out to be lists of trees. I refer you to any handbook on Sierra Nevada natural history, life-zones chapter. My mental scrapbook, though, still carries some underlined experiences I'd like to share. While crossing a high pass north of Mount Lyell, we walked across a frozen lake on the 15th of August. I want this recorded on the plus side of California geography for those foreigners who imagine we suffer in an unbearably hot wasteland, relieved only by orange trees and movie stars. The thunderstorms that had circled teasingly around for two weeks moved in to pour and soak. We watched amazed as solid sheets of water washed down granite slabs on the sides of Merced Canyon as spectacularly as the famed waterwheels of the Merced River.

A couple of things happened in our camp above Nevada Falls.

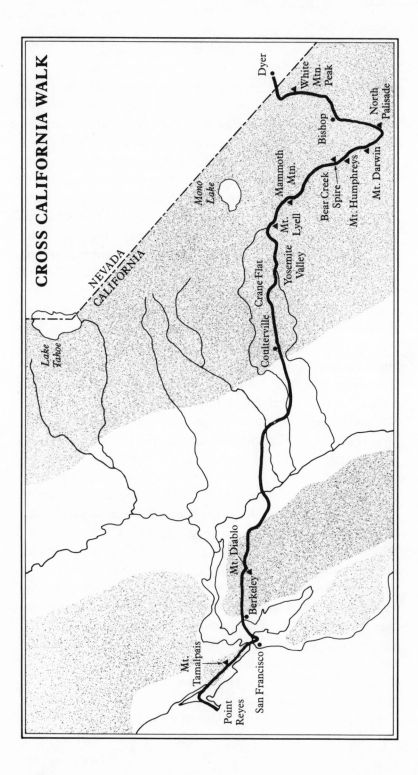

CROSS CALIFORNIA WALK

NEVADA
CALIFORNIA

Lake
Tahoe

Mono
Lake

Dyer

White
Mtn.
Peak

North
Palisade

Bishop

Mammoth
Mtn.

Bear Creek
Spire

Mt. Humphreys

Mt. Darwin

Mt.
Lyell

Crane Flat

Yosemite
Valley

Coulterville

Mt. Diablo

Berkeley

Mt.
Tamalpais

San Francisco

Point
Reyes

Just as we were turning in, well after dark, a party on horseback came and began to make camp next to us. Puzzled by the late arrival, I asked what kind of travelers they were.

"We are hunters," the man said.

Since there is no hunting season in Yosemite National Park, I waited quietly for more. He said solemnly, "We are hunting for my son."

The main search had given up a month before, so speed was not a factor, but the terror and urgency were still fresh enough. It affected me like a blow to the belly—reminded me that tragedy can come to the mountains too.

On a lighter note I will tell a bear story. Su woke in the middle of the night and opened her eyes to see Smoke standing in the dark just beyond the sleeping bags.

"It's his plumbing," she thought. "He'll be back soon."

She snuggled down again but jumped up when she felt Smoke's elbow near her. Then she saw the man in the fur coat drop to all fours and shuffle off through the forest. The bear had poked a long fingernail through the back of my pack and into the powdered onion soup. I doubt if he enjoyed licking his finger.

Yosemite Valley richly deserves its reputation as one of the premier places among the planet's mountains. I've had many fine experiences there, but on this trip the most satisfactory waterfall fell from the showerhead of our Camp Curry quarters. Bobby motored over in his new car to pick up Su and to bring my lowland gear. I substituted a cane for my ice ax, discarded the rope, cut the kitchen down to fit into a small rucksack, and changed to lighter shoes.

To commemorate motoring to Yosemite Valley via the old one-way-traffic entrance in 1937, I found the abandoned road and followed bear tracks in its dusty surface to high above Crane Flat. I bedded down between two behemoths of a seven-tree row of giant sequoias. The strongly felt sentience of the mighty guardians of my little nest purveyed a stronger medicine than any cliff bivouac, and that night I became a druid.

My mountain climbing friends wondered how I would fare in the dread Central Valley. Happily. And it was not all dreadful. I talked to farmers and farm animals, learned to turn off my highwayside ear and tune in to birds, watched insect tracks in the soft dirt of the road edge, and enjoyed a new (to me) entertainment called "color TV" in soft, cushy motels.

After leaving the mountains, I seemed to encounter small comedy regularly. Most of these happenings are not worth recording, but I will tell of the wine tour. It was Sunday. Tasting room open, winery closed. I told the tasting-room attendant only part of the story—how my regular Bishop climbing partner Hal Klieforth had turned me on to wine, how we had settled on Franzia because of its superiority (actually because it was a bargain in Bishop at the time), and how Franzia was the only winery on my route stretching all the way from Nevada. He excused himself to make a phone call. The president personally escorted me through his factory.

Across the Central Valley it felt good to get into the hills again near Byron. After a delightful bivouac atop one of the golden-grassed, sensuously shaped, dome-topped hills, I drew up later in the day to the summit of Mount Diablo. Here was a two-story tower whose upper floor was filled with the machinery of a full-time fire lookout. The bottom floor echoed with emptiness save for a pay telephone. I leaped to the machine and dialed Bishop. While listening to the ring and waiting for Su to get off her pottery wheel and answer, I exulted in the view of a line of cumuli marking the distant Sierra. In the other direction I could almost see my destination. Practically the whole route was in view.

"Hi, Su. Where do you think I am?"

"You're on top of Mount Diablo."

My schedule was working.

Walking out of Walnut Creek, I came to a sign listing freeway rules prohibiting pedestrians and cycles. Twice I tried to outflank the freeway and failed. I'd have to just go on it anyway. But I could not afford to break my vow and ride in a wheeled police car! What to do? Cycles! That was the clue. I hurried to a motorcycle shop for advice. They told me that California law permitted passage over a freeway, regardless of prohibitions, if there was no alternate route. "But," they said, "on your walk from Orinda, you'll be killed by heavy construction vehicles using the space between the freeway and a concrete wall."

The warning was enough. Their predicted fate was even worse than riding in a patrol car. What then?

"Well, maybe if you get up very early and walk by starlight. Construction starts at dawn."

I made it. First daylight found me following deer tracks in the dust on the shoulder of the Fish Ranch Road off-ramp. I reached the top of the Berkeley hills in desolate gray fog that hung in the eucalyptus trees. A car stopped across the empty street, and a woman leaned out and said, "You can see by the sign on the side of my car that I work for the East Bay Regional Parks authority. I was sent out this morning to find and photograph a walker."

"You've come to the right place. I've just walked here from Dyer, Nevada."

After making my way down the hill, over the green lawns of the campus, and in and out of the library and bookstores (now I could tell prospective employers I'd been through the University of California), I checked in at my hotel. As previously mentioned, the phone was ringing; a very prompt, on-time walker, I.

On the crossing from Berkeley to the San Francisco peninsula, highway laws again fouled me, but I was prepared this time. I already knew of the prohibition against walking the Bay Bridge and contracted with my good friend Bob Swift to sail me across the bay. Motorless boats were okay, and the trip's purity was preserved.

San Francisco is a preeminent walking town. While Su deployed the car to Point Reyes to provide transport at walk's end, Tex Mock, a rockclimbing friend from Bishop, joined me on a thorough all-day city jaunt featuring an ascent of the east face of Telegraph Hill.

Thirty years ago three Oregon mountaineers spent a hungry day strolling Market Street with only enough money left to fuel our Ford for the return to Portland. Worse than the prospect of shriveled stomachs was the distinct possibility that we'd miss climbing Shasta and Thielsen if we couldn't finance our feed. Good old Hubert put the bite on a Chinese friend of his for five dollars, which pieced out our food budget for the return plus two mountain climbs. In dreaming up this thirtieth-anniversary dedicatory trip, I intended to press five dollars on the first Chinese person I saw as a substitute for Hubert's unknown friend. The idea was noble, but in practice, timidity and cupidity stopped any such extravagance.

Su now joined me for the final phase of the trip, which included walking across the Golden Gate Bridge, passing through Sausalito and the coast redwoods of Muir Woods National Monument, climbing over Mount Tamalpais, and beach walking to Point Reyes. The first evening out of the city we were encamped on Tamalpais sipping port after supper on a boulder overlooking the fabulous skyscraper skyline, when we heard a crashing of brush and the call: "Smoke Blanchard! Smoke Blanchard!"

"Who knows you are here?" Su asked. It turned out that Dean Meyer did, a brother of my old expeditionary partner Bruce, and one Bert Ballmer, Mill Valley City Manager. Bruce had told his brother, "You'll find him; his schedule says Tamalpais tonight." It surely would take a man of Bruce's positive personality to make such an optimistic statement. Optimism kindles luck, and at the first stop the searchers made on the massive mountain the first shout was answered by the man they sought. Why were they looking for me? Perhaps because Mr. Ballmer was also a correspondent for the Mill Valley paper. They asked if I would grant them an interview. I had to start by saying I'd turned down the major newspapers of San Francisco when they requested the same thing a day or two before: publicity shy. However, since they had sought me out so successfully in the dark of night on the wide slopes of the big mountain, how could I refuse?

They said they didn't know what I looked like, and, since it would be rude to turn a flashlight on my face, they'd just shoot me with a Polaroid camera and look at the instant picture. Before I could figure out this ploy as a newspaper trick, they were examining my photo by flashlight.

There was a rotogravure page from the paper in the mail when I reached home, describing me and my trip. It got trashed at some point, which is probably just as well.

On the forty-seventh day of the great walk, I struck the beach nine miles north of Point Reyes. Halfway from there to my final destination, a grand victory-celebration picnic was being prepared by good friends and their families. I was joined on the final four miles to Point Reyes by my favorite Alaskan snow stompers, Nort Benner, Jules Eichorn, Dick Kauffman, and Bruce Meyer.

I've taken other long walks almost as totally pleasurable, but, as I climbed up the cliff from the beach to Su's Volkswagen atop Point Reyes, I said to myself that any life which includes walks remotely approaching the happiness of this one must be judged a great success.

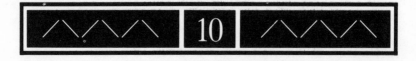

Death Valley

9 May 1977

Dear Cousin,

This is one of the hardest letters I've ever written. It has been a year to the day now. Sometimes still, a year later, it is so damn hard. I'm at the same typewriter stand. There is a fine storm in the mountains. Only the Little Egypt Pinnacles show below black clouds. Su's paintings hang on the wall behind me. And no Su.

I'm surviving fairly well, but a long spring of convalescence from an operation has weakened my mood. Now the significance of this date bears down on me so very hard.

It's been a year since I've written you and almost a year since I've seen you. The visit with houseguests all over the place left no opportunity to talk of Death Valley. I didn't want to anyway. I still don't. The very title of the place fills me with dread.

The children are holding up fine, as far as I can tell. Their grandmother called to ask if I would plan something special for them on Mother's Day. I guess I told you how the company sent the kiddies and me on a therapeutic scouting assignment in Arizona in June. It was horrible. It's hard to think about it even now. There were times when I could not see through the tears to drive.

It was this weekend a year ago. We were so happy. We were with our friends and doing another Death Valley trip. This time all downhill. A repeat of the trip down from Dante's View to Badwater, which Su and I had made with Dick and Ellie the year we were married. Ellie Kauffman had trouble that time. But I was kind and waited for her. We let her rest many times. Su was strong then.

This time Su was very much overweight. The 6,000-foot descent over rough rock was hard on her. She was probably a bit dehydrated. I kept urging her to go on. We'd rest in the car going home. There were three rope-lengths to go. (We weren't roped— no need to be on that easy but shaggy slope of gravel.)

She got dizzy. Fell. Rolled. I screamed at her to stop rolling. So loud Alla heard me at the bottom of the slope. I thought she was malingering. She rolled about twenty feet. The slope was maybe twenty degrees. She was unconscious and breathing hard. Nort and I sat and watched her for some time. I went down to get a litter, so she would not risk hurting her head again when we could take her on.

Nort hollered down at me that she had a skull fracture. I climbed full of fear. Nort hollered again and made a signal to me and said, "She's going to die, Smoke."

I've heard those words a thousand thousand times since. The keys are blurry now through my eyes. She was gone when I reached her.

When I got to the kids, playing on the lawn at Furnace Creek Ranch, Glenny said, "How come you're so late? Was somebody killed?"

The kids rolled in the grass. I did too. Glenny beat his fists on the sod. I was dry of tears then. Calm, for the kids. When I fell on the grass, I could smell the rich green smell of life, probably more powerful then because of the long day on dead barren rock. Even in my grief I could feel the life.

That was then. At the present moment I feel bad. A professional mountain guide. Trained to take care. To guard against fatigue. The guilt thing was only heavy at first. It was not my fault.

The kids and I went on beyond Arizona last June to visit a friend in Colorado who had lost her husband on a mountain. She used the shocked days to build a barn. My barn was my trips. They came in July and August to Japan, and in November and December to Nepal. While on the trips, even the first one, I was able to concentrate on the job and keep out of grief.

Home is hell. There is always the coming back. The re-entry to these scenes we built together. It was just a house before Su. So very much of my life locked up with her. The mountains are still here. I've been able to climb again. To enjoy. Maybe, let's say surely, I'll get it together again. Right now, it's so very hard. The empty house. The revolving calendar. I keep telling myself that I lived in Bishop, watching these clouds curtain off the pinnacles of Little Egypt, for more than two decades before Su came along, but. . . . Maybe it's time to move on. . . .

Sorry about all this load laid on you, dear cousin. I hope this catches you before your long trip. Maybe you can come by afterwards and find me strong and recovering.

Next time my letter will be full of some adventure in this or that corner of the world. "For some we loved—the loveliest and the best / have drunk their cup a round or two before / and one by one crept silently to rest." Life goes on.

Smoke

The author performing a standard maneuver on the route up The Little Pinnacle at Scheelite, California, 1971. The walking stick is regulation equipment for late-season ascents. *Jan Tiura*.

◄ The author and Palmer Gilbert approach Illumination Rock, on Mount Hood, via the Zigzag Glacier, 1935. *Gary Denzel Leech.*

The author, wearing hickory skis with bindings made from screen-door springs and his father's golfing plus fours, poses in the glade near Mount Hood's Camp Blossom Cabin, 1934. *Joe Daniel.* ▼

The good ship *Nancy Belle* with (left to right) able seamen Gary Leech and Henry North and Captain Hubert North aboard, on the Tualatin River southwest of Portland, Oregon, 1934. *Smoke Blanchard.* ▼

Norman Clyde with a 92-pound ▶
pack at Piute Pass, near Bishop,
at the beginning of a 46-day
Sierra trip in 1952. *Smoke
Blanchard.*

Norman Clyde and his 1926
Chevrolet cloth-top, near the
Baker Creek Ranch out-
buildings, 1956. The jalopy
may have been stripped down
for sale; it had not looked this
sleek and empty since it was
new. *Smoke Blanchard.* ▼

The author and Jules Eichorn, left, en route to Bishop Pass, Kings Canyon ▲
National Park, in 1972. *Su Blanchard.*

Jake Breitenbach and the Buick that took him and the author from Seattle to
Alaska in 1958. The headlight was repaired before leaving, but not so a broken
tailpipe, which dragged all the way to Anchorage. *Smoke Blanchard.* ▼

Camp on the Vittorio Sella Glacier, Mount Logan, during the 1959 ascent; the ▲
author, center. *Richard Kauffman.*

The "Hillsborough Boys" about to depart from Portland for Mount Logan in 1959.
Left to right: Jules Eichorn, Nort Benner, the author, and Richard Kauffman.
Robert K. Blanchard. ▼

The author's son Bob ▶
Blanchard on the summit of
Fool's Needle, circa 1962.
Smoke Blanchard

Su, on the Everest Road at
18,500 feet, on the way to
Kala Pattar in 1967. *Smoke
Blanchard.* ▼

Relaxing with a kalimba (or thumb piano) in the Palisade Sierra, 1973. ▲
Su Blanchard.

Entering India just south of Lumbini, Nepal, on the 1968 trip by bicycle to
Buddhist pilgrimage sites. *Laurie Engel.* ▼

Ready for a day of climbing at the Blanchard family camp at Sixth Lake in the Palisades, 1975. *Su Blanchard.*

Equipment

Theodore Winthrop bagged it completely when he described preparations for his 1850s crossing of the Cascade Range in his book *Canoe and Saddle*:

> There are several requisites for travel. First, a world and a region of the world to travel in. Second, a traveler. Third, a means of conveyance, legs—human or other, barks, carts, enchanted carpets, and the like. Fourth, guidance by man—personal or impersonal—acting by roads, guide books, maps, and itineraries. Fifth, multifarious wherewithals.

Today, before assembling the "multifarious wherewithals," we thumb through stacks of catalogs. Winthrop could hardly imagine the complications of the gear game in this age of camping consumerism.

Trekking guide Bob Swift complains that he has never had all the exactly right things and nothing else in his kit. It is my ambition to win this game. When that regular page in my notebook la-

173

beled "next time" comes back blank, from anything more expeditionary than the casual afternoon walk, I will be ready to write Blanchard's *Bible of Travel*: the up-to-the second final revision of Dalton's *Shifts and Contrivances Available in Wild Places*.

Right now I'm approaching perfection in packing for Nepal, and need only an extension of my lifetime to come up with the ideal kit for all occasions. Here is a partial list for assorted occasions.

Starting from the top and working toeward, the Almost Complete Walker is crowned with a real ski cap. Some genius perfected this design before fashion infiltrated the ski scene. It has an eye-shading bill and earflaps to guard against sunburn and frost nip. Its light material folds to fit in the pocket when "gompa going" (Sherpa phrase for visiting a temple). I started wearing a ten-cent baseball cap in my youth to keep the parka hood out of my eyes. My custom hardened into habit, and now my eyes complain of the California or Nepal sun if they're not shaded by a cap bill.

The neat monocular, invaluable for spotting the errant trekker or separating the sheep from the goats, is worn on a thong necklace of red nylon. Next is a tennis shirt of net material.

Riding in my rucksack are all manner of accoutrements for the odd emergency. First aid, of course. Why do I say "of course"? Could be leftover guilt-mold from a trip in the Sierra when my client gently cross-examined me: "The young man who guided me in the Tetons carried no morphine. Have you a complete kit?"

"Uh, yes, reasonably complete." It consisted of a Band-Aid. The young man, I found out, was the famous guide Leigh Ortenburger. Shame on him.

And there is a line. Possibly it evolved from the coil of clothesline we Boy Scouts suspended from our belts. The Scoutmaster never told us what it was for, but since I began mountaineering in solo fashion, I've carried a light rope for hoisting the sack, for short rappels, or for rare self-protection. I've also taken to using it to tie courage into a companion at a critical exposed move. I've called it a rope, but after years of ridicule I bowed to my detractors and call it a string. A Fräulein at Sporthaus Schuster in Munich almost refused to sell me such a diameter when I told her I would rappel on it. String or rope, a 7-millimeter-by-25-meter length of nylon can save a life. Indeed, it has.

"Why carry such a thing on a picnic?" thought I, when packing for Point Reyes Beach. "No matter, it weighs nothing," I carelessly calculated. Into the sack it went. Why the nonclimber chose a different route up the sea cliff from any of the ones we experts used is irrelevant postcrisis chatter. The point was that when the cry came, there he was spread-eagled helplessly on the sheer cliff between John Fischer and me. John was closest, but without a line and unable to reach him. I sprinted up top—to the rescue with my standard picnic gear. There was another anxious moment when panic spooked him into untying the knot I flung him and he had to be instructed how to tie the figure eight while he wobbled on the brink over the cruel rocks below. He was soon up to my anchor, and I, off to receive yet another medal, or at least to add a check mark to my "next time list."

My pack looks bulky because it is fluffed out with the pile of clothes and gear the prudent traveler carries for mountain cold and storm. Always the pack will contain a set of dry clothes and a change of socks, so that I can be warm and dry at a campsite independent of yak- or porter-carried duffle. Among the many gadgets aboard I have light, zippable wind pants, which can add instant armor to my short pants, a rubber tube in my fire-making kit, which can puff mouth-blown air into a nascent campfire, and my backup goggles of the Eskimo lensless type, which Bobby manufactured as an unbreakable last resort to get someone off a glaring snowfield. Japan taught me to carry a folding umbrella and a cagoule, and now I've added a waterproof pack cover as well.

My left wrist sports an alarm watch for shaking me out before dawn. The sling from the ice ax goes around the right wrist.

Shorts. Great garb. Frees the knees. Make them out of regular trousers for fit and pockets. Pockets are generally innocent of money but useful for transporting a Swiss Army knife and small pliers. Pliers? Yeah, for untying frozen crampon straps and this and that. From my belt hangs a Sierra Club cup.

The lower part of my beautiful legs are sheathed in beautiful gaiters. These lovelies are made of stretch nylon and velcro, and are as handsome as spats. Gerry Cunningham invented them before the Gerry Company got lost in the shuffle of corporate conglomeration. They keep my socks clean and prevent rubble from entering the tops of my medium-weight mountain boots.

I just returned from a week's walking over a rugged course in Hong Kong's mountains. I carried a flight bag whose strap allowed instant conversion from an elegant side bag while I took continental breakfast in The Peninsula to an efficient rucksack when reaching for handholds on Lion Rock. Inside this do-all duffle I packed lunch, map, wind jacket, and collapsible cane.

The great H. W. Tilman, when queried on equipment, was said to have replied, "All you need is a tin cup and the clothes you are standing in, and don't ask any more foolish questions."

ICE AX

I have been using a standard-size ice ax for some time now, and it has promoted my path up and down a good many hills. I spent ten dollars out of my first paycheck to buy an ice ax. When the pears rolled in at the cannery, it was possible to hand-truck enough of them to the grader at 32½ cents an hour to start a collection of gear. My new ax looked ever so much better than the homemade job. That one's shaft came through an eye in the head like a woodchopper's chopper, and when Joe Leuthold or Ralph Calkins climbed stylishly by I would hold my hand over this shameful defect and pretend a nonchalance I did not feel. But it performed much more efficiently than the great eight-sided hickory-shafted telephone pole from Curtis Ijames's basement alpenstock rental.

The Scoutmaster had his own real ice ax, a symbol of authority which enticed us to follow him up Mount Hood with our rented alpenstocks. We were dressed in stocking caps, sweatshirts, laced breeches, and calked logging boots; we carried our Trapper Nelsons loaded with two blankets (for sleeping on top after viewing the September sunrise), eight blanket pins, a flashlight, a box

Brownie, a piece of clothesline, and twelve peanut butter sand-wiches.

Maybe my very first mountain tool was a Model-T Ford lug wrench. My cousin Ted Bloom found it in the town dump on the way up Dukek's Hill. He told me it resembled the sure-'nuff ice axes the big boys used. We found a foot of snow under the north rimrock, so we played a good step-cutting climb. On top, he showed me two of the three highest mountains in the world: Mount Hood and Black Butte. Such was the state of our geographic knowledge in 1921. Mount Hood looked higher than any mountain in the world to me, and maybe Black Butte second, but Ted said the number one mountain was on the other side of the world. Its name was Everest, and it was made of limestone. I didn't see how little animals could build a big mountain, but Ted was always right about everything else.

I petted and polished my first ice ax and protected it with a leather sheath. When Gary saw it he told me to take that silly cover off and treat it like a shovel instead of a trophy. His criticism shocked me a little. My boots had come down from sixteen inches to twelve, and the logger's calks had been replaced with the latest Swiss edge nails from Beebe Marine Supply Company, but still the awesome father figure of far-out mountaineering frowned. He told me an ice ax ranked as the mountaineer's first, main, and almost only tool. It served as his horse and saddle and bridle, his helmet and breastplate and gauntlet, his shield and buckler, his halberd and dagger and club. He showed me how the ice ax could be used to spread beans on bread, then the slice could be balanced on the flat side of the pick and this delicacy suspended over a fumarole long enough to prepare a warm brunch. Before he had finished indoctrinating me in the uses of this versatile implement, I knew I could best a bear with it. I believed a good man with an ice ax could solve any problem. That was before I had seen an income-tax form or fallen in love.

When I directed the Palisade School of Mountaineering, I tried to stuff our students with an instant ice-ax course. The school's curriculum, which I inherited, included the briefest possible introduction to the ice ax. In theory, the students could later practice the correct self-arrest until it became as automatic as foot-jamming the brake at a traffic signal. I knew we could not make a meter-long length of wood into an extension of the students' arms on a short walk up the hill on Tuesday morning. I tried. I asked them to try the walking stick function of the ice ax while crossing the meadow. I showed how the ax, held diagonally, could help keep their weight over their feet while we practiced crampon-type footwork on a steep slab. I swung the blade and cut foot notches almost as fast as we could mount a morning-firm mound of snow.

I would plead with them to tie their axes to them. Yes, I remember stories like the one about the climber taking a leader fall down a chimney on Ben Nevis and how his trained fingers and British pluck never let him relax his grip on the ax. Barnyard luck, I'd say: suppose he had hit his head? An ax sling can keep the tool attached to the tumbling climber for his later use down the hill, maybe even after he has regained consciousness. Having their axes tied on saved those guys who zipped down the Newton Clark Face on Hood for two thousand or four thousand feet. The actual lecture was accurate and precise in its figures, even if I had to make them up.

The best reason for tying on the ax: it prevents some hungry idiot from tipping it off the ledge while grabbing for lunch. This always reminds me to explain why my nylon lash is connected to the ax head by a dog chain. The dog chain prevents the nylon from parting when the ax is used to cut ice. By now the sound of my own voice would excite me into telling stories. Here is the story of what led me to think of this inexpensive, easily obtained and installed safety gadget. While pioneering a new route, I stood on an Army-surplus soft-iron piton and knocked at a suspicious block with the ax head to see if it would ring solid. The string having weakened while I cut steps on the way up, parted. Did you ever try to tie a granny or a double carrick bend with one hand? I muffed it and tipped the cussed ax off. It ricocheted down the couloir a few feet and sproinged over the edge forever. I've scrambled through the talus at the base of the cliff a score of times searching that rocky haystack, but needle I say? I never found it. Never finished the route either. Maybe someday I'll blunder upon my battered bat. It will inspire me to select the right chocks from my modern nut rack and lizard up the rest of the green-lichened razor. I'll call it "Blanchard's Arête of the Flying Ax," first ascent, grade 7-B, class 8, subechelon XXIV, very severe. I'd tell my class that story, if I could avoid the accusing eyes of my guides, who just might have heard it before.

The guides would now sneak out of earshot as I'd begin another story. This one illustrated the rule that the involuntarily descending climber should stick by the book and never attempt to devise new systems. I'd start off by telling them that keeping the ax tied to me once aided in arresting a 600-foot ride down the mountain. Of course that is hardly an arrest, but the story does illuminate some mountain principles. I hadn't tied the crampons' heel bars before we stomped down the bottle-blue ice that February day in 1935. The soft mukluks slipped out past the pivoting heel bar, and I smacked Joe Daniel, one hundred feet below on the rope, right across the shoulder blades, spinning him off too. I rolled into an ice-ax arrest and so did Joe, but the rough ice knobs ripped Joe's untied ax from his hands. The terrible acceleration when Joe lost braking power scared me into breaking the rule. I tried to invent a new arrest system, and of course we accelerated again. I flipped back into the standard method and maybe slowed us a little when we shot over two crevasses and fetched up on the lower lip of the third—scratched and out of breath but stopped.

By now we'd have reached a series of roches moutonnées on the Palisade School crawl to mountaincraft, and I'd find many places to demonstrate the use of the ice ax on rock. It did little good. Most customers remained totally unconvinced that they could ever carry their axes in their hands over rock, much less gain any advantage. As soon as clients reached rock, they would lean in and grab and forget all I'd said about keeping their balance with the ax.

The students could imagine that a man might profit from having his ax ready-to-hand in mixed snow-and-rock terrain, but that he might enjoy it—never. Besides, a backwards glance at other guides slinging their axes on their rucksacks for a short vertical pitch tended to spoil the whole thing. I'd show how I could carry the ax by its pick with my thumb and still have four fingers left, how I could jerk it up from a temporary lodgement by its sling and catch it like a juggler, and many other tricks.

I'd show the students how to sling the ice ax by just dropping it through the shoulder straps to ride against the back (still attached to the wrist sling). Then I'd remember a caution which I'd illustrate by another anecdote. I'd tell them of my dangerous trips through the liquor aisles of the Safeway with a great basket rucksack on my back. The basket worked fine for coasting a load of groceries three blocks home on my bicycle as long as I'd remember the McClure effect while negotiating the aisles. The McClure effect is my name for the phenomenon of the climber turning around on a narrow ledge and having his bulging rucksack or slung ice ax nudge him off into space. If my facts are straight, that is what happened to Professor McClure when he descended Mount Rainier with a long mercury barometer on his back. He took a wrong route down, over a steep cliff of the rock that now bears his name. He turned to yell up to his climbing mates, "Don't come down here, it's too steeee . . . !" Always turn inward, I'd say, when reversing direction on a ledge, with or without a mercury barometer on your back. You instinctively know the location of your shoulder blades or the size of your hereditary humpback, but the relative unfamiliarity of a larger-than-normal load in the rucksack or a momentarily slung ice ax could be just the tipperoffer that could send you, too, spinning down to the glacier. (I carry only a nonrigid rucksack to the grocery store nowadays; I could never pay for a shelf of sherry swept to the floor.)

Just before the tiny classroom glacier, there is a bit of talus and a short stretch of moraine, which would trigger yet another story. I'd tell about the time I blew my cool and nearly drowned my dignity in Nepal. Early one day on the road to Kangchenjunga, we came to a stream with a high bridge made of two six-inch poles, maybe twenty-five feet long and about twenty feet above the water. The others found a less scary crossing down-canyon, but the bridge didn't look all that bad, so I jumped up on the rock pier. I stepped out on the logs in high good style, looking really pretty for about a third of the distance, when a thought stopped me sudden as a shot. Frost! My foot hung in midair. I lowered my boot slowly and gently placed it on the log. A last resort would have been to flop to my belly and crawl to safety, but people were watching— mustn't lose face. Easy, I thought, I'll just back out of this situation. No good; I couldn't see where I was going. I crept—if one can creep standing up—inches at a time, the rest of the way, tap-tapping my ax carefully along the side of the pole. I balanced easily but moved slowly, slowly, because the frost I feared might skid me over to smash into the frigid water.

The important thing is that I used the ax as a sensor. Laying it, tapping it, and feeling it alongside the slick round pole told me, with nerves other than ocular, the position of my feet, the location of my center of gravity. There was no frost—the frost was in my head.

I'd ask the students to walk the sharp edges of the big boulders, holding their axes with palm on the head, thumb pointing down the inside of the shaft, fingers curled around the swelling blade, index finger straight along the outside of the shaft. They could instantly feel the sensitive nerves of the ball of the first finger joint extend thirty inches. It makes all the difference for balance.

The first snows of the glacier lie in shadow, so the frozen surface would allow the briefest course in using the ax to aid uphill tippy-toeing. While waiting for the sun to thaw the slopes for safe arrest practice, we would do some boot-ax belays. Sometimes small crevasses were open, and we'd peer into them a bit while I lectured on the many uses of the ax for dealing with the large concealed cracks of the northern mountains' snowslopes. If I could find hard ice, I'd demonstrate how to slice steps with the pick. With any luck I was able to plead old age and backache and turn over the ice-ax arrest practice to the junior guides, while I rested up for the downside route finding, and glissading.

It was a ridiculous fraction of time needed to build motor memory for using a new tool, but we hoped to show them how to hold an ax to stop a slide, and maybe they would finish by teaching themselves. They might pick up a little along the way later, on the Wednesday climb and the big Friday climb.

A cane or a walking stick is the same thing as an ice ax, almost. It performs all the walking functions of an ice ax and looks better on the beach. What an aching back I would have manufactured on the Washington-Oregon coast trips without a walking stick to poke in the tide pools. A long time ago I used ski poles without baskets when walking in the lowlands, but then I discovered the European mountain cane. I bought a bunch in Chamonix for eighty cents apiece. Now I buy them in Hong Kong, or buy ordinary rubber-tipped canes in the local drug store. I even found a folding model. This one winds down into four sections to fit neatly in a flight bag. It is just the ticket for Hong Kong hills, where the approach is apt to be a crowded streetcar or ferry.

A foldable ice ax for suitcases makes sense. It prevents those painful scenes in foreign airports—facing the steely-eyed immigration inspector after the ice ax, momentarily hooked on his high desk, crashes down to pin his shoe to the floor. I used to buy folding axes from the one manufacturer who made them. He has gone out of the business, and they did have certain defects. For ten years now I've made my own and regularly pack them into my overseas suitcase.

These axes, unfolded for use, are thirty-six inches long. I'm aware that the modern version of the ice ax has shrunk a couple of feet; but on none of the thousand mountains I've descended have I seen any advantage to folding my shoulder to my ankle bone to use such a sawed-off walking stick. Himalayan and Greenland explorer Mike Banks, whose comments on mountaineering are most memorable ("the dulfersitz is worth knowing for getting out of a second story window when the house is on fire or the husband on the stair"), said upon seeing a fashionable-length ax turn up on our Mount Mera climb, "To climb a big mountain a man needs a big ax. That's a toothpick."

I recommend a folding ax, to fit in the suitcase for travel or nest in the rucksack on the hard moves. But I warn: don't leave it in the sack unnecessarily. Take it out, walk with it, shove your weight up with it, use it for balance, lower your way down with it, get friendly with it, and make it a part of you. You need familiarity, handiness, and ability to flip the ax around instantly into a life-saving brake. It takes time, lots of time, to develop a good relationship with a new appendage. A good swordsman must practice constantly in order to wield his weapon well when suddenly confronted with Sir Steepslope.

More and more I've been carrying an ice ax instead of a cane, particularly when I'm unsure of the terrain ahead. The dangerously steep grass slope on the narrow shortcut to the Dhaulagiri icefall is an excellent place to carry a tool capable of use for self-arrest. I try to get my passengers to carry at least a cane walking stick. I tell them that it makes difficult walking maneuvers easy. It will get them across frosty or unfrosty pole bridges. It works on the smallest of stream rock hoppings, as well as on the great swaying, cantilevered, heart-stopping bridges held aloft by the invisible power of *mani* flags. It gets one safely past the shaggy slope where some exuberant monsoon has torn away a few feet or a mile of trail.

Last summer I suggested to my small scouting party in Japan that we all use walking sticks. Of course I carried my ax—necessary for step cutting. It worked out like this: the old timer said she'd never used one, didn't need one, and wouldn't have anything to do with a cane; the other three purchased walking sticks. At trip end the verdicts ran: the experienced one found no need for a stick, two were happy to have them, and the remaining member swore she'd carry an ice ax next time. That's about par for the course. For me, when I'm descending that last slippery road and heading for the rickety bridge over the river Styx, I'll be walking with that grand old steel-headed stick in my hand.

PACKS

"What kind of pack should I buy?" my friend Victoria Hamilton wanted to know.

Well, I once suggested which of her old rucksacks to bring to Japan (medium-size crunchable to fit train racks), but, when it came to heavy advice for a long solo Sierra trip, I hushed my big mouth. No good telling her to stay away from fancy suspension systems or to look for a pack, as I do, whose hip belt can be easily detached and thrown away.

I agreed to meet her at Rick Wheeler's mountain shop after her school-teaching day. Rick trundled up a sort of fabric Winnebago and guided us on a tour through its cupboards and closets. Next he laced Victoria into a pack-fitting session as complicated as a dressmaker's and no more interesting. I sulked. Packs have changed a lot since I used to spend a half-hour folding over a rectangle of heavy canvas, punching grommets, riveting webbing, and going to the shoemaker to ask him to sew up the edges.

On the day that I joined the Boy Scouts, my mother bought me the Official Boy Scout Packsack. It was a lead balloon of inefficiency even for that primitive day. It may have been a gnat's notch above my companions' horseshoe bedrolls and World War I-surplus haversacks, but not much. I carried sandwiches in it and tied on blankets for weekend walks to the woods back of Oswego Lake, but it was soon trashed in favor of a Trapper Nelson's Indian Packboard. The bust of the old trapper should rest alongside those of Robert Fulton and the earlier James Watt in the Transport Hall of Fame, just ahead of Dick Kelty's.

Typically, I was a bit late on the modern packboard scene, having been seduced into a ten-year affair with a couple of Yukon packboards in imitation of Norman Clyde. Built like wooden battleships, these six-pound brutes are almost indestructible. Even today I use one for hoisting big loads up the canyons.

Dick Kelty was among the first to make a pack that forced the center of gravity of the pack high and forward. Up to that time the whole world carried loads that rolled up hills like the square-wheeled cars in "B.C." cartoons. He built his first expedition-sized packboards for Monty Alford, Dick Kauffman, and me, for our 1961 McKinley trip. I've hauled loads in Alaska on that old frame that I can feel in my knees to this day. Despite hundreds of competitors now, Kelty got so big a jump on them that some use his name with a lower-case letter, as in: "We will be carrying heavy up to base camp, so everyone must bring a kelty."

"But I have a General Motors Tenzing Transporter, and Joe has a Mitsubishi Bonatti."

"Fine, you bring your Tenzing kelty and Joe can bring his Mitsubishi kelty and . . ."

It would be surprising if the intense modern competition could not produce packboards that were superior, or at least had different advantages, than Kelty's first successful aluminum model. There is a crying need for a frame that collapses at the push of a button and folds into a rocking chair. On one of our African safaris, the Kenya outfitter used homemade packframes that joined to become stretchers. And why could hollow tubes not do double duty as liquor flasks?

A minor problem for the manufacturers is the stubborn resistance of old timers. Cliff Jennings works for a prominent pack factory. Besides attending equipment seminars and sales training classes, he helps in design and does testing in the mountains. He was horrified when Alla Schmitz loaded his old pack for the mountain.

"Alla, our newest model is made of 87 percent polypropylbutylpoop and never leaks; and look, the wodget angles at exactly thirty-three degrees."

Alla accepted the loan of the brand new model, but started up the first quarter-mile of trail with turned-down lips. At the second quarter-mile, he grumbled the shiny new pack to the ground. "I can't carry this thing any farther!"

Cliff, realizing that the complaint came from a man who had carried packs in all corners of the world long before the founders of the fancy pack company were born, magnanimously carried his pet pack all the way back, to be exchanged at the car for Alla's old dog. No doubt the flashy new models are great, but sometimes you just can't budge a man from a Packard to a Porsche.

Pack factories practice overkill. They engineer even rucksacks into the stratosphere of high finance, and specialize the gadgets on it beyond all recognition of its basic function. On Mount Mera a couple of years ago, Bobby brought me my old klunker rucksack to exchange for the fancy blue nylon ski-carrier semi-rigid-frame model, because we anticipated boosting our own loads to 20,000 feet. I had fallen in love with that ancient canvas monstrosity. It was definitely not love at first sight, though. It was rather like discovering that one's old, reliable, but ugly and taken-for-granted, cleaning lady might be a better choice than any number of glamor-puss starlets. My old klunker is not really ugly. It is just a plain cotton working girl: buxom, faded, large in the hips, innocent of jewelry or sophistication. She has carried enormous loads on the Thursday mountain-school climbs to upper base camp. ("Our camps are not accessible to mules, so we ask you to help carry a little food for our bivouac. For tomorrow's climb, your guides will be carrying ropes and stoves and the heaviest of the food. . . .") By virtue of a liftable inside petticoat of heavy canvas, she enabled many a crude bivouac to be concluded unfrozen.

I'm guilty of a tiny bit of gadgetization myself. Su sewed in a light nylon waterproof substitute for the heavy canvas combination load-extender and bivouac sheet; I soaked the leaky canvas with waterproofing and added leather tie-on patches to better carry skis and snow tubes. (Snow tubes? Somewhere in the musty archives of the State Capitol, my application for the important position of snow gauger lies moldering. Probably I'll meet my end sitting out in the garden listening to my arteries harden before ever becoming a ski-mounted snow measurer—sad.) The main improvement was the installation of a piece of ensolitelike mattress in the space between the bivouac extender and the rucksack's back panel. Now I can throw any old thing in this great sack yet avoid back gouging.

Alas, the grand old rucksack is not long for this world. Too many scratchy granite chimneys, cliff scrapings on the hoisting line, scrunches into the narrow confines of Indian taxis' luggage compartments, lost battles with airline baggage handlers, daily draggings in and out of the tent, monsoon rains, and Himalayan miles. The sharp rock in the shoe is the discovery that planned obsolescence and cancerous plasticism have destroyed any chance of exact replacement. Stores that formerly stocked this solid symbol of common sense have sent it away with the buggy whips. Obsolete.

A pack manufacturer, startled by a couple of retired rucksacks with which I crossed ranges in Asia and Europe, talked me into shipping my old friends to his pack museum. It's better than having them become part of a landfill, I guess. It's becoming increasingly difficult to corral rucksacks reasonably free of neon razzle-dazzle. I've got two or three now that I would not be ashamed to wear in a 1930s fashion parade. I hope they last up to the day I am bundled up for shipment to the museum.

I get about two to four years out of these packs before wear or obsolescence or catalog-cultured whims dictate change. The last change misfired. A friend set me up with a super-pack manufacturer for an advertising freebie. The deal was to be consummated by telephone, but even while talking to the packmaker I could feel annulment in the offing. I was too slow-witted or greedy to quit, even after such phrases as, ". . . ten years in the business. . . after all I'm thirty years old . . . and you must get so-and-so to give you a personal fitting. . . I don't send this lightly, as, after all, the pack has been ten years in the engineering and costs 180 dollars!" When the little brown-garbed UPS man brought the pack around, I had already realized my mistake. No way could I recommend any pack that cost so much. I slit the end of the tall carton and slowly began to draw out the cellophane-covered pack. My senses first registered its extreme weight, and then, with six inches of the pack exposed, my eyes squinted protectively from the glare of its brilliant red! I shoved it back in, resealed the package, and mailed the thing with a thank-you-just-the-same apologetic and kindly-worded letter, with only a touch of sarcasm about how maybe during a half-century of mountaineering I had developed equipment prejudices.

It's such a nice, sunny, warm day that I'm going to shut off writing and ramble up to the spring on the Inyo Mountain side of the valley. And you know what? I'm going to carry no rucksack at all, just a walking stick, a cup on my belt, a monocular for spotting the odd elk, and a wind jacket jammed in my pocket—that's the way to go.

HASHISH

A timid trekker asked me if we ever had anything stolen from our camps, so often located near poverty-oppressed villages. I quelled his fears, protected the basically honest Nepalis, and compromised my integrity by declaring that I'd never heard of such a thing.

I'd heard of it all right. Jules Eichorn told a scary story about a burglary high in the hills of Nepal. In the middle of the night, his tent was opened by a slashing *kukri*. The missing gear and the obvious danger did not bother Jules as much as sleeping through the raid.

It is a sad new thing in Nepal. The Everest road, especially, is becoming polluted by minor crime. I got so paranoid I took to tying my shoelaces to the tent pole on the theory that a clumsy thief after my boots might be foiled by the collapsing tent. The thought of one or more thieves and I flailing around in a flattened tent is good for guffaws.

My group suffered a loss up the Kali Gandaki some years ago. I called it the Jomsom Drug Caper. We were camped in town, in a patio formed by stone buildings and a high stone wall on one side. As we reconstructed it later, the thief leaped over the wall just at dawn, snatched a rucksack from one tent and a plastic bag from another, and ran out by the massive wooden front gate. And where was the great dawn walker? Sleeping in, for shame; I never even heard the thief. When I emerged from my tent some minutes after the crime, the campers' complaints sent me scurrying into the first gray light to look for both culprit and swag. The Sherpas were no doubt stirring that early, but they were in one of the rooms of the house. Their natural inclination to protect their clients was fanned to incandescent temper when I reported finding one of their own tents discarded by the fleeing thief.

A pack of aroused Sherpas can easily outscramble a sedentary townsman, and they soon had the perpetrator cornered, and started questioning him with their fists. The Sirdar reached the scene before the thief got badly pummeled; I showed up at the ruckus as they hauled the miscreant before the local police. The village cop had to go wake up his superior, and the arraignment took all of the thirty minutes we needed for morning tea. We were ready to march when the official verdict came through. Obviously the man had an accomplice not yet found, as not all the loot was recovered. Still missing was seventeen dollars U.S., a gold fountain pen from an architect's rucksack, and a lawyer's medical kit taken from his plastic shoe bag. Yes, they'd like to have the stuff shipped to their respective addresses if it was recovered later. No, no use holding up the trek over such trifles: the architect figured the money was gone for good and she'd have to get another gold pen; the lawyer said he could live without his bottle of chloroquine tablets, his aspirin, and his comb and brush set.

So off we went down-canyon and turned up into the mountains toward the Dhualagiri icefall. At tea time that evening we scurried around scratching up straws and pieces of dried yak dung to throw on our pale above-timberline fire. Smiles on the wind-reddened faces huddled in parka hoods showed our pleasure and excitement at being in the heights again. We felt released from the claustrophobic canyon bottom and almost intimate with the avalanches, seracs, and crevasses of the great peaks.

In the midst of the fireside revelry, the lawyer cried out as if in pain and latched onto my lapels in agitation.

"Where is the nearest police station?"

"Why, down in the valley, I suppose. We passed one back a few villages. What seems to be your problem, Al?" I inquired soothingly.

"My God! My hash was in my medical kit!"

"Logical place to keep it. The stuff is readily available; probably some of the younger members have some they could loan you. We'll be back down in the lowlands soon."

"But you don't understand. If the police in Jomsom find my kit, they'll ship it home to Ottawa, and the customs men will grab it. I've got to stop the police from sending it home."

Al had just begun his career in government service. Perhaps it would have gone badly for him, I don't know. Few of the other trekkers thought so, apparently, for they kidded him unmercifully. He spent all the available time in the succeeding days writing and rewriting messages to be sent off from every possible dispatch point to the law in Jomsom. It quite spoiled the trip for him, because, in the week or so left, he tramped through the scenery unseeing. He spent morning tea, lunchtime, afternoon tea, and supper chewing his pencil and drafting communiqués.

I hope our trekkers did not carry through a muttered threat to hide some bits of hashish in his luggage. Come to think about it, I haven't heard a word from him since. Maybe they restrict his letter writing in solitary confinement.

12

Dogs

THE DOGS DID IT! They made me pay over a dollar for that damned magazine. It had a dog story, and I've been a dogophile since meeting a certain airedale in 1920. No, that's not quite fair. I rationalized that the travel company would want me to bone up on a couple of articles relating to my job in Nepal. I explain all this because the last time I purchased that rag I swore I would not read it again. Mountain magazines quit talking to me a long time ago.

One came out with an article on the Palisades, my playground in the Sierra Nevada for forty years. To my disgust the feature photo showed the Evolution group of mountains instead of the Palisades, with the Evolution negative reversed! You can imagine the accuracy of the text. The editor, replying to my heated complaint, offered the excuse that it didn't make that much difference!

But every once in awhile. . . . The dog article was okay. After all, I could not fault the author for leaving out some of the most accomplished pets. Any dog-owning mountaineer has taken his pooch along at some time. Fortunately dogs do not sign registers, keep summit lists, give slide shows, or write books.

The author did not mention my friend George, the famous exponent of the "spring and scratch" rockclimbing technique. He can climb almost anything. George rocket-launches his small body at precipices, bounds with a blur of levitation to a height five times his own, scampers up scary-angled slabs by over-revving his spinning claws, and reaches safety with the help of rough granite crystals and the grace of Almighty God.

He thinks he is invincible and unkillable. Since he survived a fifty-foot fall off Old Sharpie, he may lead a charmed life, but my crossed fingers ache when there are cliffs around. He is also damned tough endurancewise, as demonstrated by his lively descents from long one-day peak-bagging climbs from valley to Sierra Crest.

The magazine article mentioned some peaks whose ascents were accomplished by dogs being rucksacked over the steeper parts. This reminds me to catalog among George's assets the convenience of his eighteen pounds stuffing easily into a rucksack for fourth- or even fifth-class pitches. He rides contentedly with only a slight sneer on his face, which peeps out from under the flap.

This is the only conveyance from which he looks out. George learned from his first 12,000 miles of travel that safety lies in the dark and viewless confines of my friend Laurie Engel's purse. After all, it brought him past hazards of immigration, inspection, quarantine, and who knows what other ravels of red tape. What do the common neck-stretching, highway-smog-sniffers know of traveling across oceans, countries, and continents?

George comes by his sterling virtues through honest genes of Lhasa apso. The blood of generations of temple guardians courses through his veins and stirs his vocal chords as he goes about his daily barking chores. Laurie picked him from the cream of Tenzing Norgay's Darjeeling kennels. I coddled him through early puppyhood in Calcutta. Now he sets off each dawn on a floppy-eared jog alternating with an all-out belly-to-the-ground sprint around our three-mile cow and coyote, mule and magpie, duck and deer, raccoon and rabbit, cottonwood and willow, land and canal-water aroma appreciation course. With less predictable frequency he does major mountaineering in the Sierra Nevada and the Sierra Inyo.

Dogs have a way of buddying up. And if Bowser's buddy is a climber? A cairn terrier named Keith had a backcountry ranger for a friend. It was inevitable that he should break the "No Dogs in National Parks" rule. Keith learned to ride on the tails of his friend's skis on deep-snow patrols in the wilderness. He topped that feat, though, by about three thousand country miles, when he became the first dog to ride from California to Alaska in the front basket of a ten-speed bike!

Hosstoh, a black-and-white, seventy-pound flat-haired retriever, helped raise my son Bobby, and, along the way, managed many of the upper dog routes in Arizona, Colorado, Utah, and Oregon, as well as in the local mountains. He was a frequent companion of that intolerant mountaineer Norman Clyde. To pull off a friendship with the last man in the world who needed pets to fawn over him was a dogged exhibition of canine ingratiation.

All this is leading up to, or leading back in time to, the great Ranger and Wolf, of Mount Hood, as in: "Probably he has gone up the mountain, because Ranger and Wolf are gone."

It was convenient for five years or so to say "Ranger and Wolf," as the two often climbed together. But Wolf was never more than an accessory. He climbed because Ranger did, although he was a shade better on rock and knew it. He was big and yellow, collie crossed with husky, perhaps. He was handsome and knew that too. I liked Wolf but couldn't get any closer to him than Gary Leech or Gordon Dukes could, and nobody else wanted to approach him. Wolf was ornery, gruff-voiced, and snappy. Who wants a totally independent dog who merely tolerates man and climbs only because Ranger does?

Ranger was a nondescript, middle-sized, ancestor-mixed cur who escaped from some passing Indian's wagon in the twenties. He was supposed to be Vince Rafferty's dog, but Vince got sucked into the cab of one of Arrow Oil Company's bulldog Macks. He went tankering off across the country and left Ranger to make new friends where he found them. Vince's parents fed and cared for Ranger, but mountaineers starting up the trail from Rafferty's lodge were his heroes. As soon as he was old enough, or well before, he followed people up the trail to timberline and on up the tall white cone of Mount Hood.

He followed people up the snowfields of Hood for over a decade and racked up more than one thousand climbs. He also led people down these same snowfields when screaming horizontal blizzards tore the flaps from mountaineers' mindfulness and exposed the first frayings of panic.

People unacquainted with mountain weather have difficulty imagining the suddenness, power, and violence of a great Mount Hood storm. Because Hood is tall, isolated, and stands in a stream of warm marine air, it brews a wicked broth of winds. The upper reaches of the mountain often signal a storm some twenty-four hours before the hammer blow. This derby-hat-shaped "storm cap" is so reliable an indicator that the state highway department calls in extra snow plow crews when Hood flags its warning. A climber who would venture aloft under a storm cap would stir a nest of sleeping cobras.

The Mazama Club, citybound and chained to their calendar, once ignored a big cap and started up the mountain under calm but menacing skies. The storm struck with such ferocity that it killed one man on the spot. Perhaps he had a bad heart. The others scattered like a flock of quarks. One young man was not reported missing until his parked car was found at Government Camp a few days later. Searchers found his skis at the edge of a "wind hole." (Hood's fierce winds eddy with such gusto that they drill house-sized snow holes ringed on all sides with skier-trapping cornices.) It was later determined that the victim had broken both wrists in the fall, and the pain no doubt dictated abandonment of the skis. Then he marched down the hill, punching through the crust, surely one of the most exhausting maneuvers in the mountains. Either confused by the storm or ignorant of geography, he walked within a few feet of the Camp Blossom Cabin, where fifty people basked in front of a roaring stove. His body was found in a tree hole a quarter of a mile below the cabin, crumpled over three pitiful matches lit in a last vain attempt to get warmth from a fire.

Four feet of snow had fallen on top of that crust before they tracked him. Yes, tracked him! Some genius equipped a hundred searchers with bamboo prod poles. When their probing against the crust revealed a boot hole, they dug down to the track, determined the direction of travel, then probed again farther along the trail. That way they were able to trace the poor boy's wandering right to his last.

The storm that hit Ole Lien and I on March 27, 1935, shocked even this veteran of the braced ice ax and clenched teeth. We had seen the cap on Hood, the cap on Mount Jefferson, and the lowering overcast in between. We set out for the top anyway. There is significance behind the exact date; this was the era of the "monthly Hood climbs." To climb Hood once a month year-round seems now like a simple thing to do. Most of us had only weekends, though, and that meant four or maybe eight days a month to find a clear slot of weather for charging the summit. It was so difficult that only Ole (with four years' worth of monthly climbs), Gary Leech, and I, and maybe a few others had done it. There were only four days left in March, and Ole and I needed that climb.

When the storm struck, it knocked Ole and me off our feet, even though we were braced! We had fifteen hundred feet to go. We roped, on our knees, and went for it. Good old Ranger was along. He endured thudding ice chips as Ole sculptured a stairway up the blue ice of the Chute Glacier. Ranger saw us to the top, and carefully down-climbed the steep steps off the bergschrund slope though stung by snow pellets. Then, on easier ground but with visibility gone, Ranger saved the day by bringing us safely home.

(Climbing Hood each consecutive month for a year is not the craziest of Hood's contests. An old Hood game turns out fanatics each New Year's Day to race up the mountain to be first on top. First on top or first to climb in the new year? There is a subtle but important difference here. First on top requires a willingness to climb at night in order to win by putting a foot on the summit at the stroke of midnight. First to climb is a race *from* midnight. Two different distinctions, obviously. Some carry the game to more ridiculous extremes and dawdle away New Year's Eve in an attempt to be the *last* on top in the old year! The most-sporting event, according to some extroverts, is to party riotously up to midnight, then sober up in a cold and swift race to the summit.)

A frigid blast of hail or snow creates navigation problems, but so does whiteout in calm. I remember brailleing my way around Crater Rock in a bowl of snow milk, feeling with my ax to determine up from down. That time, too, I caught up with a party descending with Ranger and was happy to follow a canine guide.

There is supposed to be an infallible north-south compass course from the lowest point of Crater Rock to "Big Rock" at the top of the Camp Blossom Cabin glade. The problem is that we informal types never learned to carry more than the first five of the "ten essentials": coat, hat, ice ax, gloves, and a peanut butter sandwich. Ranger used a built-in mental compass. Maybe he inherited the skill from his Indian pathfinder ancestors.

Ranger had no St. Bernard genes—a good thing, too. St. Bernards, the ones I have seen, are practically worthless. I can't remember seeing any in the Pass of the same name, but Timberline Lodge at Mount Hood once had a pair of St. Bernards who had to be rescued themselves if they strayed from the lobby. Glacier Lodge in the Palisades also had a St. Bernard who never got a chance to try his famous rescue business: "Here comes man's best friend—and a dog!" His agility and daring were so conspicuously lacking that he had to be rescued from the easy descent of the Gayley Couloir. At the same time, Glacier Lodge had a malamute who followed me on hard dog routes.

Some people accused Ranger of being a one-route on-trail south-side climber, like his constant companion, Ole Lien. This nasty rumor was started by Russ McJury when Ranger refused to follow him up the Zigzag Glacier side of Crater Rock one winter day. Russ said Ranger shouted at him, "You may be a hot-shot of the elite Wyeast Club, but that route's full of flying ice feathers, and you'd be safer following a climber of more experience!" (I happen to know that Ranger had accomplished both the Steel Cliff and the Reid Glacier routes.)

It would be hard to get more experience in a short time than Ranger amassed. He would climb on Saturday and again on Sunday. No big thing; so did we. He would often make two climbs in a single day. Only a few of us did that. But Ranger made as many as three visits to the summit, by following very early parties up, dropping down to Triangle Moraine or even the big Palmer Snowfield, and then joining another upward bound party, and so on.

I was instrumental in helping Ranger to fame if not fortune. I once acted as his agent in getting him a radio contract. I had just arrived at Government Camp one spring evening, and was rummaging around in my climbing gear, when a stranger accosted me. "What is that dog doing?"

"He is singing, of course."

"Singing?"

"Yes. He always sings when he knows there is a chance to go climbing. Watch this."

I drew out my ice ax again. At the sight of it, Ranger sat back, tipped his head, and warbled out a mournful but not too untuneful climbing song. On the strength of that audition, the man signed him up to sing on the NBC national network!

It's no wonder that a dog of such talents and fame is buried on top of the mountain.

These writings often stray from the theme of mountains and climbing, but this one has gone to the dogs.

13

Ecology

TIME TO CACHE OUT

An old ecology message preaches: "Take nothing but photographs, leave nothing but footprints."

Sound advice. I've had no trouble with the first half of this admonition but have often failed the second part. Caches are my sin. The urge to conceal things shows up in dogs who bury bones and in financiers who send money to Zurich; mountain caches, though, involve more than miserly hoarding. Since teen-age days, when I used to store dried potatoes, erbswurst, figbars, and Maggi's soups in a bread can hidden in the rocks above Oregon's Wahtum Lake, I've figured a cache could guarantee freedom of the hills: a chance for spontaneous take-off, pausing only to snatch a rucksack hanging from a nail by the front door.

For nearly a quarter century, we maintained a cache at "the fort," in the Palisade group of the Sierra Nevada. This was Bobby's name for the great house-sized boulder he liked to play on as a small boy. I selected this boulder for a rain shelter, one of my typical stupidities. The long hours I spent with a broken shovel and a railroad bar digging dirt and prying rocks to excavate a decent-sized space under the overhanging side could have earned me the price of a tent. I chose this boulder, also, for its location a day's walk from roadhead for Bobby, when he was just past toddler age. That's the truth, but not the whole truth. I, too, wanted a short walk. The boulder snuggled under Temple Crag, the first real mountain up Big Pine Canyon and my favorite peak. I wanted a short walk, a steep mountain, a pure stream, nearby fishing, privacy; all these were available on the far end of the old Gayley Glacier moraine near Third Lake.

At the height of operations at the Fort, five large garbage cans were tucked under the big rock to preserve the bedding from squirrel nests, the pots from rust, and the food from fat birds. All those cans, bottles, sacks, jars, and packages came up the canyon on my back—peanut butter, rice, macaroni, rye crisp, kipper snacks, beans, tea, sugar, dried fruit, salt, and flour. Sometimes we took inventory, but on some odd wrapper that seldom made it down the hill, so the menu of leftovers offered a smorgasbord surprise. (When we moved the Fort cache in 1974, I found a can of Sir Walter Raleigh tobacco left over from twenty years before, when I quit smoking—an improvement consummated at this place.)

At first approach along the bleak moraine, visitors might judge the site stark. The level roof of the great boulder is the only really flat ground, timberline winds have beaten the few trees to scraggly and careworn forms, the black crags beetle above, and there is no grass or sign of water (from the camp itself the lake is out of view). Later our privileged guests would notice the rocks we'd tumbled around to simulate sofa, table, bench, and easy chair for kitchen, pantry, and parlor. And they would find that water ran cold and pure in the little stream from Gayley Glacier, that no mosquitoes droned in the soft morainetop breezes, and that a limit of fish leaped five minutes away in the lapping lake.

At dusk the low light softens the harsh rocks. The cooking fire, stoked by centuries-seasoned pine, produces odors to make the stomach gurgle, the hollow under the boulder seems to cuddle us, and the very stones become cushiony. The flickering fire shadows outline old and true friends on the sheer walls of the great boulder; the stars begin to burn overhead. Almost as directly above, the black wall of the great North Tower of Temple Crag watches— leaning over the stew. In those days I would not have traded for the most elegant mountain mansion.

In spite of the manifest advantages—the almost unlimited wood supply from old avalanches (I never felt the necessity to make a wood pile), the pure water, the overhang that hid the cache cans, the fishing, the privacy, the quick access to the heights (we could actually shout back and forth to the eerie summit of Temple Crag on wind-free days)—the grand old Fort began, early on, to fray and show some tatters of its faults.

I had originally selected the site with the idea of taking refuge under the boulder. This we did on a few occasions when summer thunderstorms showered down on us. It was a cramped and dirty experience. The main idea, though, was its supposed advantages as a winter camp. No good. In my zeal to approach within arm's reach of the great mountain's 3,000-foot wall, I failed miserably at geography and geometry. To my dismay, I found that the all-day shade of a summer north-wall Temple Crag climb was a clue to what happened when the sun went deep into Mexico for the winter. The Fort enjoys only a few minutes of real sun in winter, as the life-giving orb sails low through the pinnacles of Temple Crag.

I first became aware of this on a winter solstice trip with my flat-haired retriever, Hosstoh. Hoss was a veteran of many rock climbs, though his seventy pounds had to be boosted once in a while, and always ranked high on the invitation list. We arrived on the shore of Third Lake on a calm evening when just a dusting of snow decorated the ice. Out we went from the north bay. All went well until about the midpoint, where we encountered bare ice windswept free of snow. Hoss skidded. Much too dignified to exhibit panic, he just sank gracefully to the ice, turned all four sets of claws up, and remained motionless. I squatted and shoved. As it happened, I was shod with tricounis, and they slipped like so many miniature ice skates. Dropping to my knees, I found that the wool knees of my "truck driver's greens" froze to the ice, and we went on thus tractioned. Hoss never resisted and never helped. It is a fair distance across half of Third Lake, but that is the way we crossed—kneeling pusher and toes-up slider.

The next day we got only a dab of sunshine for twenty minutes. Off the ice, Hoss used his toenails again, and I dug with my fingernails into the goodies in the garbage cans.

We might have simply declared the Fort a summer camp and carried on, had it not been for a series of disasters that forced us to throw in the towel. The record snows of 1969 avalanched over the camp and broke the six ancient albicaulis pines we depended on for shade. Larry Williams's Mountaineering Guide Service set up a semipermanent bivouac within the drainage of our glacier stream. Larry's successor, Bob Swift, camped his climbing-school clients on Third Lake. Unlike fishermen, rockclimbers go everywhere, and they began to wear a trail near our camp. A search party carried a dead climber (not from the school) right through the middle of our camp. And then we got booted by the environmental preservation kick. The Palisade School of Mountaineering and their predecessors always had caches in the mountains. They had so many that some are lost to this day, since superguide Don Jensen was killed on his bicycle in Scotland and will never return to find them. For two of the four years I directed Mountain Travel's climbing school, we used to cache the heavy items each fall to save hauling. When my chief guide suggested that we should heed our own teachings and be the first to obey the canons of good outdoorsmanship, I directed that the great cache, so handy and well-hidden, be torn down and hauled to the valley.

When it came to my own private stock, freight whose transport cost could be calculated on my very own perspirometer—that was different. Maybe the time has come to disband the aristocratic elite who thought themselves privileged to hold private stocks in public woods. Norman Clyde had caches not only all over the Palisades, but throughout the Sierra; how he would have howled if anyone suggested they were environmentally out of bounds. Maybe the Sierra Club is right: maybe the wilderness belongs to all, and private caches are a violation of a modern mountain ethic.

The old ways hardened in my soul like the cholesterol in my arteries. What they don't know won't hurt them, I rationalized. I dismantled the Fort cache, with some show of thespianism to throw the Sierra Clubbers off my trail, and sneaked the containers upcountry. I went looking for that ideal combination of pure water, wood, shade, view, access to the peaks, and a secret-panel closet for the cache cans. It's not easy to hide things in the crowded "wilderness." And now a type of ecology zealot who makes a hobby of discovering rumored caches comes to dog our tracks.

For the moment the cache is safe. No one will think the wall safe hides behind the portrait of Grandpa. If garbage cans can never be seen, how can they offend? But if they are discovered, I swear I will remove all foul evidence of man's temporary occupations of the heights. I will be pure indeed.

There is, though, the other canyon: that nameless, perfect, hidden, secret, serene, absolutely unvisited speck of heaven to which one can climb with light rucksack and expect an undisturbed bed and board with chosen friends. Maybe some day you can join, sign the ceremonial slab of granite with your blood, and accompany us to the new hideaway. The last one before old Smoke becomes a guaranteed cacheless paragon of virtue.

SHOOTING DUCKS

It is a common, if not universal, conceit among outdoor people that the wilderness must display no sign of previous use by our species. I have always resented evidence of my fellow man's presence in wild places, although it would take no great woodsy Sherlock to track me around.

A duck, in Sierran lore, is a small cairn of two or three rocks that marks routes. I consider trail ducks unsightly and unnecessary: a species of mindless vandalism. I shoot them down with my walking stick. If I take care to tip the stone trailward, I not only destroy unnecessary landmarks, but do my tiny bit to make the wilderness way less of a boulevard. The Forest Service, during one of their policy flip-flops, announced their intention to remove trail signs from the wilderness. I took it as encouragement for open season on ducks.

The eastern Sierra is open and obvious, but people regularly get lost. We could call it the Duck Mentality. The fault lurks in the minds of duck builders and duck followers. Pathfinding in the mountains, which should be an exercise in geology, seldom needs street signs, house numbers, x and y coordinates, or ducks.

The worst example is the road to the Palisade Glacier. The CCC built the trail to the glacier in the 1930s. It used to be maintained by the Forest Service and has only recently undergone benign neglect. The path is as wide and smooth as any sidewalk, yet ducks bloom like polomonium. (Perhaps we have no ducks in town because the street cleaners remove loose stones?) They make as much sense as city street signs repeated every few feet. Their very irrelevance, though, serves somewhat to preserve my temper.

What burns me down is that, where the trail ends on pristine granite pavements, there's an ugly proliferation of these superfluous vulgarities. True, the trail is not blasted into the stone. The footing changes to solid rock, impervious to lugged boot tracks. But one does not need to plot the course on the smooth granite by watching for footprints. The slightly inclined sheet of granite is bordered by a rough hill of moraine boulders on the right and a vertical drop on the left. Except for this glistening highway, whose smooth beauty only the cairns mar, there is no other possible road. Navigation here is not so much an exercise in geology as a minimum test of rationality. As the climbing-school instructors advise, "If you are stumbling in the moraine boulders on the one side or in danger of falling off the cliff on the other, may we suggest you try the clear place in between?"

The school's chief guide, Bob Swift, grew so tired of losing battles with the mad duck builders that he gave up trying to knock them down. He joined them. He built ducks each time he went up the hill, taking care to lead any followers into a swamp or over a cliff.

The greatest strain on my tolerance for the foibles of others is the criminal stone graffiti erected on the route to Camp Robin Hood. We use the camp to springboard climbs on Mount Winchell, Thunderbolt Peak, and the buttress route on North Palisade. This pint-sized patch of flowers and grass on a bench above Robin's Egg Lake is one of my favorites. Nearby is "Sherwood Forest," a copse of twenty-inch albicaulis pines. The way to this high outpost is as beautiful as the destination itself: a series of granite slabs and domes, interspersed with miniature meadows, tiny groves of trees, and the odd snowpatch. The route culminates in a meter-wide sloping ledge high above the ice floes sailing the green fiord of Sam Mack Lake. Damn the vandals who desecrate the sanctity of the wilderness by man-marking this exquisite route. They'd carve initials in a cathedral. A single out-of-pattern stone in God's erosional happenstance stands out as an eyesore, and three pebbles in a pile scream "Kilroy was here!"

So when sharp-eyed Glenny calls, "There's a duck, Dad, can I kill it?" I always grant him permission with a verbal pat on the back for spotting another. For shoot them down as we will, we never seem to kill them all.

This vendetta, I must point out, does not extend to foreign countries. Routes on Japan Alps cliffs carry paint marks. A white four-inch circle means "on course," and an X sometimes accompanied by the *kanji* sign for "stop" says "Watch it, man, you are in danger of going over the side!" When storms cut visibility to near zero and rocks begin to glaze with ice, you bet your sweet life I appreciate man's marks then.

Japan also exports bamboo garden stakes to wholesalers in New Jersey, who reship them to Bishop, where I've gathered a few thousand for planting in Alaskan snows to indicate paths in a whiteout. If all goes well, the glaciers grind them into aesthetic purity.

Passengers on Nepal trips often ask how we find our way about. Well, we are not exactly Dan'l Booneing our way through an unknown wilderness. Nepal is inhabited and civilized. Out in front we have a Sherpa, who may be lost himself, but easily finds his way by asking a local resident. Sometimes the local yokel exchanges information after asking his Nepali equivalent of "What-cha-doin'?" (Our 1971 cook, Penuri, gave a reply to this one that pleased me so much I used it as a title for one of my Nepal slide shows: "Just walking around, buying chickens and eggs.")

Because our trekkers get scattered out of sight of each other in a two-mile-long caravan, I give them a speech about trail following before leaving Kathmandu. "Please, let no one leave morning camp or noon stop without my permission. I will designate the Sherpa you are to follow, or lead myself." (Except when mountaineering is a problem, I almost always dog along in the rear, ostensibly to scoop up casualties, but really to dream along at my own leisurely pace without fear of being run over by ambitious trekkers.)

"By the second day you will recognize our loads amongst all the freight moving up and down the road. If you see a basket with peanut butter cans peeping through the holes, best follow it. Your own duffle bag would be a good thing to follow. Later on you will begin to recognize the individual porters who are walking with us and distinguish them from other carriers.

"You will come to many road junctions, but there are no signs in all these hills. At a fork in the road, I suggest you look in the dirt for an arrow scratched by the lead Sherpa. Often the way is so obvious to him that he forgets to mark it, and you may find the arrow a few paces up the correct road. Ordinary citizens go barefoot, so the print of a lug sole means that one of your fellow trekkers is ahead. If these tracks lead down a level road, it may mean that your predecessor is unwittingly heading for a farm house, and you will soon meet him returning. 'Our road is the steep road' is a code to keep in mind." (It works nearly everywhere in Nepal because roads follow ridges.)

"I will teach you the name of our destination for each day, which can be a help in asking the natives for a pointer. Perhaps the second most useful Nepali noise after *'Namaste'* (hello) is *'Yo bato, mul bato ho?'* (Is this the main road?). On the Everest road, a mere puzzled look and a pleading 'Namche?' will set you right. If all else fails, just stop and yell. Some kindly native will hear you, and, if you are not actually at the very first of the string, he will already know from the gossip where you are supposed to be going."

Sherpas have a well-earned reputation as premier mountain men, and the passengers like to think of them as expert guides. Nepal is a big country, though, and many of our routes are new to the Sherpas also. The sober and serious trekker feels put off when a Sherpa gets lost. Especially if said Sherpa is the famous Nawang Dorje and he answers the tourist's fret with a wide grin and a twinkle: "I never no been this road, sir." Or even worse: "I been this road once, sir, but I much mistake forget."

Last year one of my passengers pooh-poohed my trail-finding instructions because he had a compass. This common ignorance of mountains and misreliance on the machine was irritating enough, but when he "found Mount Everest with the compass," I blew up. He pointed to a hill twenty degrees off azimuth, 10,000 feet too low, and thirty-five miles too close.

"A compass is the most absolutely useless piece of junk you could possibly carry!" I raved, guiltily aware of the secret hiding in my rucksack. It was no time to confess that my emergency kit contains a compass, even if it was for use on fogbound glaciers.

Compasses, markers, and even ducks can be useful in some parts of the world. As a last resort, guidance can be sought in the brain. In Colorado, in Himalayan hills, or in the Hodaka peaks, I must acquiesce to the customs of the natives. But in the eastern Palisade Sierra, my own backyard, I need not restrain the swinging ax; I can declare open season on silly stone statues.

14

All Kinds of Advice

HOW TO KEEP YOUR HEAD

"Must we wear these hard hats?"

I gulped back my hatred of the heavy, dignity-destroying protective devices, and gave the young guide the standard liability lecture. As director of the climbing school, I had to emphasize to guides and clients alike the danger from skull-cracking stones.

I can hear a cynical old guide mutter, "If God had wanted you to wear a mountain helmet, he would have made you with a stainless steel skull." Pain washes over me as I think of Su, killed by a blow to the head in a place where no one would think of wearing a helmet. I think of vacationing recently in mountains known for the solidity of the rock, mesmerized by the outside of my companion's head and by the sparks from the inside, yet not forgetting to warn her to throw an arm over her head in case we heard falling rock. Better a broken arm than a broken head.

A boyhood spent in volcanic mountains taught me a proper petrophobia both for stones falling from above and loose ones at hand. Shaman Gary Leech drove deep inside me the rockclimber's

207

chant, "Watch that rock." Watch it. Don't tug on it. Eye it, observe whether it is part of the mountain or a disconnected potential head-smasher.

When I came to the climbing school, I tried to pound caution into the students: "The Sierra Nevada is world famous for the quality of its rock. However, when people say there is never a flawed face-splitter waiting at the top of a pitch, they are speaking of Yosemite. It might be true there. Here we climb in high mountains. High mountains all over the world are frost-riven. Loose rocks lie everywhere. Watch that rock! Look at it! Test it with the eye and never, never with the hand. See this stone? . . ."

Wednesdays we used to take the clients to the "Great Red Wall of the People's Republic of Fifth Lake." (The locals get carried away in the name game.) It was a chimney exercise halfway up Mount Rogers. Early in the day we guided the students up a short, easy, chimney-wedging move, with a thirty-pound granite klunker sitting bare-faced on a smooth slab at the exit. We'd not thrown it off because it was useful as an illustration. I would wait until their clutching fingers came within two inches of disaster, and then scream so loudly they would all but fall off. Strong medicine, but it worked.

Every rock. Every hold. Look at it. Concentrate. Remember. Be alert and aware. Be aware that the population explosion has come to the mountains. Our species is everywhere. There are always heads below. A careless foot on easy ground can start a stone.

Once, coming down Mount Robinson, I whirled on a student, "What do you mean you couldn't help it?" I had jumped, and it had missed me. When I am going down first searching for a route, below a group like this, my nerves are strung like piano wire. "Listen! Do you hear Bob and Chris coming down? Of course not—the guides move silently. I can climb loose rock all day with them in perfect confidence. True, they are more skilled. But mainly, primarily, they do not, will not break heads from carelessness!"

You, leader, rig anchor and belay securely, and lay out the rope with care. Follower, that snake of nylon slithering up to the belayer may spit stones at you.

It is almost a decade now since the accident I'm about to describe. Leo LeBon, travel company president and experienced European Alps mountaineer, showed up at the climbing school with a couple of office hands in tow to take climbing. Famous mountaineer Allen Steck's well-trained daughter, Sarah, climbed on Leo's rope. Carla McCarthy came as my partner. Carla had trekked with me in the Himalaya, but this would be her first steep rock climb.

Off we went to the Fingers Route on Mount Robinson. All went well until the second pitch of the difficult midsection of the upper wall, when Carla forgot her one-sentence mountaineering instructions and pulled on a loose stone. Leo, leading the second rope, saw the whole thing. He said she reached high up and pulled off a big one, which caught her square in the forehead. Later, he made much of the fact that my belay was perfect and Carla not further damaged in a fall. Of course. That's what a belay is all about. Why should he even mention it? I could scarcely feel it, and there was not the slightest strain on my stance or on the good nut securely anchoring me to my perch.

We eased Carla down with her bulging forehead and blue-black eyes. Dr. Gil Roberts, who has patched people from there to deep in the Himalaya, fixed her head, and she was left with only a scar or two on her hand to remind her of a potential disaster luckily escaped. It's sad, though. Flesh is so soft and rock so hard. The rules of our game are equally hard, and the penalty for violation is the awful pulping of the weak housing that encases our spirits.

Fifteen years ago I helped carry two victims of loose rock from the base of a peak in Rock Creek Canyon. Their blood had sprayed over the unyielding ledges down the 800-foot fall, pooled at the crunching landing, and still oozed from the quiet lumps as we trundled the litter to trailhead. It was a most sobering experience, destined to mold in my memory for some time.

A letter just came from some friends who are shortly off on a long canoe journey in the Canadian Arctic. I have written them about the dangers of rounding a bend in the swift current and suddenly butting heads on a "sweeper" that can dump them into cold water. I said I hoped that they would swim ashore and climb the riverbank cliff with a care for "watch that rock."

"Watch that rock!" means, of course, keep a sharp eye for a leaning spruce tree or a darting taxi as well.

HOW TO BEAR UP BRAVELY

"Do you have any bear stories?" she asked.

My dear, you must be new around here; I've got more bear and wild animal stories than Carter's got pills. The only bear stories I don't have are small bear stories. There are no stories about small bears.

Traipsing around the east side of Yosemite National Park or the coastal side of Alaska, one is apt to bump into bears. I'll start this one out with TV, though: not an unlikely conversational beginning these days, though I've yet to own one of those machines.

A few years ago I motored up the San Francisco Peninsula to old expeditionary friend Nort Benner's house. The big old mansion was empty except for the master—an extremely rare occasion. He served me some sherry, and we plunked down in front of the color TV to watch an hour-long special on the world's weather.

"Man could be altering the climate," the announcer intoned.

Maybe factories are putting out too much carbon dioxide. The "greenhouse effect" causes warming, an appealing notion to Nort that chilly evening. He started huffing and puffing to exhale more carbon dioxide.

And now an announcement of interest to us glacier lovers: "On the other hand, it just could be that man-made dust screening out the rays of the sun will result in a cooling trend."

I kick at the floor. No dust there, but I guess Nort knows what I mean, because in the midst of his huffing and puffing, as the commentator gets further into the mechanics of man's goofing up the atmosphere, he says of my gesture, "Like kicking at bears, eh, Smoke?"

Well, now, I hope you are not getting the idea that old men spend all their rocking-chair time in reminiscing. It just so happens that

Nort was referring to a certain kicking-dust-at-bears episode in the Canadian Rockies a couple of decades ago.

I was first up that morning, as usual. Just up and finished dressing when up walks the bear and frowns at me. As I say, I'm dressed, and in those days that means I've got a Leica slung on me—and there is Mr. Bear standing gruffly for his portrait.

I try to get him to smile while focusing with the old-fashioned two-holed finder. I say to myself, "He looks awful damn close, but that must be this magnifying rangefinder. Oh, oh, I'm looking through the other hole!"

Yes, he *was* close, too close and too obviously frowning. In fact, he was snarling as though he was being photographed without a signed model release.

Meanwhile, Nort woke up to find himself in danger of being tromped on by clawed feet, and was himself frantically clawing, to get out of his sleeping bag. It is difficult to retreat when encased in nylon and down. Being down in front of a bear is hard to bear.

To shorten the suspense, I played the hero and saved the day— by scuffing dirt in the bear's face. The big animal beat a retreat while I helped Nort get out of bed. Emboldened by our escape, we tried to round up the bear and chase him past Jules's bed for a picture, but our furry model had decamped.

HOW TO AVOID THE EVIL EYE

Someone asked Niels Bohr, the Nobel Prize winner in atomic physics, "How come you carry a lucky rabbit's foot? Surely you cannot believe in such things."

One of my favorite Nepal trekkers, physics professor Bertram Gale Dick, reported that the great Bohr's reply to this potentially embarrassing question was, "Of course I don't believe in it, but I have heard that it works whether you believe in it or not!"

I like to think of the world as a machine. Cogs may slip, wear, jam, but the gears will break down into discrete pieces and never dissolve in mush. Yet. . . .

School taught me that the world ran logically, that I had no need to carry some water-worn pebble, bit of driftwood, whitened bone—some amulet to curry fortune's favor. It's true my earliest outings were protected by a talisman—clothespin carved and marked in the shape of a man, which peeked from the pencil pocket of my bib overalls—but I left that back in kindergarten days.

I straightened my shoulders with scientific superiority when my lawyer friend, Ben Priest, showed me his good-luck tranquility stone at the start of a Japan Mountain Walk. He had purchased a smooth, shiny, freeform carved rock as a feely, a pacifier, a helper to aid him in dealing with whatever frustrations might arise in a foreign environment. He faced many devils: outlandish language, obstinate steeps, vexatious weather, and an intractable leader. Ben has a soft voice and a disarming manner, which helped me to conceal my cynicism.

"How naive," I thought, as we stood there smiling at each other, my left hand grasping the *ju zu* beads in my pocket.

I purchased the neat, well-made beads at a temple in Nara. The attached little plastic ball has a hole that, held to the eye, magnifies a picture of the Todaiji Daibutsu, Vairocana. This practical tool can establish instant rapport in any Buddhist country. It is good to watch a broad smile slowly wreathe the craggy face of an ancient Tibetan lama as his squinting rheumy eyes peer through the little hole and resolve an image of Buddha.

On a trek to Himalchuli, Thelma Hapgood, who studied anthropology in Edmonton, Canada, explained to me the proper pronunciation of the famous Vajarana mantra, "*Om mani padme hum.*" To test the Sherpa pronunciation of the sacred syllables, I went to my duffle to get a silver neck charm with the words carved on it. Just happened to have it along. A small purse carried it and another set of beads that I bought in Khumbu a few years back. These flat wooden beads are unusual and aesthetically pleasing. Also in the purse was a tin badge from the Lumbini Preservation Committee, which I meant to sew on my coat. (I'd kicked in some rupees to help make a park of this holy place.) Tsering Onchu helped us with our reading problem, but he showed more interest in my trinkets. When I also brought out the Japanese rosary beads, he said, "Esmoke has all the Lama's weapons!"

We like to walk to the left of all Buddhist monuments as the Sherpas do. It's a courtesy to our hosts, I tell the trekkers. It doesn't hurt.

The first of the *mani* stones on the Everest road stands on top of the big hill at Thulo Pakha above Lamosangu, but few trekkers notice them. On the early portions of the road, *Om mani padme hum* tends to show up in unfamiliar Sanscrit, or Tibetan weathered too badly to read.

The sacred writings on the *chortens* below Chisapani Pass read plainly enough, but the doctor from Seattle slipped by unobserving to the right of a sacred stone on a trip to Everest in 1971. We stopped overnight on Sikhri Khola, and the leeches were thick. Dr. Ron Beck bunked with me in the Sierra Design hexagon tent and fussed a great to-do while pulling up the sill and scraping both tent and sleeping bag free of blood suckers. First thing in the morning, he turned to look at me with scarlet-streaming face. After the initial shock, I taunted him with the theory that the leeches had punished him for violating the precept on walking to the left of *manis*. Some days later Ron passed a large *stupa* below Takshindu on the wrong side and became violently sick that night. This time I forbore kidding him.

Coincidences? Consider the story of Dave Lincoln. On the way to Everest a month later, my party included young Dave—a sober, quiet graduate student with a Lincolnesque build, who soaked up all the etiquette lectures and took care to treat the other man's religion with perfect respect. We camped at Buldanda on narrow terraces that needed a bit of grading for tent sites. I worked with the Sherpas to cut grass and brush and fill in some shallow, round holes. The old woman below hopped up and down; she screamed at the Sherpas. In their usual arrogant way they hollered back at her, till finally I got Ang Temba to investigate. Two things troubled her. The shallow holes marked her newly planted orchard, and she was annoyed by David Lincoln's sitting atop a great moss-covered boulder. The Sherpas sent up Gombu, a tall, pious, pig-tailed, prayer-chanting Tibetan, who ice-axed four inches of moss from the stone, revealing *mani* writing. David came down immediately, and we soothed the old lady's feelings with a biscuit-tin present.

Around midnight the whole camp, except the Sherpas, who slept a couple of hundred yards from us, was awakened by people shouting and tripping over tent guys to rouse the doctor for sick call. David Lincoln took no breakfast. Strain showed in his pale face as he walked unsteadily near the doctor all day. We served him a little weak tea for lunch. At evening camp he retired the minute the Sherpas pitched his tent. We brought him one bowl of thin soup for dinner. He recovered fully the next day, and that was the end of the incident. The end, except that Penuri came round to me in the afternoon a couple of days later and asked, "Esmoke, did anyone get sick a couple of nights ago?"

"Yes, why?"

"Because that old lady put a curse on the man who sat on the *mani* stone!"

At the end of one of the Japan Mountain Walks, my people honored me with a ceremony. They presented me with a fine silk painting and asked how I managed to operate the walk through the mountains so smoothly. I explained it was easy because I carried these two things in my pocket. I drew out my current set of *ju zu* beads and a brand-new miniature electronic calculator.

HOW TO FIX AIRPLANES

Latter-day trekkers learn that influence from the Lukla airstrip reaches up several days above the green bench above the Dudh Kosi River. October clouds boil up like a cold breath from the storm dragon's ledge lair at Lukla.

The Everest trek went well, though dampened by the tag-end of the monsoon. All the passengers were happy; most of the twenty who started out reached the high viewpoint called Kala Pattar. But as we came down the hill, vibes from far below chilled us: rumors from Lukla of passengers stranded at the airstrip and food running short. Weather prevented planes from getting in, and passenger lists grew.

The Sherpas say, "The sight of an airfield makes the trekkers weary." Nowadays, with almost all trekkers opting for the thirty-eight minute shortcut to Kathmandu, available plane seats become a matter for panic. Hanging around the monastery at Tengboche were some hippie-style trekkers who had gone down to Shengboche, some of them all the way to Lukla, only to run afoul of weather delays and lack of reservations. (Old-time Dologhat trekkers may not recognize Shengboche as the name of the new airstrip at 12,000 feet. I tell my passengers, with tongue in cheek, that it's an ancient Sherpa name for a legendary god, invented by the press agent for the nearby Japanese hotel.) Our group went down into the rain and rumor of the lower canyon.

Both precipitation and idle talk were at their thickest when we sloshed into Lukla. A couple of days later the rains relented; we were all ready to go. As the three planes swooped down onto the field and smartly right-turned to stand safely crosswise to the slope, like skiers dismounting from a chairlift, I went around telling my people: "You are as good as in the hotel's hot bath now."

But Grant Rogers muttered, "Never count a take-off until you're airborne." Since he had found this out the hard way by running off the end of carrier decks in World War II, I filed the advice in a corner of my head. In a few minutes his caution was dramatically justified. An innocent bystander did it. It is hard to call him innocent, but technically he was.

He was one of "the Swedes." We first noticed the Swedes nearly a month earlier, three days from our starting point at Lamosangu. They had a Nepalese guide and only two porters, and said they were bound for "somewhere below the Everest Base Camp, to fool around with some caves." They seemed like nice boys, tall and shy. So shy, one of them never spoke, one seldom spoke, and the one who spoke English avoided me as if I had halitosis or too much curiosity about cavers who carried mountain gear.

I had a right to be sensitive about small, secretive parties who pretended innocence and came to Nepal with tarps not quite con-cealing piton hammers, ice daggers, mountain helmets (sans light clips for caves), and jars of suncream—for underground explora-tion. My bosses Mike Cheney and Jimmy Roberts had lectured me sternly just a few weeks before about obeying the latest govern-ment edicts on climbing. The French had sneaked up a nonper-mitted mountain, and the government frowned so severely on this they swore they would enforce the law stringently from then on. Any transgression of the strict rules they had set for our upcoming Mount Mera trip could jeopardize the whole operation of the com-pany.

The Swedes sort of followed us for two weeks. It was as if their roly-poly Nepalese guide did not really know the route. He was a nice fellow, and we got along all right, as long as we stayed away from discussion of immediate plans. But can anyone trust a round Nepali?

So here came one of the Swedes, the one who mysteriously wore rubber boots all during the march in. The one whose brother was in the hospital in Kathmandu after acclimatization failure during their sneak attempt to climb out of the Shangri Glacier. Here he came: no ticket, no apparent anxiety to ride out. He was just an innocent, helpful bystander who leaped up to close the door of the middle plane in the line—and broke off the handle!

What a bumbler! What a rubber-boot wearer in the mountains! Innocent or no, the pilot wouldn't go. The handle was broken.

"Hey, Ted, you're a mechanic for Pan Am, hop down here and assess the situation."

Ted wormed his way through gabbling Sherpas, porters, hang-ers-on, passersby, French trekkers, Japanese tourists, German climbers, airport officials in mufti, and two long-overcoated, rifle-bearing, capped, and badged members of His Majesty's military.

"Tie it with a rope and take off," Ted expertly prescribed.

Not unnaturally the pilot, facing Ted agreeably, replied, *"Na-maste"* (greetings), and went off to the dark and evil-looking Ti-betan hut for an omelette. He had plenty of time. It was going to take the first plane a couple of hours to make the round trip, especially when they had to scare up a genuine RNAC mechanic and spare door parts. It is no wonder that the pilot hesitated to go out on a limb and take the word of a foreigner on anything so delicate as his job.

Nevertheless, we fumed all this time about why they couldn't just taxi or push the planes round, use the one-foot clearance to pass the stalled aircraft, and let at least part of us escape this unlucky Lukla. Especially as clouds down-canyon again threatened a delay. A week this time?

Ah, but the plane returned, and an "engineer," complete with tool kit, deplaned and soberly and importantly inspected the damage. "Tie it with a rope and take off," he pronounced. Away, away we happily flew to Kathmandu.

Do you think that was all? Listen! These trips are run on schedule. They are sweated over as much as a year in advance with all kinds of correspondence catapulted around the world, occasionally even leaking over the Sierra into Bishop.

"Please be advised that the said reservations for a party of fifteen requiring seven doubles and one single have now been adjusted to read six doubles and three singles, as per your letter numbered blah, blah, blah. . . ."

Our original plans showed two days of sightseeing in Kathmandu. They were now altered by the rain delay at Lukla, and further problems that could cancel or alter our Indian tour loomed.

But there in the domestic-arrivals lounge at Tribhuvan Airport, there in the thick, steamy, four-thousand-foot air of Kathmandu, was good old Dawa Norbu, thinking all the time. Dawa Norbu, our agent's office manager, had heard of the broken-handle delay, foreseen the difficulties, and swung into action. He had all the bags moved out from hotel to airport (the schedule called for going to Varanasi that day), pressed the tickets and passports into my hands, and told me, "You can make it, Smoke. While your passengers eat, get your group's papers cleared through ticket, baggage, immigration, and customs, and you'll be right back on schedule."

"What about my wallet?" some practical thinker complained.

Valuables had been left in the safe instead of with the luggage at the hotel. It was a complication even the great Dawa hadn't foreseen. Each member with goodies in the safe had to personally sign for them.

"Susan," I said, "take 'em down quick in a taxi, scoop up the cash, and bring my papers. I'll go to India with you and help." I was supposed to stay in Kathmandu and await the next group, but this was building up to some emergency, and I could just as well meet the next group in Delhi.

"Oh, damn, Dawa, Su can't get my papers. They are locked in the suitcase. The key is in my pocket. And the suitcase is at Manik's house. She doesn't even know where that is or how to get the papers!"

We zoomed off on a mad chase by taxi, and stopped by Manik's and the hotel. Passengers milled around and needed whipping into a hurry. We screeched back out to the airport, swerving through Dili Bazaar's balanced-pole pottery porters; poor humped-over women barefooting cordwood to the city; troops of graceful saried schoolgirls parading informally lunchward; taxis; cars; trucks; overloaded, bulging-at-the-seams, black-smoke-belching buses; throngs and throngs of exotically costumed members of a dozen races going about their business; kids rolling hoops through vehicular traffic; goats darting across the street; sacred cows meandering—the usual scene.

Like a chase scene in a Keystone Kops movie, all this chaos crested to a crescendo in the Indian Airlines office at the airport. I will sum it up in two sentences, quoted exactly as I remember such a traumatic experience: "But hurry, sir, the plane is waiting for your group!" And the second sentence? "I'm sorry, sir, your group's papers are not in order, so you are not permitted to board!"

Well, it was resolved. Quickly, but not easily. I signed a bond to repatriate the group if India would not accept our outdated visas. That meant to fly them back to Nepal: a matter involving a thousand dollars and unthinkable delays and foul-ups. I had no time to think, and less than fifty dollars in my pocket.

Good old dependable Su. She herded the passengers into the airport lounge while I conned immigration into accepting us through the gates of India at Varanasi. In an hour and a half we were bathed, rested, relieved, and beered in the bar of the Clark's Hotel. Deep in cushioned luxury again, everyone was happy.

The third definition of *adventure* in my dictionary reads: "A bold undertaking, in which hazards are to be met and the issue hangs upon unforeseen events. . . ." We in the branch of tourist business labeled "adventure travel" like to tease our customers with the possibility of risk but do all we can to avoid unforeseen events. However, in trying to fix airplanes and otherwise adhere to schedules, we sometimes run into what my dictionary lists under *adventure* as definition number four: "a remarkable experience."

HOW TO HAUL LOADS IN THE MOUNTAINS

Grouse Mountain is a foothill peak we often choose to climb simply because its one or three-hour routes call for no great rucksack loads. Some youngsters, though, have had their first experience of shaping their shoulders for mountain burdens on that rocky eminence at the base of the Sierra.

Dave's daughter babbled happily about finding her name in the summit register book: "Dana Lee Sharp, age 1¾ years." My old expeditionary partner had rucksacked Dana to the top of Grouse Mountain more than once. This time she made it under her own nine-year-old power.

After lunch Dana reminded her father of his promise to let her carry the rucksack on the down-go. There is no simple way down from the summit rocks, but Dave handed over the sack without comment, except to mutter something about shortening the straps. Dana carried that man-sized sack all the way down the cliffs, down the scree, across the bench, through the gorge, over the snow-bent birches, across the creek, and up to the car.

I told her to be careful about saying "Let me carry your pack; it's light and will readily fit on top of mine." Many times I've been caught without a Sherpa near, and made this ridiculous offer in an excess of machismo and good spirit. The trained leader will not burden his back with a stuffed frame pack; he eases along until he finds the faltering trekker with only a teardrop pack. Now the barb is set. That streamlined twenty ounces of nylon may enclose a pirate's swag of solid glass-and-metal camera parts.

Dana missed the lesson. She is a veteran of scores of rough trips with her father but still too innocent to gauge charity contributions with a beady eye on the tax deduction.

Bob Swift, a guide of many ploys, invented the game of "light pack—heavy pack." In order to win this game it is only necessary to restrain bragging long enough for the opponent to open. If he opens with, say seventeen pounds, it is obvious that he is playing "light pack." And if the opponent comes out with a figure like eighty pounds (not an uncommon number), then he is into a game of "heavy pack." Of course, once the game is identified, the second player can remain one up without even mentioning numbers.

"Some people like to be prepared for every emergency, but, by accepting some risk and using the modern lightweight equipment, I find I can really scale mine down." This might be the answer to one-up the man with the seventeen-pound load.

Or, "Ah, but when you carry a full double rack of hardware and stay out a really long time, as I do. . . ." Something like that for Heavy Pack.

The native's loads are one of the fascinating sights on Nepalese roads. How they can hump those loads so heavy and ill-balanced is beyond understanding, much less imitation. Many times I have seen them carry a measured one hundred kilograms and often more. Diesel oil goes up the road in five-gallon cans. A child will carry one, a strong woman up to four, some men stagger along with seven! Much of the material for building the Everest View Hotel went all the way up the long road without benefit of Lukla airlift. Come to think of it, I've seen loads going by Lukla and over in eastern Nepal that wouldn't fit in a mountain plane.

Once I found a sick Tamaung porter along the road and tried to help him by trading off my thirty-five-pound rucksack for his mountainous load. He could carry better than I, even if he was sick. Thinking about this at home, I decided to try the head-strap (*namro*) method over a longer distance. We were bringing a forty-five-gallon garbage can up the canyon for a squirrelproof bread box, so I stuffed about twenty kilos in it, hung it from my head, and took off up the trail. What an aching-neck experience that was. I couldn't see where I was going, and, before I got to Fifth Lake, I didn't care.

Another time, last December, I found myself sitting alongside the kitchen boy on a *chautara* (pack rest). Kitchen boys carry enormously bulky loads of pots and pans with the tea and coffee and catsup and peanut butter for the sahibs' noon stop. The *doko* itself is next in size to a cow feed basket, and the pots are mounded two feet over the top and lashed precariously with shredding jute string.

When he wasn't looking, I cranked my head under the *namro* and staggered to my feet, leaving my rucksack on the pack rest for him. I got along fairly well on the steep stone steps, except that it was hard to balance. I swore I would go to the next *chautara*, but on a sharp switchback turn I nearly lost it; the boy grabbed the load as I was going over the side.

It is tempting to say that the solution to the problem of hauling loads in the mountains is to let the other guy do it. Complications arise, however: the burro goes astray, or the yak grazes off trail, steamrollering the side-mounted duffle against a rock. After I had finally learned that a machismo-inspired load in my rucksack could deprive someone of his job, a legitimate reason for heavy hauling turned up: six of our porters had to discard their loads to carry a sick passenger down. The thought of the other bearers so overburdened shamed me into adding most of my duffle goodies to my already too-heavy rucksack.

I tell my passengers in the Japan Alps that only day packs are necessary, since choppers transport food and bedding to the *yamagoya* huts. "Well, we will be two weeks on the trail, so throw in an extra shirt." My extra shirt often translates as a considerable wardrobe, not to mention first-aid kit, hardware, spare gloves, chess set, and a pocket stereo with twelve tapes.

There is no real hope of traveling perfectly light in the mountains. It is good to try, as long as you realize that, like proving a unified field theory, mastering *kanji*, or routinely brewing the perfect cup of coffee, the game can never be won.

HOW TO MAKE MONEY IN THE MOUNTAINS

"Why don't you pick up rocks when you are in the mountains? Sooner or later you would strike it rich."

I've been told this a hundred times, and it still doesn't make any sense to me.

What is the necessity of a reward? Must a person reap tangible or specific benefits in order for any activity to be worthwhile? Is climbing only justifiable if one can show a rock, a fish, a mounted deer head, a gold-plated ice ax, a list of firsts, a name, a reputation, or any kind of cash of the realm?

I did pick up a rock once. Gary said to me (I don't know if he was scientifically correct), "Smoke, this is Precambrian rock we are climbing, right? It has been exposed on this peak for millions of years. It has been struck by innumerable meteorites, and all we have to do is keep our eyes open and . . . there!"

He reached down and came up with a melon-sized stone, pitted and burned looking. It was the perfect picture of a cooled sky missile. Gary carried it all the way down and I stole it. I knew he would never get around to doing anything about it, and in the confusion of unloading him at the bus station in Salt Lake I sneaked it out of his gear.

I took it around to the MacKay School of Mines in Reno and got the verdict: "Valuable if the ore body is very large and quite close to rail."

15

Picnics

A QUESTION about mountain guiding that I'm often asked starts out, "Uh, since, as you say, your trips include almost as many women as men, uh . . ."

Mountain climbing and adventure travel are romantic. I have hinted that mountain-mobilized good health and spirits may spark flirtation between the members. And the guide? Of course. Prominently, even spectacularly, he poses as a hero, spouting exotic and newly vital wisdom. It would take an extraordinarily repulsive specimen to play the role of guide or tour leader without looming as an attractive father figure to some of the group. And the guide, like the Lord Chancellor in Gilbert and Sullivan's *Iolanthe*, becomes "highly susceptible."

Cheryl Arnold still keeps the startling beauty that once sent her on a tour of South America as "Miss Ice Follies." Other guides called her "googoo eyes" and avoided her hypnotic crevasse-blue sparklers. She mesmerized me. She is a dedicated, compassionate nurse who contracted hepatitis working with Mother Teresa in India. Her adventurous spirit has taken her on a thousand-mile Arctic canoe voyage and up a 22,000-foot mountain. She enjoys discussing religion and arguing philosophy. Her aversion to opera only prevents a cloying perfection. Best of all, she liked me.

I took her on a climb up the Little Scheelite Pinnacle, made day-long by our sitting together on the belay stances holding hands. She asked many questions. She wanted to know why I liked trekking and what it was like to walk to Everest. I answered her in the letters that follow.

WHY I TREK

Some trips have a way of flipping over in midcourse, and such a one is this. We've been hobnobbing with some of the world's best mountains for a short and cloud-hung day or two, but most of our march to and from the Sanctuary has been in rain slopped over from the monsoon. The anxiety of watching each greasy stone footstep has been aggravated by leeches. Would you believe eight at once? On one shoe? Eight leeches bobbing and weaving and reaching ankleward. Bend over to get them: aversion to creepy crawlers makes for a clumsy grab. Panic scratches the backbone. This time catch them, but one flicked around and hung to my thumb. Collected two more on wrist from rubbing by a bush. Umbrella falls in mud. Rain down the back of the neck—and so it goes. First tourist-trots of the season, a slight head cold, clammy clothes, and drippy skies add to the general blah. All this evaporated like smoke from a puffball this afternoon.

I'm writing this, sitting leechless and dry on top of a mountain. A little mountain, a cow pasture hill, but this is the first time in thirteen days I've been out of my tent after tea! And it isn't raining! Camp is in a green bowl of goat-and-cow pasture 500 feet below me, and on the other side a mile-high cliff plunges to the Kali Gandaki. I can see the river emerging from its celebrated gorge, but the great peaks are hidden in storm. Momentarily the clouds shift and the sun burns on the white top of Dhaulagiri, sparking a faint ambition that has been simmering on the back burner and needs only sunlight on snow to bubble a greed for high mountaineering deep within me. Now it has gone, as clouds recapture the world. They tower in castle cumuli, and fog blots the view to the river. But the fog is a warm breath of India and cures the damp blues instantly. I'm sitting wooled in fog now, but the page is dry, the ink is not smearing, and my oft-used umbrella is folded and furled. I climbed to this window of freedom through pines. Wonderful trees. Of all the woody-stemmed plants of the world, pines are the ones that speak of dryness, of sunshine, of breathable air. Jungles are fine, but the smoky hills, the distant shafts of sunlight, the glimpses of snow, are like the sound of hacksaws slicing through the last cell bar. I've been imprisoned too long in moss and fern and zero-visibility leech swamps.

One of my passengers asked me the other day why I trekked and what I got out of it. It was almost the same question we discussed on the Scheelite Pinnacle last summer. I put the passenger off with, "It's my job; I like it." I'll see if I can write you a better analysis of what I'm up to over here.

I get out of it health, sufficient wealth to maintain some kind of genteel poverty at home, and good friends. Good friends, of course, are the best advantage. Salary is least important. I've got to have it, but surely I could earn this small amount in the states more easily. Health is not to be sneezed at.

This feeble joke put me right off. I have descended to the tent to dig out my loose-leaf notebook for better arguments. How do you like these? From the *Apocrypha* (Ecclesiasticus 51:70): "Health and a good estate of body are above all gold and a strong body above infinite wealth." And here is another from Confucius: "He who needs only coarse food, water to drink, and as pillow his folded arms will find happiness without further search." Yes, I get out of trekking a set of strong legs. You once called them gorgeous!

I am now writing several days later. I meant to mail the letter from Beni, but they were having a big ten-day celebration. The streets were full of people dressed in their finery, the bands playing, the stores all shuttered, and the post office deserted.

I have been thinking about why I trek. Although I have to have a job, and it is wonderful to have one that gives me good friends, good travel, and good health, it is not really the reason I keep trekking. The real reason I trek is because of the charge. Because it is a drug trip. Because I get turned on. For several excellent reasons I have never sampled psychedelics, but I know what it means to be turned on. Some things on the road turn me on as if I'd swallowed a neon sign. Now this intoxication doesn't keep me lit constantly, as I tried to explain in the first part of this letter. It is a sporadic but more or less frequent semi-satori that fills me with wonder and delight. That's the word I want. I took delight this morning in the dew diamonds strewn by slanting sun rays down the short green grass of the road. I stopped to stare with delight at a pair of slant-heads. That's my name for water buffaloes. They stand with their heads tipped back. I don't know what they are thinking behind those big black eyes; I wasn't thinking anything profound myself, just how grand and fine they looked. I couldn't help bowing slightly and muttering, "*Namaste.*"

Luckily I am a strong walker, and it is no trouble to catch up with all but the fastest trekkers. Lucky because I can seldom walk along without finding reason to stop and savor another scene. This time it may be a field of marigolds so bright they nearly blind me to the pleasure of ruminating over a roadside cattle trough. A dry hollowed log, its cracked and wrinkled outside and rough-chiseled inside, have an ancient, grizzled, but so natural, look. This contrasts sharply with the transient beauty of the flowers, obviously painted by an artist too splashy with his golds and greens. Today's diet was a multipage menu of delights.

All morning we followed a river. There is no foot-dragger like a swirling, rushing, boiling, sometimes lazing, often whirlpooling, mostly boulder-beating river. Should I sit on my walking stick head for five minutes here to watch the lapping backwater or surge of narrow chute? Would five hours be better? Moving water must be one of the most hypnotic of the Great Magician's tricks.

After noon stop, we climbed up a good, hot, sweat-oozing-down-the-nose mountain and topped out among shiny-leaved oaks with half a sky full of glacier-draped peaks.

There seems to be no logic to the category of things that stop me. The list of turn-ons I find along the road includes not only pines and waterfalls and buffaloes and marigolds, but also any view from a steep cliff, all bridges, the iridescent sheen of a rooster's feathers, drum sounds floating up out of a deep valley, children's laughter, shouts of a plowman to his team at furrow's end, any and all bamboos, allelomometism (I looked it up and wrote it in my notebook; it is the wheeling of a flock of birds in unison without an obvious leader), fat, purple fir cones. (If the trees stand below the road, these top-branch juicy-looking fruits are brought to eye level.) And that lower-altitude tree, the sacred *Ficus religiosa*, common name *bo* or *pipal*, turns me off the road to sit at the *chautara* (pack rest), to recuperate in leafy shade and contemplate *pipal*'s old and gnarled bark.

Speaking of old and gnarled things, I always stop at an old, wrinkled-faced native with white whiskers. He smiles back, I wink, he laughs, and we both pull our beards in camaraderie, good fellowship, and the recognition that we are congratulating each other across the language barrier. We are members of an exclusive club and full of years and wisdom.

That's enough raving. When my friend asked why I trekked, I didn't answer him this way. He didn't want to know anyhow. He just wanted to tell me that he came on the trip to see if he could walk, found out that he could, and please, please, would I congratulate him.

Yes, the mood of this trip has changed. A few days ago, I didn't think of writing down all the good things about trekking. I'll bang this in the box when we go through Beni on the way down. You should get it in three weeks or so. By that time, I'll be off on another trek and thinking that rain is not so bad. Leeches? I can do without them.

DEVUCHE TO NAMCHE

Cheryl, your sense of appreciation and enthusiasm are among your best qualities. I understand how you can say that your trip to

Everest over the Teschi Lap Cha was a grand experience, even though the big storm that pinned you in Gorakshep for ten days cost the life of one of your crew. I too have enjoyed storms, even rough ones that have struck down other mountain travelers. But I wish you could look back on better Nepal memories. Not only must the death of the porter (who died by disobeying your leader's orders) cut bitterly into your experience, but the Khumbu part of your trek involved too much snow on the road for it to have been anything like what we look for on Nepal treks.

I'd like to write you about a typical day on the road when we do *not* lose crew members or wade through thigh-deep snow. Since I describe a stretch of road you walked under less happy conditions, I thought you might enjoy this.

There was not a trace of light in the sky from the coming sun. Only stars, black night, and blacker mountain hid the last crescent moon as I crawled from the frosty tent in the little round meadow at Devuche. Old Kipa had just started the fires, and it was quite shivery until I could start warming the inner man with cup after cup of steaming, sweet milk tea. What a constant delight, on those winter mornings, to witness the fading of the stars and the growing light: the dawn of freedom.

We got under way early because even the kitchen fires would not warm toes. There was a good, but short, uphill march through birch and fir; that is the best warm-up because, like the warmth of the tea, it comes from the inside out.

Tengboche is one of the wonder places of the earth. The second clang of the big gong (the first was long before daylight) was just fading into echoes when we clomped across the hard frozen meadow under the grim *gompa*. It was especially spooky, as winter had sealed off the gangs of trekkers and seemed to subdue even the resident yaks and equally silent red-robed monks. It was crescent-moon time, scheduled for study.

No Tibetan traders dared the frost and spread their wares on blankets for the few groups who trek in cold season. (When I tell the avid shoppers among my November groups that they can get the same old junk fresh from the antique factories in Kathmandu, they think it is sour grapes because I don't like to shop. On one trip to Namche near the end of trekking season, we met Tibetan traders on the steep road near Puiyan. One of the heavy shoppers stopped with me while Sirdar Khancha talked to his trader-friends from Namche. Khancha's interpretation of the purpose of the traders' journey perfectly corroborated my theory: "He tell member 'very old, Tibet'; he buy, Kathmandu.")

The Mani Rimdu religious celebration was over. Gone were its pomp and pageantry, its gongs and cymbals and horns reverberating across the then-crowded meadow, the colorful crowds of locals, the foreign visitors from many lands, the stomp and wail of dancing choruses, the solemn marches of the life-consecration ceremony, the whirling dances. Some say the wonderful eight hours of lama dancing should rank with the principal peaks of Nepal.

At the first Mani Rimdu I attended, my natural skepticism kept me skulking in the rear of the audience. We were scheduled to leave that day, Darjeeling bound. The Sirdar whispered we'd better walk right out in midperformance, as "Khumjung some long and dark time much fast come."

I headed for the gate, but George Yntema grabbed my arm and said the Head Lama was beckoning to us. It looked that way, but how could it be? George said he must know that we were the only two foreign Buddhists around, but just then the Head Lama clashed his cymbals to announce the next act, the band began to play, and the dancers emerged from the shadowed *gompa* door—we must have been mistaken. I glanced once more toward the balcony where the band and the Head Lama sat behind a beaded screen. And then! The great man himself drew back the beads and definitely signaled us to come. We climbed the stairs and approached the sanctum. The Head Lama laid down his cymbal, opened the curtain, draped prayer cloth *katas* around our necks, uttered the single word "Goodbye," and returned to his throne.

This time I made it through the gate, but practically staggering. For some distance down the road this agnostic old skeptic reeled in a fog of awe.

George had known nothing of Nepal when he received an invitation to join his friends on a trek. He looked up Nepal in an atlas and, finding it next door to Tibet, looked up Tibet in the New York telephone directory. There he found a lama, studied Tibetan diligently enough to be able to join old Gombu in daily chanting on the trek, and was already a practicing Lamaist. George thought my awed reaction was perfectly natural.

Many times since I have talked with His Holiness N. T. Jangbo, the Head Lama at Tengboche, on the road and at Kathmandu, where one of his projects is an attempt to finance a hotel for Sherpas. (Contributions accepted by the East Willow Alpine Club, Bishop, California.)

The winter trip I am describing, we did our *gompa*-going, as is the custom, on the way up. After our group audience, I was invited back for a private audience. "What did he say, what did he say?" My passengers, so recently impressed by the air of divinity that cloaks this small, quiet man, besieged me. Nothing profoundly religious, I confessed. He apologized about the sanitation of the grounds and asked me to bring him some flashlight batteries next trip.

On the return journey, I took care to lead the pack away from the *gompa*, around the left side, the correct passing side of the *mani* stones and walls. Some travelers never see anything and could walk into a cesspool or a sanctuary with equal unawareness. Down, down the long hill, my heels banging the frozen gravel worked such warmth into the body that I was soon ready to strip off mittens, muffler, overcoat, and sweater. Not quite shorts weather those days, but at least I could strip to one layer of wool. "Going bushes" made an excellent occasion for doing this striptease.

Ah, "going bushes," that delightful interval, that regular relaxation, that perfect chance to pull out of the chain-gang tromp. One can adjust the pace, and fall back in behind some group of grunt-ing porters or yakking passengers or jabbering Sherpas, to find a little patch of peace and silence on the road after the ritual of the little patch of privacy in the bushes.

Off I went again, untroubled by the sight or sound of others, my only companions the standing-at-attention cones of the firs and the winter-curled leaves of the rhododendrons.

Dominating all was the snowy meringue-topped mile-high face of Kangtega. Mountains have presence. No doubt the lamas, searching for a pious and proper location for the monastery, con-sidered isolation, firewood, and water, but also cranked into their computer the view of sacred Mount Khumbuilya and Kangtega.

The steep face of Kangtega can hardly hold a flake of snow, so the Phunki glacier is fed by ice tears from the overhanging brow far above. (Aspirated *P* is a difficult sound for an American speaker to hear, so he may be excused for thinking this small gla-cier has been titled with our slang word *funky*.) Geologists used to be puzzled about the disappointing size of Himalayan ice streams flowing from such tall mountains. The answer to their puzzle is in three parts. The bulk of the monsoon precipitation falls at mod-erate or low altitudes, and the peaks receive relatively little snow. Second, the great power of the sun at these latitudes subjects such snow as they do get to sublimation. And third, the celebrated steepness of the peaks allows snow to avalanche down to melt levels.

Phunkitanga is just a wide spot on the road, a gas station and MacDonald's in the form of a Nepali tea house and six prayer-wheel houses. For trekkers coming up, this is the first view of whirling *manis*, and they are duly impressed. It is at the bottom of the long grade up to the monastery—a good place to let the radia-tor cool while photographing *mani* wheels. On the return the trek-kers slog by with nary a glance. How soon the traveler becomes jaded.

The prayer wheels are spun by a tiny stream that emerges from a spring, which we sometimes use for water at lunch on the way to

Tengboche. The spring starts so near the road that I fear pollution, so I can't use the little joke I play on the customers at Devuche: "Of course I'm drinking it; do you not see that it comes spinning purified through the wheel? It is holy water and cannot hurt."

Over the bridge. A moment to stare into the surging waters of the Dudh Kosi, which here were almost free of the near total grip of ice we found in the more-shadowed gorge above Devuche. Water is holy whether chained in ice, working a *mani* wheel, or tumbling free.

I began to catch up to the passengers. Poor passengers with road-locked eyes and trip-end worries, will you not at least give a glance for religious monuments or for those frequent stones whose carvings turn all the pious to the left?

Here is one who will lift his eyes long enough to discover what is in front of him and will agree to follow another man's custom in another man's country. Moreover, he is a concerned, compassionate Catholic who enjoys rite and ritual and is sympathetic to heathen ways as well. "What do the stones say?" He begs the old prophet for insight.

He touched the right button, for the hill fairly melted under our flying feet, or mine anyway. He may have found the gravel of words an additional underfoot hazard while I expounded on one of my favorite subjects. Soon, for me at least, we reached the village of Trashi, where a few minutes' wait brought sun and lunch.

I got caught in another conversation and could only make an attention-divided devotion to the daily miracle of the life-giving sun god bursting full-formed over the high crags. What an instant reprieve from deathlike cold, experienced so emotionally in these mountains. A blinding light, then the whole body, starting to cool from cessation of walking, glows with the warmth of life.

Everyone wanted to go to the Everest View Hotel for a dinner of luxury after twenty-two days of trail food, so I gave clear directions how to find the junction. As usual, there were some who were too nervous to hang back at my postlunch warm-up pace and, sure of their pathfinding, forged ahead—missing the road. I set others on the right path and, leaving my rucksack as a marker for those still following, "went bushes" at the junction. Not really—this was my way of gaining a little time to sit quietly in the forest. I don't see how one could select a more beautiful site for meditation. Besides the smiling peaks and deep blue skies, there was the faintest breeze rustling in the firs, the shining bark of birches hanging loose and translucent in the marvelous light. A nine-colored Danfe pheasant (otherwise known as the Himalayan monal, *Lophophorus impeyanus*) ran by, giving an extra flash of beauty to the scene.

The doctor and I went to Khunde hospital to distribute medical supplies from our box. On the way back from this spectacular viewpoint, we rummaged through the village of Khumjung looking for my Sherpa friends. They were all "upon a trekking trip," but I hoped to find their wives about. Da Puti's husband has the Dumje duty this year. This is a religious party at which he must host the entire village at the cost of a year's salary. I thought it would be sporting to help out by buying one of the excellent carpets from his wife's loom.

Then over the hill to Namche. This hill is the same one the hotel is located on, although the trail still follows the ancient way through open meadows and patches of fir amid mossy *manis*, safe from the profane prowlings of shabby hippies and camera-hung Japanese tourists in suits. The hotel entrepreneurs must have instantly recognized the finest viewsite in the world.

Everest had withdrawn into clouds, but seeing it would be a back-over-the-shoulder, familiar-old-stuff peep anyhow. Ahead was the abrupt glory of the vast, black-rock, ice-hung wall of Kongde Ri. On the right side, Teng Kangboche pointed the way to the two white giants marking Teschi Lap Cha, the pass of many memories.

All day long my ego had been tickled by the passing Sherpanis saying, "*Namaste* Barasahib, *namaste* Esmoke, *namaste* Gaga." I was twenty-two days out on the road, over three months from home and Su, and these moon-faced gals were looking mighty good. Good enough to give the old sometime bachelor such a glow that even the sternfaced policeman at the Namche checkpost smiled when I reported there. Up and down the cobbled streets of Namche I was greeted by tangle-haired Tibetans, by merchants peering over their *ghee*, biscuits, tins of rice, piles of tennis shoes, matches, and soap, even greeted by passing porters. "*Namaste*, you many times Namche come." Such hospitality gave me a rosy feeling—and a head start for the invitations to *chang* drinking.

Somewhere in midrevelry, after *dahl baht* dinner with our Sherpa crew, the passengers arrived from the hotel. We were invited to a party at Sirdar Khancha's house. We were guided by young Tsering Ongdi, who was on the way up the hill "to search a cow." In the smoky evening-dark house, with a beaming chorus of children, sisters, aunts, uncles, and grandfolks about, Khancha and his good wife served us many cups of warm *chang*. It must have been freshly made as it did not seem to inebriate us, although two got lost on the way back to the tents and arrived amid much laughing and crashing about.

My day ended with a most peaceful folding of hands over well-fed and liquored belly in the soft candlelit solitude, lulled by the whisper of dry snow sifting down the tent roof, tuning my little radio to a BBC program of music by Dvořák that built to a climax repeating the "Going Home Chorus" from the *New World* Symphony. I drifted off to sleep thinking that even better than a great day on the road from Devuche to Namche was the prospect of going home.

16

Guiding Secrets

FIRST STEPS

"How did you get to be a leader?" comes shortly after "How do you do?"

What does it take to be a guide or mountain tour leader? A first requirement is to be able to masquerade as a mountaineer. I was a passable imposter a very long time ago. I turned down my first chance at guiding when I found it was to be Everett Darr's honeymoon. Everett, still nervous from a fall he'd taken on central Oregon's Three-Fingered Jack, needed someone to belay his bride. I was too shy for that one but picked up my first guide fee the following year, in August, 1937, for taking a party up Mount Hood. No big deal? Two of the four of us were wooden-legged men! My uncle, who worked for the Oregon Artificial Limb Company, talked a one-legged fellow worker and a customer, who was a one-legged logger, into hiring me. The logger was more active and did better, but the other man kept up, and we made it over the Chute Glacier to the top in 7½ hours. I still have a fading box-brownie summit photo showing the two men standing alongside their prosthetic devices. I'm alongside them, with my leg folded behind me and a sock in my pants as a pretended stump.

What does a trek leader do?

He keeps his passengers from losing the path, going over the side, falling in crevasses, water-soaking their lungs, overexpanding their brain cells with the dreaded high-altitude cerebral edema, stumbling into the last stages of hypothermia, blistering their feet, or coming down with the aches or the plagues. Hazards are expected on the North Face of the Eiger or the East Ridge of the Little Scheelite Pinnacle, but the above-mentioned dangers, and more, are encountered on the plain pedestrian paths of the ordinary adventure trekker. We have no special knowledge beyond that pointed out in a hundred manuals of mountaineering and pointed up by a thousand near catastrophes in the actual practice of our profession. We watch for signs of anoxia and rush the victims down in the Nepal night, scream at the lightly-clothed climbers in Japan's Kita Alps who risk death by wet cold, plead with the latrine-users to hunker low and prevent camp contamination, warn walkers to tape up the first hot spot on the feet—the usual things.

We also like to combine herding with a bit of teaching and preaching to make it easier and more enjoyable for those paying our freight. We instruct our charges, point out a peak, or help them with a handhold. We often act like a guru, psychologist, philosopher, or even priest.

We recognize that a first step on the road to making passengers happy is to select those predisposed to muscle-powered travel. Ideally, we would screen them by a test walk, though this is rarely possible. We hope that their answers to questions on the application blank will provide clues. In practice, the only reliable information we can get is from the leader who observed them on past trips.

Beginning trekkers often ask, "Am I strong enough to go?" Yes, they are, if they are at all sound of wind and limb. Few of our passengers are athletes or laborers; we tailor the days to fit the capacity of those who make their living in offices.

Sometimes the clients do not read the brochure's fine print. A passenger collared me at lunch on the first hill. "Are we going to have to walk uphill on this trek?"

"Yeah, man, that's almost a definition of mountains, and since this is a walk in the Himalaya. . . ."

"Well, then, I quit!"

Allen Steck, my company boss when I led an organized Mount McKinley climb, asked how my people were. "They were great. Well, that one guy. . . ."

"What did he do?"

"Nothing."

"Nothing?"

"At the end of each day he would just fall over backwards (he must have had an indestructible packboard), lie supine until the tents were up, then crawl into his sleeping bag and hand up his cup for dinner."

"He should have gone to climbing school."

He did. He must have missed the lecture on sharing the work. It was spelled out in the trip brochure, but in fine print.

We screen as best we can, but character and personality are not instantly obvious. The proof is in the pudding, and the pudding is out on the road.

It helps if a guide is sometimes mean. No kidding. It is one of the points of contention we have with our boss. When the boss proposed replacing mountain guides with Sherpa guides (confusing two entirely different connotations of the word *guide*), we had difficulty imagining the easygoing Sherpa men being effectively mean when an emergency required this quality.

Ray Genet, the famous Mount McKinley guide, may have used a chart less lily white than my own. He asked me to work for him once, and, to my regret, I never got around to it. I did learn some pointers from him, though.

"Do you get many customers from referrals, Ray?"

"Don't be silly. Some guy wants to brag to his bar buddies in Louisiana that he has climbed the highest mountain in North America. Do you think he's going to tell someone else how *he* can do it?"

"If you have those kinds of individuals, how can you get a group to work together?"

"Easy. I build a strong emotion. What's the strongest emotion? Hate. Who do they hate? Me. I work 'em like mules. Shout at them. Any back talk, they dig latrines. They band together to hate me. They are charged with hate, and it carries them up the mountain."

"How do you get a barfly from the South to haul such terrible loads, Ray?"

"Listen, Smoke, you've got to start out right. Work them just this side of exhaustion. Load 'em heavy low and they'll carry heavy high!"

I can't summon quite this degree of toughness in guiding, but Genet's ideas worked well for him and his parties. His toughness was legendary and was demonstrated in numerous acts of heroism, such as saving the lives of his fellow members bivouacked at 18,000 feet on McKinley in midwinter. (Ironically, this iron man, so experienced in cold and storm, was killed by exposure high on Mount Everest.)

The leader normally gathers his group in a stateside air terminal, with the help of a sophisticated manifest listing every particular of each member's travel documents and plans. He seats them in the lounge and bids them relax while he checks them in.

He then practices upside-down reading with his left eye, as he watches to see that the clerk pulls the correct coupon for each ticket. He counts the luggage with his left hand. (The manual says it's worse to lose a bag than a passenger. Bags don't cry.) He loosens his necktie with gulps of his Adam's apple. (He should free a hand to tighten it. Dress codes for leaders make sense. A necktie can get you into a head office as surely as an ice ax can get you into a keyless can of sardines.) His right hand is shaking the hand of the latest trekker to arrive. He should have his right eye addressing this man, but he still must keep a lookout for the one member who has not yet come. "Wow! Is she one of our members?"

Lucky the leader who has an assistant along. In all the constant counting and checking of the details of the trip, a skilled assistant can act as the leader's good right arm.

Arrival in a foreign city headquarters can be confusing enough to make the leader want a whole corps of assistants. In Kathmandu he has them in the form of the local agent. In other cities the hotel may help by posted advice:

(NOTES FOR THE SAFEGURD OF THE GUESTS)

BE CAREFUL; NEVER LEAVE OPEN THE DOOR FULL AND HALF.
Please close the door when you are in your room and also you leave the room for a moment.

PLEASE DEPOSIT YOUR VALUABLES AT THE CASHIER COUNTER.
We are not liable for the loss in case of robbery.

BE CARE OF VICIOUS SWINDLERS
Swindlers dangling with guests around our hotel at night have no relations with us. Beware and do not be cheated by their skillful enticement.

Sometime before leaving the hotel, the leader gives his speech, or many speeches, in which he tries to orient the members to their new environment and settle the dust of their fears. He tries, not always successfully, to anticipate the many questions that will come later.

Nepal trekking trips work so smoothly the leader has little to do. The leader is along as liaison officer between the passengers and the Sherpa crew. The leader confers with the Sirdar, who will have the complaints passed down along the chain of command to the erring crew member who offended Mrs. Gotrocks. The company used to say that the leader should be able to lead 5.9 rock climbs; at any rate, he is able to give commands when mountaineering judgment is called for.

The first evening he works out arrangements with the Sirdar for the efficient operation of camping and walking life on the road. He tells the passenger how to get into his sleeping bag, how to keep his candle from incinerating him once he is in it, and other lore.

Tent assignments usually follow the rooming list, which is made up by some genius in the office. Matching compatible strangers is a problem an office magician does by telephone-voice character readings with ninety percent success. People often ask if tent-switching occurs on trekking trips. This is getting into trade secrets of trip leading, and I must reply, "No comment." I will mention that I have discovered that two left-zippered sleeping bags of the same model will mate if one is turned inside out. And I will mention that we had a married couple on the last trip who met on a previous one. And I will tell of the young couple who came with different last names but the same home address, same hotel room, and same tent; they announced, after thirty days of close living under rough conditions, "When you write to us after the trek we will have different addresses!"

If this idealized leader we have been following on paper is named Smoke, he will be up long before daylight and will awaken the passengers at first light. Wake them for "washing watah" but not for tea in bed. Shame on the very thought! Members are expected to be up and about, pronto, for an early start.

So I have announced tea in my regular loud call, "*Cha, chu, ohma* ready!" which never fails to make the Sherpas laugh. And now the trekkers gather around the tea table in the center of the camp. I have removed the stools so they can be packed and the porters can get away, and so that the members won't linger but will mix up their hot drinks, chug down a little porridge, and be off.

Then the questions start. For the purpose of this outline, let us take the easy ones first.

"Will there be anything worth seeing today?"

"No." (This is related to a question frequently asked of travel agents: "Is it worthwhile going to . . . ?")

"Will there be any pictures today?"

"No."

"Is that an important mountain?" (Probably related to: "Are you anybody important?")

"No."

Put down in black and white on unforgiving paper, these questions look a little odd and unbelievable. I have heard them all, and more than once. The answers are obvious.

Now the questions become closer to most trekkers' hearts, and they come thick and fast.

"What is the elevation of that peak?"

"What is the name of that pass?"

"How high do we climb today?"

"Downhill hurts my knees; will there be downhill today?"

"I hate level; is there much level today?"

"Will it be a steep climb today?"

"How many miles do we walk?"

"What do they call the village at lunch stop?"

"Will the wind blow?"

"Will it be cold?"

"Should I wear my sweater?"

"What if it rains?"

Trekkers come with their thermostats screwed too tight. Their comfort range is so narrow they spend much of their time checking their temperature and adjusting their clothing. Rain is even more of a strain than heat or cold. At the first sign of the slightest mist, before the tough-skinned, insensitive-souled leader or Sherpa feels any moisture, all passengers are likely to be enshrouded in colorful nylon.

"Can I make it with just one water bottle?"

"One should do, but by all means take it. If you should see me drinking out of a stream, please look the other way and pretend you did not see. All water except what we supply is poisonous!"

They do not carry water for liquid replacement. The water bottle is a security blanket. Security is the name of the game, and reducing anxiety, I think, is a big part of the leader's job. But let us see how a Sherpa answers the questions about the steepness of the road.

"Will it be up or down today?"

"Some up, some down, some long, some short, some like my arm!"

He means that, since we are walking in Nepal hills, we will be dealing with mountain geography. When driving in your car, do you worry about whether there will be left or right turns?

"Do we have to climb *up* to lunch?" a member asks a Sherpa who spends his whole life walking up and down hills.

"No up." Sherpas sense the city dwellers' hillophobia and attempt to calm them. If the road has gone up and down several times in the last hour, and the passenger asks about the road ahead, the Sherpa may estimate it as "level like this." He doesn't always understand how this may put the wilting member off. Level is a safe, familiar concept to passengers. When they tremble at the 50,000 feet of vertical gain on the Everest Road, I point out that if they return to Dologhat, there is 50,000 feet of loss and the average is zero. Arithmetically the road is level.

"Besides," I argue, "when you get truly into condition, you need to carry a bubble level to tell if you are going uphill or down." This is almost literally true. When one turns around in Kathmandu and heads up again for a second trek, he is likely to be in such fine shape that only the speed of movement and close reading of body temperature can determine if the course is up or down. A fine-tuned body feels no trepidation on either course.

The first trekkers ready to go are given instructions to follow the lead Sherpa, and soon the others start off. While I am drinking my eighth cup of tea, the Sirdar comes around to suggest a change in tomorrow's route.

"He walks like this, Gaga," imitating the wobbly walk of a less-agile swivel-chair type. "Better we go lower road."

Sherpas are acutely aware of the delicate nature of the crockery we are transporting. Apparently one of the first English phrases a

Sherpa crewman learns is, "I carry, sir." They see that trekkers have difficulty in hauling much of anything.

A passenger complained to me that the Sherpas were carrying Roger's pack. "Oh, I'm sorry, I'll get someone to carry your pack," I told him.

"I can carry my own pack!"

"That's okay, it's no problem. It's part of the service. I'll speak to the Sirdar."

"But," he started blubbering again. I knew what was eating him, but pretended not to know and kept needling him obliquely. He was an older member who always kept in the front of the line and wanted to upstage the middle-ager at the rear. But trekking is not a contest.

People often ask me what the Sherpas think of them. Perhaps rich people who come from some distant place and pay to walk around for no apparent reason must seem strange to the natives. Of course, Sherpas have long been making their living by catering to weird people, so they may be more able to understand than other natives.

John Fischer guided for many years in the peaks near Bishop and recently bought the local climbing school. He has expanded it greatly and has begun teaching technical climbing to the Sherpas both in the Sierra and in their homeland. He showed up one day with my old friend Tsering Onchu.

In explaining to John why we greeted each other so effusively, Tsering Onchu said, "All Sherpas like to work with Gaga." Maybe so—I like Sherpas. I'm easy on them, not demanding; I carry more than my share.

How do the other leaders lead? I don't know. Never worked with any on the long road. I've seen them in camp, when our paths crossed in the hills, and a little bit around the hotel. We seemed to operate in much the same way.

The boss used to worry about how the leaders were leading, and sent off "green sheets" to the passengers to check up. One satisfied client wrote to the company: "I would follow Smoke Blanchard to hell and probably will!"

When customers were asked to criticize the leader, it was easy to find something wrong. The company valued this feedback, but the leaders cried so bitterly, it abandoned the tattle sheet.

Sherpa Ang Lhakpa Mote advised me: "It is my duty and your duty, Gaga, to make the members happy." He is absolutely right. How to do it is the problem. To keep them happy—untouched by traumas major or minor, reasonably congenial, minimally frustrated, skimpily informed, constantly entertained, educationally broadened, and with anxieties allayed. To bring them back alive and well and enthusiastic to go again is a Matterhorn of a challenge. Probably the reason Ang Lhakpa says, "I like with Gaga," is because I try to fill the passengers with sound mountain advice, such as: "Pack your down clothes in your rucksack to use on the descent. For the ascent you will want to wear your up clothes."

Sherpas have difficulty understanding our ways. Instructed to clean up the camp, they find the passenger's half-eaten food lying around, the jam, butter, and sugar uncovered, his cup, half-full of coffee and cigarette butts, overturned on the tea table. Is it any wonder the crew throws tin cans in the bushes behind the kitchen? Once we came down from a half-day climb to find this message chalked on the plywood table: "PELIS CEP TABAL CEUL-ING." What a shame that a junior of the kitchen crew had caught us with a dirty table, which we should have had the decency to keep clean.

Nawang Dorje said Sherpas climb for the same reasons Sahibs do. At first, this tickled his interviewer, who thought he had discovered equally high-flown motives among the natives as those the foreign mountaineers profess. "For money," Nawang Dorje then said, "for the same reason all you book-writing climbers do it. Otherwise, it's silly!"

I'm sure the Sherpas' respect for leaders is partly based on their empathy with our motives. We, too, get paid for walking. (Vic Yarbro, Bishop boot-repair man, was a steady sort, totally locked into the Puritan work ethic, with twenty-five years of seven-days-a-week self-slavery behind him. He would scarcely talk to me when I traveled overseas like some kind of depraved over-rich tourist. His attitude changed 180 degrees when I went to work as a tour leader. He delighted in announcing to customers in his shop that "Smoke gets paid for going to those foreign countries!")

Sherpas may not understand tourism and tourists, but they are keen judges of human nature and quick to spot any kind of phoniness. They saw right through the passenger who sneaked off alone on acclimatization day, strolled along the lower dry glacier, then bragged to his woman friend about scaling a pinnacle on the crest at 20,000 feet. They didn't believe him either.

And they had no sympathy for another 20,000-footer who wanted to gather glory to take back home. This one leaped from the plane in Kathmandu with clenched fist, vowing that he would go to 20,000 feet. I had to send him back at 15,000 feet from mountain sickness. Back down at 12,000 feet he had recovered enough to demand, "I want a Sherpa and a porter, and I want to go to 20,000 feet."

"No, George, you aren't acclimatized," I reasoned.

"What's the name of that mountain and how high is it?"

"Khumbuilya, about 19,000."

"I want a Sherpa and a porter and I am going to climb it."

"No."

"Why not?"

"First, because I say so. Second, it is a sacred mountain, off limits. There are a lot of other good reasons, but mainly because I say no."

"I've failed!"

He failed, all right. He failed to understand what he was supposed to be doing there. He kept telling me that he could not face the home folks. (Sounds like they had problems also.) I made a beautiful speech, which I should have tape-recorded to play to any group that needs to be reminded that trekking is like a picnic. There is no way to succeed or fail, win or lose, on a trekking trip.

The 20,000-footer developed some psychosomatic ailment and left the trip.

There's always a fairly heavy language barrier between crew and leader, and maybe that's all right. We communicate what is necessary for safety, health, and happiness, and let the rest of the gossip go. I'm not sure what the Sirdar meant when he asked me, after some mild problem with the passengers: "What that man name?"

"Damn it, Ang Temba, we've walked thirty days with these people, and you ought to know that man's name."

"What that man name?"

"That's Mr. Blank."

"Bah! What *that* man name?"

"Geez, Ang Temba, you surely ought to know *his* name, even if you couldn't manage the other."

"What that man name?"

"That's So-and-So."

"He good man, he mucha strong!"

He is a crusty old man, that Sirdar, one of my favorites. (They are all my favorites.) Ang Temba also has some pithy remarks for members. On drinking: "Morning time drinking, falling down!" On Himalayan fauna: "We never no see yeti, but they much coming out when *chang* drinking!"

It is not surprising that Ang Temba couldn't remember the passengers' names. PAX names, I should say. That telex travel term has now made it into the Sherpa language, as in this recorded statement from a Sherpa friend: "I Muktinath going—with fifteen PAX." Our names are difficult for Sherpas; they seldom bother learning them. One time, the Sirdar informed me that "Husband" was in camp, that "Buzz Buzz Camera Man" (a movie maker) had turned back, and that "Yellow Man" (the color of his parka and wind pants) and "Long Doctor" (the tall doctor, as distinct from "Crazy Doctor") were still coming up the mountain.

Farmers along the way often ask our Sherpas what the purpose of our march is. We come from such different worlds that a common question I am asked by my Sherpa friends is, "How far do you have to walk from your village to carry firewood home?"

When I told my friend Ang Tsering that we had met a party of Israelis trekking the Kali Gandaki, he said, "Ah, yes, Israelis. They're Moslems, aren't they?"

JUST A BIT MORE, WE'RE ALMOST THERE

Well, we've got the PAX all out on the road. It is time to go. We'll never see the front runners. They will arrive at lunch camp on the heels of the lead Sherpa, so they can brag that they were never passed or that they reached lunch stop in so many minutes. Maybe they hurry so they can sit and read a novel. We had four of these speeders once who sped in order to have more time for noon bridge. This bridge is not prayer-flagged architecture flung over a canyon. It is a card game. At Gorakshep one of the players announced that, this once, their game should be suspended out of respect for the mountain scenery.

Do people trek to play cards? Maybe. They go for any and all reasons. Our people come from professions as numerous as you can count on the fingers of two hands. Their individual quirks of personality and character are as numberless as the sands of the Ganges.

On a trip of fifteen people, there are really fifteen trips. While I was studying glacier crevasse bridges through my monocular on a spring trek under the Ganesh peaks, a birder asked me if she would get any chance to see a glacier along the way. She had seen 150 species of birds. I had seen many fine glaciers and a half dozen mubs (miscellaneous unidentified birds). Experienced travelers know that one travels around inside his own skull.

Everyone has a right to his own trip. Tourists disinterested in scenery puzzle me, but that's okay. Hong Kong tourists come to shop; I just wish they would raise their eyes from the merchandise once in awhile. I once saw some tourists, not my walkers, taking coffee on the roof garden of a Hong Kong hotel. As the lowering sun gold-plated the waters of this world-advertised beautiful harbor, they placed their chairs with backs to the view to watch TV! Non-scenery people ignore views. Even scenery people, those who will watch a waterfall or a rainbow from the trail, won't look out of the window of a moving vehicle. We schedule rides in trains, boats, and cable cars specifically to observe the wonder places of the earth; most passengers refuse to look out. Sometimes it frays my patience.

In Bhutan our parked taxi waited ten minutes for one of the passengers to finish shopping. When the passenger in the back seat complained, I shouted at her. I pointed out she was in the capital city of one of the most glamorous of all countries, that the citizens were passing by in their most colorful costumes, that artifacts coveted the world over were displayed inside the shop, that she was free to step out on the uncrowded sidewalk in lovely sunshine to watch clouds play among the forested mountains, that she could practice deep breathing the pure air. She leaned her back against the window and took up reading her novel.

Do we get many odd types? In fifteen strongly motivated people from out of the mysterious blue yonder of a mailing list of several thousand, of course we do. I am a little odd, and I suspect you are. Difficult types? Yes, once in awhile we have to ask the company to send Mr. Obnoxious with another leader next time, to spread the work fairly. My assistant on a commercial expedition, perhaps suffering from high-altitude-anoxia irritability and surly from trying to fit his pace to that of a tired client roped to him, growled at me, "You tow this son of a bitch for awhile, I'm tired of tugging him!" On the first China trip my assistant and I knew every member from previous trips. They were all tremendous people. But, still, because they were so exceptional, we had to take care to keep some apart from others.

The boss once asked me, "Why don't you tell them about the flora and fauna of Nepal like the other leaders do?" I don't know how I got out of that one. I can only remember the names of four conifers, two goats, and a bear of the Himalaya.

I do know the names of the stars, and thereby gleams a tale. Richard Thompson pushed open the glass door of the customs lockup at Kathmandu, looked at me, and complained, "Oh no! I thought Ray Jewell was leading this trip."

"I'm sorry, the leaders often get changed around after the catalog comes out. You'll just have to put up with me again."

I found out Richard worked as a mathematician in the space program and spent his spare time grinding reflector lenses. There, if he had a telescope and I knew a constellation, we'd find a mutual interest. I told him we had a month of fine weather ahead, and could surely catch old eclipsing Algol at its tricky variable twenty-minute minimum. Its period of two days, twenty hours, forty-eight minutes, and fifty-five seconds would force many of these dim periods into daylight hours, but still, with a month of fine nights. . . . No doubt the old Arabs who named the Winking Demon were more patient watchers, or had no need to jump in the tent to escape Himalayan temperatures—anyway, we never caught it. The next time Richard came trekking he brought a computerized chart which caught Algol cold. Some stars are able to aid and abet friendship from one hundred light years away and renew it every 2.867 days.

To most passengers, watching the same stars they could see at home is not worth leaving the lantern light for. I'm keen on glaciers and run people out on the Khumbu or the Dhualagiri at the slightest show of interest. I swing my ax and slice steps, prod around for crevasses, gesture and rave and lecture as much as I have wind for.

Mostly I instruct in just plain walking. It discourages me to see a trekker, after thirty days on the road, come down a flight of stone steps baby-fashion, with just one foot leading. It saddens me even more to find that trekkers tire themselves by inefficient walking. Some will not listen. What can they learn about walking when they have been two-legging since they were toddlers? If they wobble while rock hopping, freeze on the steeps, lunge breathless at every up, jelly-knee after the down-go, and come into camp excessively fatigued, there may be a chance for improvement.

People walk awkwardly in the mountains because they neglect pacing and balance. Pacing can be improved by remembering that the heart is an engine that needs to be operated with a sharp eye on the tachometer. Change gears with the road and load to keep the motor running evenly, and it will serve you well.

For balance keep in mind the principles of physics. Your center of gravity must be directly over your feet. You learned it when toddling across the living room floor and made an immediate sitzmark in the carpet when you forgot the unforgiving principle. This is the secret to cycling, skating, running, rockclimbing, dancing. It is what the ski instructor really means when he shouts, "Bend zee knees." Holding the ice ax diagonally across the body reminds the mountaineer to check lines of gravity when traversing slopes less level than living-room floors. The skilled rockclimber whispers to himself each morning, "Weight over feet."

Besides keeping you firmly on the mountain, keeping weight over feet will bring you down again less fatigued than the spring and struggle system will. Watch an old alpinist walk. Even from a distance, you can recognize his "rocking-chair gait." Look at the tops of his boot toes, all granite-grazed from the habitual relaxation of the downside foot.

Coming down? Watch the Sherpas and porters. Passengers say they run down. Not really. They flex all their joints: toes, ankles, knees, hips—keep them flexed. Think of your hinges as well-oiled, keep them bent, and let them go. Never lock up your joints and punish your springs.

I call the whole thing, for want of a better name, WOFMIR: Weight Over Feet, Moving In Rhythm. That's all there is to it. The Chinese philosopher Feng Yang said, "To walk thousands of miles over hundreds of mountains is, indeed, no easy task." It is made easier by lifting them up and planting them—WOFMIR.

To keep the weight over your feet, you do not have to *watch* your feet. One of the most exciting views on the road to the world's highest mountain is the first sight of Mount Pumori as it looms over the snout of the Khumbu Glacier, signaling our entry into the intimacy of Everest. The gently winding path from Dingboche offers not the slightest obstacle; it could easily be followed by a blind man without a tap of his cane. Passengers' eyes are glued to the ground. Judy Cameron, veteran of eight treks with me, is shocked. She knows I'm mean, but she knows, too, that Pumori will disappear in five minutes and we will not see it again until after lunch. Some passengers, anoxiaed out of going beyond Lobuje, will never see the Khumbu at all.

"Aren't you going to tell them, Smoke?"

"No."

We have been walking toward and talking about these sights for more than two weeks now. This morning I did stop them to point out two eight-thousand-meter peaks. The jagged spires of ice that have been floating by on our left, the ragged rock pinnacles peering over us on the right, the yaks in the valley below, the frozen lake under the icefall upcanyon, the snout of the Khumbu, and Mount Pumori will have to await invention of boots with mirrored toes.

This watching the feet bothers me. I rave about it a good deal. I try to instruct them, tell them they can cultivate the expertise to walk over almost any ground by only occasionally checking three steps ahead. The mind will catalog the information and inform the feet. It becomes, after awhile, as if there were eyes in the boot toes. I show them how I can walk up stone-step switchbacks blindfolded. I try all sorts of ways to enable them to get more out of the trips by not missing scenery while they're moving. I will admit feeling shaky about this now, since a man on someone else's trip looked up momentarily and went over the side to his death. And I remind myself that each of us is on his own trip. Everyone has a right to his own trip, and if his walk through the mountains is not for scenery, then let him watch his feet.

It's time to worry about the frontrunners getting lost. They receive a heavy lecture about trail-finding and are instructed to stay behind a Sherpa, but the way is long and winding, and sooner or later they get out of sight of the crewmen ahead and make a wrong turn. ("Crazy Doctor" strode out of camp one morning and started on the road back.)

Getting lost in a country without signposts is easy. On a typical trek in Nepal, we almost surely will misplace the odd trekker. It is no problem. He is easily found, although it may take awhile. Six of them spent the night in a native house one time. We learned of this through the hill grapevine and worried not, but I was a bit put off when one of the straying members wanted reimbursement for the trifling sum they'd spent for dinner.

The good guide keeps his swivel neck oiled and constantly looks back to count. "This is a small, shallow bergschrund with a safe snow bridge. It is only safe, though, if you step exactly in my footprints!" I looked back and counted four. Strange, there should have been five. Bob Swift will never let me forget it. He helped to pull her out.

Inattention of all kinds can lead to getting lost. Charley had quarreled with his wife and stomped off in a huff ahead of her. He was so preoccupied with the righteousness of his argument that he walked right by the camp that was being set up. By the time I got there, he'd had enough of a head start to get over a pass. Rather than make him return up the hill, we sent a Sherpa with a mini-camp and orders to catch Charley and camp him at the bottom of the big hill.

What about my leader function as guru? Our trips in Nepal are staffed by Buddhist crews, and we often march through Buddhist country. I like to expound something of what I know about this philosophy, not only for cultural interest, but in an attempt to use these ideas to reduce anxiety. I reckon anxiety the sharpest pebble in the walker's shoe.

I quote the Buddha: "Rough is the ground trodden by the hooves of the cattle, thin is the couch of leaves, light the yellow robe, sharp the cutting winter wind; yet I live happily, with a sublime uniformity." Obviously, he didn't screw his thermostat too tight.

Another Buddhist saying: "The way is not difficult, only avoid choosing." I take that to mean that one should not be constantly checking, as my trekkers do, to see if they are hot or cold, if their muscles are straining as they go up or downhill, whether at the moment they are comfortable. They risk squeezing that portion of life they judge satisfactory to a small fraction.

"Why don't you join our campfire discussions?" a trekker on one of my early treks asked.

"Because I get sick and tired of listening to how the laundry is drying or how the Nepali intestinal bugs are behaving," I told her. From that day on I've not neglected my evening guru duties.

Certainly it is a prime job of the leader to stir the social soup. Among the members we have a marvelous collection of talents, experiences, and thoughts to share. I often prod my groups to assign one evening to each member to speak on any one subject, with the entire time devoted to the lecture and a question and answer period. I particularly enjoyed the one that started: "I am the second-biggest tomato canner in all the world! I am very rich and very important! But I don't want to talk about food processing. My daughter brought home transcendental meditation, and that's what I want to talk about." He was great.

Anxious trekkers come down with numberitis. Its symptoms are an excessive concern with capturing reality in an arithmetical net. Victims pester me for statistics to write in their journals. My somewhat evasive answers are not motivated by meanness. I try to jar them loose from the notion that the mountain experience can be reduced to numbers, that once mountain scenery has been recorded with a label in a notebook no further participation is necessary. I try to teach them that it is rude, meeting an icy spire, to categorize, file, and forget it, so that one can get back to discussing his automobile.

Alan Watts said, "Cultivate good manners toward all sentient beings, including vegetables and even lakes and mountains."

I try to teach them *relative* heights of the different peaks, some mountain geography, geology, and glaciology, some feeling for perspective and scale in mountain viewing, some real love and lore of the magnificent land forms we are marching through.

Hours are the best measure of distance in the mountains. I give trekkers an accurate estimate; miles are meaningless in rough terrain. Yet people insist on miles and will yield to no such hanky-

panky as metric conversions. "Okay, this trek is 250 miles—
twenty-five days at ten miles per day. Full days we march ten miles,
half days five miles." Despite the intended irony, some people accept these highway scale figures and write them down in their notebooks with only the faintest doubt about their accuracy.

There is a rumor that the mathematicians in one of the engineering offices of the East Willow Alpine Club are devising a new
approach to the numbers. Some people say it is a comprehensive
system, which deals with slope angles, distance, climbing difficulties, heights, weights, temperature, temperament, etc., but
uses only one unit of measurement. This is to be called the *bulchi-
tro*, and works on some kind of natural logarithmic sliding scale
that varies with the individual. Meanwhile we must do the best we
can.

I've been most of a chapter chopping the passengers, when
really it is these same passengers that make the leader's life so
worthwhile.

When Grant Rogers goes on vacation, he likes to get completely
away from managing the small factory he owns. He is big-bellied
and big-hearted and likes to laugh and to make others laugh. He
enjoys playing the buffoon. He amused us on the way to Everest,
telling stories of his drinking days. He also told us war stories, like
the time he dropped the bomb that sunk an enemy battleship, flew
back triumphantly, but missed getting his medal when he blun-
deringly led his squadron to a landing on the wrong carrier.

On the long, hot road up from the lowlands, we all envied the
animals and wished we could wallow in cool, brown ponds of stag-
nant water; Grant waded right in, clothes, rucksack, and all, and
sat down alongside the water buffaloes. His clowning brought
laughter, but when he turned serious, we admired him. Grant
Rogers said of the natives in our crew and those we met along the
way, "I came to see the mountains, and I saw the people; they are
taller than the mountains!" If he would broaden his proclamation
to include the passengers, I couldn't agree with him more.

Sometimes, after a new guide or tour leader gets over his astonishment at wafting wallet-free over the earth, he might be heard complaining, "Guiding is not climbing, and tour leading is not touring." So either he quits or discovers that the new game is also good. It can be fun to prance about through alpine steeps or air-terminal lobbies leading a parade. It is fun much of the time, but it is not always easy.

Most young people have travel ambitions, which they quickly forget as work, career, and family responsibilities push dreams deep into the subconscious. Years later, when they meet a man who gets paid to travel, an ember from long-banked fires may light a fleeting thought: "Could I do that?" Ray Jewell, who traveled as a passenger on Mountain Travel's first commercial Nepal trek and quit his physicist job to become a world-champion adventure tour leader, says, "No."

About three days into remote country on one trip, a passenger said to me, "I've been watching you. I see that the Sirdar does all the work. At the end of the trip I'm going to ask you a few questions. Then I too am going to lead trips and get paid for it." He never came around to ask me questions.

We had no mountaineering difficulties on that trip. Luck was with us, as we averted several potential disasters. On the last day of the trek, the doctor and I stood watching some of our people stagger down the wide, gently sloping road. One was three-trip-certified accident prone. She had survived, so far, with only a broken wrist from falling down temple steps at the start. One young man had had his brain's balance center severely affected by coma from an automobile accident. ("Say, Doc, sign this silly medical application for me, will you. I want to go trekking.") Two young women tripped gracefully in high heels but exhibited rigor mortis when laced into boots; their walking improved little during the trek. The Sirdar watched them closely in hopes of returning these fragile dolls to the shelf. He pulled up to talk to the doctor and me and said gravely, "We bery lucky, sir, we bery lucky." We got them down out of the hills all safe and sound. The nontrekking part of the trip ran into washed-out bridges, immigration snarls at obscure border posts, misdirected baggage, overbooked hotels, visa irregularities, AWOL and inebriated bus drivers, an all-India air and surface transport strike, the complications of Calcutta, and so on.

I have said that taking care of passengers is not easy, but when the leader draws a group who are full of fun, who laugh or can be made to laugh, the job becomes a breeze. To take care of PAX is to keep them laughing? Maybe. I must be doing something right; here is a petition handed me near the end of a trek:

Dear Man of the Mountains:

We, the undersigned, do respectfully request a prolongation of said Manaslu trek to extend beyond the previously specified time of December 27th.

We have agreed to become a permanent band of nomadic Himalayan trekkers.

Always the mountains!
Otherwise: mutiny!!

TAKE TWO ASPIRIN AND KEEP WALKING

"Every year on this date I set a new height record for myself." That was the elderly trekker's opener one morning just before sunrise.

"Damn," I thought to myself, "how am I going to find something to satisfy this old geezer?"

Down in Kathmandu he was muttering into his goatee about the mystic altitude numbers that attract so many to this highest range in the world. Attract and kill. His muttering turned to moans when I explained to the group at our pretrek meeting that we could not go high, as planned.

He grumbled, "Why has this trip been changed?" Tut, tut, he should have read the fine print in the supplement: itineraries are subject to change.

"His Majesty has not seen fit to open the Kali Gandaki."

"Why does he not open it?"

"We are not privy to the King's designs."

"Then where will the trip go? How high will we get?"

Damn these oldsters. So often, when their skin begins to wrinkle and their hands begin to tremble, they set out to prove that there's fire in the old furnace yet.

Now here we are on top of the ridge, with the summit just a bit above and nothing higher around. We are looking at an eight-thousander (8,000 meters) across the canyon, but it's out of reach. How can I find him something high to climb?

And then he opens the snake cage: "It's my heart. Some shallow and irregular beat; I tested it by walking around a little after tea yesterday. It's kind of bad."

We have no doctor along this time. I am the doctor. Would that demoralize you? It petrifies me. I know about my lightweight first-aid kit and about the vacancies in my head where the Red Cross course leaked out. I wonder if my cardiac case knows; he probably suspects. He has his pills and has lived with his condition (now he tells me) since long before the trip.

My involuntary-doctor's assignment weighs heavily enough without this near crisis. I've just seen my third patient this evening. The Sirdar sends ailing villagers to my tent. Go look up the *Barasahib*. He's the leader. He has a medical kit. He has compassion too, but it's not a strong medicine. Now comes the third village father; he has a small boy in his arms. The boy has a terribly cut finger, and the whole hand is swollen. Take him down the canyon to the hospital, I urge. The father would prefer a nearby hospital, just two miles from here (which would avoid a week's down-canyon walk), but the Sirdar says, "I saw their village hospital last year. It's just a house, two or three bottles, no good." The poor little kid may lose his hand.

My heart patient is okay now. He'll make it. We are down to a low elevation and easy roads from here to the end of the trip. He doesn't need any of my pills. He can diagnose and treat himself, he says. He damn well better. In spite of his symptoms and my worry, I cannot slow him down. He still flails his ancient knobby-kneed bowlegs in nervous flutter up each hill.

Maybe I worry too much. Sometimes I think I'm foolish to carry all this gear around: rope, first-aid kit, flashlight, spare mitts and goggles, extra clothes to keep them warm, emergency food, climbing hardware, fire starter, whistles, flare, and signal mirrors. They make my rucksack so heavy. Whatever could happen to trekkers on such ordinary walks?

Out on the road a year ago, the trip doctor spooked me by pointing to one of the older trekkers and saying, "That man is having trouble with his heart and may not make it." On the following trip, different suffering trekker, different doctor, I was told the same thing. It begins to sound like a broken record and is no easier to listen to.

On yet another trek, the doctor came around at Khumjung and said, "Oh, by the way, Rudd has a twinge." The Khunde hospital was nearby, so it was easy to run him up there and put him on the EKG machine. The machine was broken. Along came a pair of doctors, touring the high country on a TB program, with a small portable EKG machine! They hardly knew how to operate it, but our doctor was a cardiologist, and he was soon reading a long tape of mumbo jumbo.

"Well," he equivocated in his best doctor fashion, "it doesn't say 'yes,' and it doesn't say 'no.' Let's take him on up and watch him."

We took old Rudd all the way up to the top of the little peak at 18,000 feet. He had no more twinges. I got mine later, down below, when Doctor John was jabbering away about how medicine is an inexact science, cardiograms not all that reliable, and, "Anyhow, I figured old Rudd would just as soon knock off on Kala Pattar as anywhere."

Only three days before, Sirdar Nawang Dorje had given me his verdict on another potential victim: "She die, no die, I no know." Lili's problem was exhaustion near dusk at 19,000 feet.

So far, knock on wood, I've never lost one on a commercial trip. I was not so lucky on a private expedition many years ago. My climbing partner went over the side. He'd lost a mitt and was suffering from exhaustion and panic at the end of a long push in midwinter blizzard. We were not even roped. I felt warm and confident and only wanted to press on to a better bivouac. And he was lying down, sliding toward the cliff.

I screamed with horror, "Look out, Fazzi, you'll kill yourself!"

I wanted to shock him into keeping back from the edge, but, as if my warning were a command, he dug in with his elbows, pulled himself to the brink, and rolled off. He doesn't haunt me as much as I thought he would, but I still see, sometimes, his Leica camera revolving on its strap slowly around his body as he tumbled through space. I dug a snow hole and came down the next day. It cost me ten black toes from frostbite. They still give me fits when it's cold.

I have a seventy-one-year-old trekker next month. We will be going above 20,000 feet. He's been with me two times before. Excellent fellow, good condition. But seventy-one? To 20,000 feet?

"What a cinch," I'm told almost each trip, "walking around in the Himalayan hills and getting paid for it. Wish I had your job."

Yeah, maybe so. Mostly, it's pretty much of a snap. There's seldom anything that goes wrong, but sometimes responsibility can be the heaviest load in the leader's rucksack.

Pilgrimages

"Why not go by bicycle?"

The instant I thought of it I knew I had the key to a long-time ambition to visit the holy places of the Lord Buddha. My walk a few years before from Buddha Gaya to Sarnath convinced me that I needed something more than my poor feet to move across the vast plains of India.

I conned my friend Laurie Engel into going along by emphasizing the flat terrain connecting the pilgrimage places recommended by the Buddha himself. She had never owned a bicycle, and I had not ridden since childhood. "That's okay," I told her, "we'll use standard one-speed Indian bikes."

There are many religious places visited by devout Buddhists in India and Nepal, but the prescribed and popular four are the birthplace, death place, first speech place, and inspiration place of the Buddha. I list the holy places in geographical order, for that is the way we planned to approach them, to avoid backtracking. Pilgrims travel in these modern times by train, bus, and sometimes by private car.

260

We bought our machines in Delhi and hauled them by train and bus to the Nepalese border, within a half-day's ride of Lumbini, Nepal. The literature makes much of the fact that Buddha was "born in the shadow of the Himalayas." Well, sort of—Dhaulagiri can sometimes be seen from Lumbini.

One of the old tales reads:

Now at the time the Lord's mother traveled from Kapilavastu toward her kinsfolk's city of Devadaha, the pleasure grove of sal trees called the Lumbini grove was one mass of flowers from the ground to the topmost branches, while amongst the branches and flowers hummed swarms of bees of the five different colors, and flocks of various birds flew about warbling sweetly.

Dr. A. Fuhrer, an archeological surveyor writing in 1897, thanks so-and-so "for allowing me the use of two valuable elephants without which it would have been an almost fruitless task to explore the dense sal forests in which these interesting ruins are hidden away."

Sal trees are few these days; the famous gardens are reduced to level fields of brown grass. Laurie and I, though, were still healing from the cacophonies of Delhi, Lucknow, and Gorakhpur, and the very bleakness was soothing. Although we were sympathetic with His Majesty's Government's Lumbini Development Plan, even to the extent of reaching into our purses to help, we couldn't help feeling a little sad. The profusion of trees (our rupees guarantee the planting and care of one), the marvelous waterways, the relocation of temples, the coordination and control of business, the accommodations for pilgrims and tourists—all looked wonderfully bright and orderly on the huge colored drawing the project manager, Mr. G. B. Subedi, showed us. Still we worried. Development has become a dirty word for Americans.

We joined a long, distinguished list of pilgrims to Lumbini. The Emperor Asoka erected a pillar in 244 B.C. fixing the location of the Lord's birth. In my saddlebag I carried a 1972 translation of the Chinese monk Fa-Hien's book describing his trip to India and Ceylon in 399–414 A.D. and his visit to Lumbini. He quotes from the guidebook *he* carried: "The lady, having entered the tank to bathe, came there-from by the north gate; she proceeded seven steps, gave birth to the Prince. Fallen to the ground, the Prince took seven steps. Two Dragon-Kings washed his body."

The tank and the tree, or, I should say, *a* tank and *a* tree are still there. We looked, stared, photographed, stumbled about the temples in our stockinged feet, bowed, and took off for town. Our duties done, contemporary life called us.

The single short dirt main street of Lumbini looked like nothing had changed since Asoka granted the village tax relief in the third century of the Buddhist era. We spent most of the day watching ox-cart trains, people walking through town with loads on their heads, passing cyclists, and rickshas. We ran into a Nepali we knew from Kathmandu who invited us to tea and eggs. After a late supper of Indian-style cooking which looked appallingly unsanitary, we walked home by starlight, utterly content with the peace and quiet of Lumbini.

Early in the morning we wobbled off and followed deep ox-cart ruts in heavy dust. Actually, most of the way we rumbled on rough pavement. The single-lane road carried few cars, but buses and trucks regularly chased us across narrow brick shoulders onto gravel or dirt. Occasionally we rode a dirt trail alongside the highway and pleasantly roller-coastered until sand or a ditch halted us. We had to dismount in the larger towns also, for hordes of pedestrians, cycle rickshas, motorcycles, trucks, camels, and cars made an impenetrable maze.

We routinely jumped up at first light and pedaled off before sunrise, wearing gloves and scarfs. After ten kilos we were warm enough to pedal in shirtsleeves and hungry enough to look for a breakfast stop. On the back fenders we carried sleeping bags, minimum spare clothing, camera gear, and a half-dozen oranges.

We used the sleeping bags in hotels that often came unsupplied with blankets. The natives told us not to camp out in the states of Uttar Pradesh and Bihar, where we would be easy targets for *dacoits* (bandits). We therefore had to schedule each day to bring us to some kind of town. We had crude maps and rudimentary Hindi, so we always had some idea of where we were going. We took care not to aim for a town too far away, lest we violate our most solemn rule: we must feel free to stop for any reason at any time—to photograph, to take tea, to eat, to rest, to talk, to stare; any excuse was valid.

In spite of the large population and the many villages, long vistas between groves gave us a feeling for the vastness of the country. Middle-class Indians travel by bicycle; when we heard a squeak and creak behind us, we knew we had gathered a following. Soon curiosity overcame language problems, and high-pitched Indian-accented questions poured out in English: "From what country do you come? What is your native place? Where are you going? What is the purpose of your journey? What are your qualifications [education]? How many sons have you?"

At first the normal shrill, brash Indian manner irritated us, until we reasoned we couldn't criticize Indians for acting like Indians. Their loudness and curiosity are natural. We found out they are simply chock-full of concern and kindness.

I had put off visiting Kusinagar because it was the death place of the Buddha. It might be like visiting a tomb. It turned out to be one of our favorite places. According to the scriptures, it was also a favorite town of the Buddha. His last words (paraphrased a little): "Don't be uptight, old buddies. This is a nice, peaceful, and friendly town in which to die. I'm over eighty. The old bod is worn out. Don't blame Chaundha. He didn't know the mushrooms were bad. Carry on the way I taught you and let each man work out his salvation with diligence."

First thing, we met a professor in the postgraduate college there who guided us about the small village and introduced us to his students and faculty friends. He also took us home to meet his family and instructed us how to eat native food in a primitive restaurant. He laughed and jabbered with us and treated us like pampered pets for the two days we were there.

Our *dharamsala* (a religious rest house, an empty cell with one bare rope bed—two rupees or twenty-four cents U.S.) had a pump in front where Laurie washed her hair. She sat to dry on a row of sun-washed steps and wrote a letter:

> . . . There are seven children around me, watching my every move. Right now the only thing moving is my pen, but still they are fascinated. You'd think this pen is performing feats. Fourteen eyes all watching me write. One little boy who speaks English interrupts to show me the monkeys standing on the wall. Earlier today we tried to coax them out of the tree with sugar cane. I have to go to the bathroom, but I'm afraid there will be a crowd of children following me to the latrine. It won't be the first time I've had an audience. I've learned to go Indian style on the side of the road. Made a bargain with the children that if they went away for awhile I would sing for them later. . . .

Later was after dark that evening, and this became one of the most memorable times on the trip for Laurie. The children dragged her off to their cabin and sang and danced for her and clapped delightedly when Laurie sang "Yankee Doodle."

Meeting people, as always, was the grandest part of the trip. How they did swarm around us at each tea shop! It was a dull stop without twenty to a hundred curious people. On two occasions the cops had to clear the crowds. "They have not seen men like you before, sir," one policeman explained.

Tea shops teased us regularly: a chance to get off the bikes, to sit, to talk, to rehydrate. We carried a small water bottle, but pedaling produced much thirst. The sugared drink of the tea shops didn't quench either. By custom tea is taken with rich milk, heavy on the sugar. It is still the custom; Laurie never succeeded in changing it, though she tried hard enough. We learned to request black, sugarless tea in several different Hindi phrases. One proprietor, finally convinced that he had heard us right, and that we were sincere, explained to the observers that these foreigners wanted their tea without sugar. Usually by that time I gave in, but Laurie stayed with it. And she got it. Got it set down in front of her, but while the tea cooled, or even as she lifted it to her mouth, some well-meaning bystander quickly dumped a teaspoon of sugar in her glass!

Those glasses gave our sanitary nerves little shivers. By the time the cook, the waiter, and the helping hands of the nearest customers had fingered inside and out, the entire glass was fully decorated with grease. We thought we could beat the system by requesting our tea in one-shot, railroad-style, throw-away pottery cups. That didn't work either. Cook picks two off the stack—dusty—taps rim down on filthy table—still dirty—sloshes water from bucket and dries with shirt tail!

After a few days, we just drank the water and ate all the food set before us. We had a tricky little iodine-crystal set which is supposed to purify a thousand gallons of water. A thousand gallons wouldn't go very far toward cleaning up much of northern India. The iodine could never purify the water, tables, pots and pans, the hands that fuel the stove and pat the *chupatties* in the same motion, the cups and saucers, or the smallest portion of the environment. Never mind the saucers—they come filled with *subji* (potatoes and cauliflower) curried completely out of danger. We even took to grazing through the marvelous markets after vegetables for our salads. Indians cook everything to death, so we survived by buying the makings in the market and mixing the salads in our hotel room. We blew on them in lieu of washing.

Sarnath, the site of Buddha's first speech to his five friends, Kaudinya, Bhadrak, Vappa, Mahanama, and Ashwajit, sits dreaming in the quiet, peaceful countryside away from the crush and babble of Varanasi. Tourist literature written by Hindus emphasizes that Sarnath was the seat of religious, philosophical, and political discussions many hundreds of years before the Lord Buddha showed up to "turn the wheel of the Law." I don't doubt it. We felt there might well be some kind of sanctity hanging around a place that has been holy for three millennia.

These vibes sent us around to the temples and on ritual circumambulations of the great *stupa*. True to our natures, however, we spent most of the Sarnath day lolling on the grass of the garden and snacking our way through food stands under banyan trees.

The next day we battled heavy traffic on the Grand Trunk Road, heading east over the great Malviya bridge across the river Ganga. The ramp going down from the bridge was so rough we had to stand on our pedals to keep from being bounced into the holy waters.

Hotels were few, and rustic to the point of being ridiculous. Most of them had baths, but an attached bath in a rural Indian hotel is an empty room with a bucket. Bedrooms often come equally bare, but we always succeeded in getting a *charpai* (rope bed) sent around. We tried to stake out these luxury quarters early in the afternoon so as not to panic when dusk fell.

First we wheeled the bikes into the room, even if it meant boosting them upstairs. We wanted them where we could guard them during the night. Then we would padlock the door and walk out on the town. We shouldered our way through the crowds, drooled over vegetables in the markets, gaped at elephants and camels, stared at lazily creaking ox-carts, nibbled on goodies from food carts, and inevitably fell into conversation with some English speaker attracted by a crowd of the curious at our restaurant.

We once transcended the language barrier. A noble old graybearded ragamuffin, carrying all his possessions knotted in a cantaloupe-sized ball in his gray blanket cape, stopped to stare at us at a tea shop. The cook said the fellow was bound for the Kumbh Mela, so I started talking to him in English about that famous festival, now at its 114-year climax. Not a word got through, but that didn't bother him. He sparkled his eyes and widened his grin and gabbled away in Hindi. We carried on a spirited dialogue with goodwill substituting for communication. Our conversation lasted long enough for Laurie to change lenses several times as she photographed him.

Any kind of pilgrimage or religious exercise gets instant sympathy in India. Buddhists, though, are so few that our flags gaily fluttering from the handlebars went almost unrecognized. "I have knowledge from this flag that you are Buddhists," a dark-faced cyclist greeted us. This meeting was good for tea and directions to a hotel. When we got to Bodh Gaya, a monk humbled us by announcing we had the colors wrong. He gave us correct flags, but Laurie says she is keeping her bicycle flag because she watched it for so long, and, besides, the green stripe could be for ecology.

I must say there is no litter in India. Poor people throw nothing away. Laurie said she appreciates the lack of industrial rubbish in rural India, but she did get a bit too much of the hygienic customs. Mornings on the subcontinent start with a whole nation performing their toilet within sight and sound of all. The gurgle of gargling will always bring back India to us. "One vast latrine," was Laurie's unkind comment.

Fa-Hien's book tells of danger on the roads from wild elephants and lions. We suffered from the modern counterparts in the form of trucks and buses. When I walked along the "GT Road" (the Grand Trunk Highway) from Bodh Gaya to Sarnath on another trip, I paid little attention to motor vehicles because it was easy to walk alongside in the grass. Since that time, much of the "Jiti Road" (Indian pronunciation) has been double-laned; even so, the traffic wore us down. Trucks passing each other and speeding cars whose Sikh drivers demonstrated fearlessness to impress their sixteen passengers kept us choking down our hearts. One time a truck caught Laurie on a narrow detour where she couldn't get off the road. As the huge vehicle swerved dangerously near her, the evil-looking one-eyed ruffian driver leaned out, gestured, and shouted at her, "Welcome!"

We were glad to get off the main road and head through quieter country to Bodh Gaya, the place of Buddha's enlightenment. The road now stretched more than three weeks behind us; to detail the anecdotes would fill a book.

We found Bodh Gaya full of tourists and pilgrims; at this holiest place of all, devotees had taken advantage of the cool season to flock in by the hundreds. Merchants raked in rupees in their rows of stalls, and hotels and rest houses bulged. Almost crying in desperation we grabbed one bed in a State of Bihar dormitory.

We paid our respects to the main temple and the tree (now fourth generation) under which Buddha sat. Actually, Buddha chose this tree because it was already considered holy, but his experience there spread the fame of the *Ficus religiosa* worldwide. We thought the modern Thai and Japanese temples much more beautiful than the principal one built in Hindu style. As at Sarnath, we soon sought secular pleasures: long lazy walks through the bazaar, munching and lunching at tea stalls, idle jabbering on a bench under a great shade tree, and sipping tall, rich coffees.

A young woman from Berkeley (who happened to know one of my fellow mountain guides there!) recommended the evening chanting at the Japanese temple. Three Japanese priests did their spooky, fascinating thing with gongs, bells, and clackers. The evening ended with some audience-participation chanting, which was attended only by a group of hippie-looking westerners. I had closed my ears and opened my eyes for the way out when someone handed me the pamphlet they chanted from. My head cleared suddenly as if by a cool mountain breeze. The words were the familiar Zen text, "Trust in Mind," but in that setting the message rang more clearly than ever. It seemed as if, in spite of the 2,500 years it took for the historical Buddha's ideas to seep into China, percolate through Far-Eastern minds, and trickle into the brain cells of Europeans and Americans in India, the old original thoughts that Gotama rediscovered here on the Diamond Seat still lived.

To paraphrase again, it seemed that Gotama the Buddha was saying: "This is it, man. You are it. You cyclists are composed of the same force, matter, or spirit that inhabits and empowers the rest of the universe. You are nothing special. But nothing else is any more special, from the sands of the Ganga which clogged your bike tires in the ox-cart ruts to the 'Sky Ganga,' which is what Indians call the Milky Way. All the same. Work out your salvation with diligence."

Catching a hint of Buddhism was a psychological climax to the trip. Arriving at the fourth holy place was physically the avowed climax of our long chug on the bicycles. No doubt we could have soaked up more Buddhism, but we had contracted to sell our cycles to friends in Varanasi on a certain date, and we had a train schedule to meet. It would have been possible to taxi to the station in the city of Gaya, but by then we liked riding so well that we never considered it.

In some ways, the last morning's ride was the best. We followed a lovely, almost traffic-free, narrow, winding road among trees on the banks of the Naranjara River. There were even hills with enticing rocks on their steep sides. Did Buddha never raise his eyes from his meditation seat and become even the least bit distracted by the thought of rockclimbing?

Now where did that thought come from? We were bound for the first leg of a train and plane trip halfway around the world, which would take us back to California rocks.

Here in California, there are many rocks and rites to be pursued, but our thoughts go back again and again to the time when we rode through the scented plains of India.

THE BUDDHA'S BRAINS

"It is said that the Lord Buddha cut open his head and handed out his brains. . . . The place is called Mani-cchu, and there will be 600 of us going. . . ."

Old friend Manik Tuladhar had thus come up with the perfect plan for a leader who had been down from an Everest Base Trek long enough to need a little shaping up after a week in Kathmandu. I had spent much of the last trek expounding on the meaning of *mani*, and was also in line for a refresher course in religion.

Mani is usually translated "jewel," as in "The jewel in the lotus." Mani = jewel = mind = brains. Bloody brains! Honest to Buddha. We would also visit Mani-ling, where the bloody jewels were washed. What nonsense. But a rare opportunity to go trekking with 600 people. I jumped at the chance.

Nuns of Kathmandu Vihara organized the pilgrimage and chartered a string of buses to take us to the roadhead. Nepali buses may be a notch above Indian buses, but that is not a hard notch to transcend. Despite our large Buddhist flag flying gaily from the foredeck, we still groaned along in a fair imitation of a lurching, swaying, creaking Indian bus. The dirt road added choking dust to our bottom-bruising, knee-knocking, mobile torture chambers, but at seventy-five passengers per bus we were arithmetically efficient.

In a ramshackle town at the foot of Kathmandu's northern hills, we disembarked our motley horde of housewives, merchants, nuns, monks, students, giggling kids, and one lone Caucasian trek-leading mountain guide in the barely bus-admitting narrow street. As I stumbled my bus-crumpled legs into walking speed on the cobbled path leading out of town, I thought I heard a voice say, "Trekking equipments." Maybe not—I often think I hear my native tongue when some days out of earshot of the President's English. Trekking equipments we had not. There were a few toy rucksacks with cloth straps. Most people carried their gear in oversized purses, string bags, or rolled-up sleeping bags under their arms. A few had hired porters to carry a great basket with bedrolls piled on top. Many carried nothing.

Everyone wore his or her downtown Saturday best: beautiful ground-dragging saris for the ladies, mod high heels and similarly ground-dragging exaggerated flare pants for the young gentlemen. Dignified Newari businessmen came in peg-top trousers, outside-tailed shirts, formal jackets, and distinctive caps. Only one elderly gentleman showed up wearing an elegant rucksack and everyday work clothes, but I *felt* right.

Manik told me that this road through Sangu was one of the old roads to Tibet. It had a wide, well-beaten look. Although much of the whole country had a generally run-down appearance, the temples and religious monuments along the crumbling, low stone wall bordering the road seemed unusually hoary. I could almost hear the chant of an ancient road to a high, mysterious land.

The road dips slightly into a small, dirty watercourse and then begins a serious climb up the almost-barren mountain by stone steps. These steps, chiseled and set with great precision, led steeply up to a small temple with a sign giving the out-of-date admonition: "Leather shoes beyond this point prohibited."

After an hour of rapid walking, we mounted a long flight of steps with carved-stone railing, flush-set rosette holy stones, and a miniature *chorten.* An ornate pagoda dominated a temple complex on top of all this.

Another flight of steps brought us up to the temple courtyard in a four-sided, hollow-square, two-story building that surrounded a spring trickling out of a stone well. Steps led overheated trekkers down to where they could fill jugs with drinking water and cool their feet in the overflow.

There was a modest scramble for sleeping spaces, in which Manik, his son Bnaya, and I fell behind, but eventually we found a few square feet of empty space in the hall on the second floor, to which we later dragged a grass mat. Our window, screened against the monkeys that ran along a ledge outside, afforded a good view of the courtyard. It also had shutters, which we later closed because of rain. We could just stretch out on the floor without being trampled by people constantly parading by us to get to the rooms down the hall. These quarters were far too barren to linger in; we went out again to see what was happening.

For us the highlight was a visit to the temple that housed the head of the holy man who dug the well. It is said that the keeper of the temple appealed to an astrologer for help when drought cut off the water. "You must sacrifice a man of thirty-two marks of merit." In all the country there were but two so qualified: the temple priest himself and his son. The old man found the way out of this dilemma by playing a trick on his son. He told his son that the god's advice for breaking the drought was to kill the *worst* man in the country. He said this man would be found lying on the road covered by a sheet. His son was to chop off the man's head without lifting the sheet. You guessed it, but his blindly obedient son did not. He cut off his father's head. My friend took me to the innermost holy room to view the two-foot-high head of this most dedicated man, which had somehow turned to stone.

Manik returned to find sleeping quarters for his wife and daughter, while I sunned myself on a ledge and watched a pack of extraordinarily repulsive monkeys. Their nauseating looks and behavior were only a shade more tolerable than those of the band of mangy curs who also frequented the precincts. Both animals were there because of the laudable doctrine of kindness to animals. Also, monkeys are identified with the god Hanuman.

Manik related a story. "The king was at Pashupati in plain clothes, and the Chinese diplomat shot the monkey with a silencer, and the king say, 'Catch and bring to me,' and he expel him instantly."

They employ dogs to eat human excrement, which pollutes the back sides of any temple. The ugly temple dogs produced such instant revulsion in this lifelong animal lover that I fantasized reducing their numbers with a rifle. I have never hunted but could imagine a murderous pleasure in blasting these diseased, pus-draining, leg-dragging, unfortunate fellow creatures. They should be put out of their misery, but what a shame to find myself the victim of spontaneous thoughts of violence. What a shock to feel hatred surge into what I hoped was a calm and reasonable mind! Such were my thoughts visiting this holy place as the invited guest of these harmless, peaceful people.

I had time before dinner to tour the grounds and look for tomorrow's road, to inspect some caves, and to circumambulate the pagoda temple. As the harsh light softened into evening, the dirt and general aura of decay, disrepair, and discouragement faded and dimmed; the pleasing shape of the pagoda stood silhouetted against a pure sky with one star.

Manik had said that this temple was "a very holy place to the Tibetans." I noticed a thin and wobbly line of *mani* wheels dispiritedly inhabiting only six feet of the thirty-foot front of a kind of *dharamsala* for the desperately impoverished that faced the temple front. But down this front, from the peak to just over the iron-grill door, was draped a lovely gold metal tassel, which began to sparkle faintly as devotees lit open-dish oil lamps ringing the old pagoda. As the keeper of the keys came around, clanged back the chains and bars, and lit holy fires in the inner shrine, even the most cynical outlander felt his iconoclasm soften, felt the faintest flame somewhere in his spirit, and happily went off to seek supper.

The dinner menu fit our spartan quarters: *chupatties*, spiced bean sauce, tea. We ate sitting on the floor, pulling in our feet as other pilgrims tromped the dusty boards of the hall.

It was my second populous dinner party recently. The week before, the engraved invitation read: "The Managing Director Mr. Saradindu Malla & Maharajkumari Rama Malla of Hotel Malla request the pleasure of the company of Mr. Smoke for Garden Buffet Dinner." There may have been *chupatties* and spiced bean sauce in the great garden too, though they would have been difficult to sort out amongst the goodies spread on tables around the football-field-sized garden. There were four bars, a huge department of cakes and sweetmeats, sections devoted to the roasting of whole pigs and sheep, and on and on. The occasion was a convention of the Indian Travel Agents Association. I met many elegant ladies, suited-and-necktied bigwigs, ambassadors, and imposters, and stuffed myself with too much of everything. Although I now found myself in a rather different travel scene, I felt just as mellow.

A fine, flashing, rain-drumming thunderstorm interrupted an opening ceremony and sent us jumping to close the shutters. I slept, or thought I did, despite an all-night party directly below us. Every time I'd wake and curse these rude (could they possibly have been drunken?) noisemakers, I'd drift off again. I dreamed of a most sensuous and worldly experience: such is the depraved nature of this religious pilgrim. The hard floor might also have intruded into my subconscious, as I dreamed of piles of soft sand in the corner of our loft, to which I dream-dragged my bed. All things end, and this night fortunately ended quickly. My watch reported that reveille sounded at 2:45 A.M.

For breakfast we made a cup of instant coffee from Manik's film

can and hot water from some distant charcoal fire buried in the
bowels of the mysterious, shadowy old building. After candle-
bearing figures scurried about for an hour, the scheduled *puja*
started on the dot of 4:00. A kerosene pressure lamp gave enough
light for the devotees to assemble cross-legged on mats in the
courtyard, while the monks and nuns led the chants. The storm
was over. Stars blazed in the clear, black sky-roof of the courtyard.
The chanting was pleasant. I could recognize and appreciate, despite my iconoclastic mood, the ancient Pali phrases of *"Buddham
Saranam Gacchami, Dhamman Saranam Gacchami, Sangham Saranam Gacchami"* ("We take refuge in the Buddha, the Dhamma,
the Sangha").

The day before I looked for the road up the hill, but there
seemed to be no path running up the steep mountainside. I soon
found the answer. The *puja* was over in just fifteen minutes, and
Manik asked me to follow people surging toward a door in the back
of the courtyard. We stumbled through a pitch-black room and
were ejected into a garbage-strewn path on the far side of the building. There were only a few flashlights to help the stars, but of
course I had my own, which I used carefully to insure excrement-
free walking till we got away from the back of the temple. A pressure lamp flickered far up on the mountain.

Away from the building, I concentrated on my balance, to keep
from using my hands as the others were, so steep was the road.
About every sixth man carried a flashlight, which he directed to
the cliff side of the road as we stumbled steadily upward into the
black night. It took an hour to get off the steps onto a ridgecrest
where faint daylight now gave some clue about where to walk, although I kept my light in a handy pocket. From time to time, the
road swung to the east side of the crest long enough to give a view
of sun shafts coming up behind Chobo Bamari and Gaurishankar.

Whatever happened to the worship of the sun? In all races and
climes it has been the natural object of reverence. Stars, too, are a
part of the same essence, but the sun is so visible, immediate, life-
warming, and powerful as it rolls over the Himalaya that I won-

dered why we did not all stop to pay homage to this supreme god. You may say it is not a god—that although the sun controls the planets, fructifies the earth, and brings forth life, it is, after all, only a ball of gas and cannot be propitiated or petitioned for help. Right, it is just a ball of gas. "That is the way things are," as the Lord Buddha announced 2,500 years ago, restating an ancient truth. A ball of gas—but important. Returning from a little clearing just off the trail, I found that at least one other pilgrim rushing along to Buddha's brainwashing spot had paused to make *gassho* to the rising sun.

We were passing through an area of small trees now, but the road was still very wide and deeply incised as it continued steeply up. The surface of the path alternated between ugly dirt and disintegrating granite the color of chicken gravy; the grade was unrelenting. The dry air contained just a hint of heat to come. No real summit could be seen.

Young trekkers streamed past me in droves until I fell back toward the middle of the pack. I did remember my age and did not try to compete with them. (After a Kala Pattar trek, a friend explained the secret of his good performance: "I wasn't about to let that woman beat me!" His remark revealed a sad case of male chauvinism and a total lack of trekking experience. A mistake like that on 18,000-foot Kala Pattar could have blown his heart, had "that woman" chosen to race. He was overweight and underexercised, and she was a trained and conditioned athlete. She told me later, "I hung back so Paul wouldn't feel bad.") As I was beginning to chafe in my soul a little, the road swung right, and we rounded a clump of trees to come upon our destination.

The tiny lake was so plain and sad-looking to contain such reverence, but it was indeed the sacred Mani-ling, as a collection of small *stupas* proclaimed. This was the place where the jewels of Buddha's brain were washed. Some people had already started their *puja*, which consisted mainly of decorating the *chortens* with flowers and foods. Others gathered in family groups to eat lunch. It was still early enough for Manik, his family, and I to circle the frosty grass lake border to seek a spot in the sun. This meal also was *chupatties* and spiced bean sauce. A little plain, perhaps, but, as Sancho Panza observed, "Hunger makes the best sauce, and, since the poor are always hungry, they eat with gusto."

After some time we started down, first on the same road and then down a steeper one, much eroded. Traffic and water had worn ruts in the dirt and the crumbly rock. Grooves three feet deep and six inches wide made slow going. The women's skirts caught in the sides; the old men, some partly crippled, found it difficult to hobble through. Brush inhibited detours, and traffic backed up bumper to bumper. Brush soon gave way to rocky, almost barren hillside, but the slope became steeper, and channels worn shoulder-deep needed bypassing. I was able to shake out impatience with a down-rushing detour, overtaking strings of trekkers but never coming near the front walkers. The hill was brown and dull, but Kathmandu could be seen across the heat-haze distance.

Manik had told me that part of the purpose of trekking in such a large group was to gain protection from leopards. This sounded like nonsense but gave the hill some interest, and I happily skipped down to a viewpoint overlooking a canyon where a couple of hundred of our pilgrims milled about.

The jam was caused by a small cliff, whose difficulties were obscured by people thick as bees. Then I saw that the main hive was a crowd swarming on the rocks of a small stream and around a *chorten* that marked the second phase of our pilgrimage at Mani-cchu. This was confirmed by a most graphic bas-relief concrete slab that pictured, in living color, the Buddha's brain operation. The surgeons standing on either side of the Buddha were dressed in white. No doubt this color represented priests, but, by their demeanor and above all their choice of scalpel, I tagged them old-time Oregon loggers. They were opening Buddha's head with a two-man crosscut saw! As for Buddha, I thought his usual benign expression was tinged by the faintest awareness of pain. But then I realized that I had no right to impugn the accuracy of the sculptors. The pain was in my own head from the picture of bright-red blood running freely across the Buddha's cheeks and soiling the jackets of the loggers.

The doctrine of Transmission of Mind has a long history, and libraries have been written on the subject. My memory of The Diamond Sutra, Asvaghosa, Hui Neng, and Huang Po struck no sparks of recognition of such literalism, or even symbolism. A hundred more pilgrims passed me as I ruminated. Young ones splashed in the pool and rummaged for lunch, while their elders lit incense, chanted, and bowed before this stark rendition of a noble concept. Manik could only mutter, "It is said."

Utterly baffled by the philosophical and religious significance of the ceremony, I washed my mind with action by scampering down to the creek bank. Oops, have a care there; it was not a difficult rockclimbing problem and looked easy for the young blades in their flare pants, but I didn't want to sail off the pitch and splash ingloriously in the pool. I clambered carefully down, leaped across the creek, passed the *chorten* on the prescribed left, and took the path toward home. We had descended so far on the western side of the mountain that a long traverse was necessary to regain the temple.

Late in the afternoon we trudged wearily down into the valley heat to meet our waiting buses. Manik said many inquiries about me passed back and forth along the line of walkers. Always it was: "Who is the old man?" Ouch! That word *old*. *Other* people are old. I felt better when Manik said that the common comment was: "He is very strong." Not too strong, though; I fell sound asleep with fatigue and contentment on the bus ride back to Kathmandu.

18

East Asia

HONG KONG

"Let's walk on up the trail. Fast enough to get out of the line of fire. But not so fast that we *become* the line of fire!" I advised my companions while out walking in Hong Kong hills. No, this is not a typical instruction. It did happen though, and I'll tell about it soon.

Walking in Hong Kong hills? Of course. If anyone questions the worth of walking in Hong Kong, let him glance out the 747 window as the big bird circles the peaked islands and settles down on Kai Tak Airport under Kowloon Peak and Lion Rock. Cliffs! Where there are cliffs, there are bound to be walks. That's how I discovered them. That's what inspired me to budget time away from the million sights and sounds of the streets. I discovered tramping through forests that were quiet except for birdsong, monkey screech, and deer bark. I strode windswept, narrow, grassy crests high above empty jade-green bays of the dreaming South China Sea. I climbed carefully down a rock rib and looked down on ocean liners and even jet planes as I felt for a foothold on a piton. I barefooted across a white sand beach and walked all day without meeting any of the five million who live nearby.

These walks can be as short as an hour or as long as a week. They can be flat as a floor or steep as you wish. Most of them will begin with a sea approach across waters jammed with craft from sampan and sail to container boat and battleships. The distance from sea to trailhead is always short. The challenge is in finding the way through the pig farms which often lie athwart the trailhead. With several months' exploration behind me now, I can generally find my way about, but last year on a solo trip I got lost in fog on top of a mountain.

Please think of Hong Kong as a prime locale for walking if the following story does not frighten you. Politics change rapidly, and some of the conditions of this 1979 story no longer obtain.

My friend Laurie Engel and I, having co-led a South China trip, stopped on the way to a Nepal trek for rest and recreation at a favorite resort on the outer island of Macau. While exploring sea cliffs, we were intrigued to discover evidence of illegal Chinese-refugee immigrants. In spite of the advantages of communism that Laurie and I thought we saw in the People's Republic, poor or disaffected mainland natives apparently see a chance to get rich in Hong Kong and take desperate and devious routes to reach a foothold in that land of opportunity. From clues we found on seaside rocks, we reasoned the illegals must swim ashore from small boats, to meet friends who provide nonmainland clothes, as well as guiding and hiding services. On a cliff top above a secluded cove, we found piles of discarded mainland clothes, plastic and net flotation devices, and a rock with rudely painted Chinese characters warning of danger on the main road. We found and followed a brush-tunnel trail leading up and over a pine-forested mountain and down into the back alleys of Coloane town. Laurie pictured romantic gloomy-night cops-and-robbers scenes, but the real stuff was better. I'm coming to it.

On the way home from Nepal, I stopped off in Hong Kong for a fortnight's walking in the rocks and small peaks of the New Territories Islands, to scout trips, and generally enjoy myself. Bob Benner, once my assistant on a McKinley climb, and his wife, Donna Kay, stopped in Hong Kong on their way home from Nepal trekking, eager to join me on a walk.

We were on a narrow trail halfway up Mount Stenhouse, on a ridge of a grassy open hill far above habitation, when two men appeared suddenly before us. They oozed out from behind a rock and acted furtively. Their clothes indicated mainland origin; their faces registered fear. They tried to communicate, but we had no mutual language. The one who seemed most frightened produced a ballpoint pen, and when we fished a scrap of paper from a pocket, he scribbled a one-line note. I reckoned it must be a message to a confederate. My *kanji* was not up to doing instant translation. I wrote "Hong Kong?" in Chinese. He reached into his pocket and showed me a calling card that I *could* read.

I just had time to translate the address when up and over the cliff above the ocean roared a helicopter with its door open and a man at the ready with a rifle. The chopper landed downridge out of sight. The two men squeezed under a nearby boulder in an effort to hide. A pack of people we had not yet seen burst from some bushes near us. Eight men from the chopper came running over the hill in pursuit of figures fleeing up the mountain. We retreated "fast, but not too fast!"

Anxious prickles probed our backs as we huffed up the hilly road. Donna Kay afterwards described this as the vivid imaginary feeling of a bullet smashing into the backbone.

Fortunately the trail to the peak veered off the direct course chosen by the sprinting fugitives, and when the police hollered "Europeans?" we knew we were out of danger. They had already caught the two men under the rock plus five women who began a pitiful wailing.

As we stood readjusting our breath and watching the pursuit with selfish relief, I counseled Donna Kay, who held the note, to throw away this potentially incriminating paper. A policeman appeared under the small cliff we were on, looking around for possible hiders. Donna Kay kept her arms at her sides, opened her fist, and let the paper sift out as unostentatiously as she could. As the corner of my eye caught a flutter of white, my curiosity and ambition flared. It would be fun to try to translate that note! But I had just been telling Donna Kay, who had difficulty concealing a prejudice for the underdog, that we were American citizens, guests of another country whose affairs were none of our business. If we couldn't root for the right as defined by law, then at least we could and should be neutral; besides we still didn't fully understand what was going on. Presumably we could be stopped and searched. I really didn't think they'd search us, but, in arguing thus to the frightened, but outlaw-sympathetic, woman, I waxed so eloquent that I frightened myself and didn't try to sneak past the eye of the police to retrieve my notebook page.

The small path led us around very large boulders and up to the grassy, pointed summit of the mountain. Cliffs hid the chase from us. No one was in sight between us and a tiny, insignificant port on the distant shore below. Half of the island was on display, a marvelous view of jutting rock capes, white sand, and blue-green coves, with not the slightest indication that a thrashing melodrama was being played out on those peaceful, wind-waved, grassy slopes.

A shout drew us to the cliff edge. Two policeman were capturing two runners. Three people sat down. One stood guard near a ravine of trees.

"There's somebody in there; look at those trees move!" Bob exclaimed.

"Of course they are moving in this wind," Donna Kay poohpoohed.

My monocular showed some leaves moving more than the wind was moving others nearby. The policeman yelled, and a blue-clad figure emerged from a cleft or cave hidden by the grove of trees. He yelled again, and another came out. Before long, the two guarded a score.

I was thinking it would be impossible to catch them all if they decided to break and scatter, but then the police hollered up, "Tell them we need help!" Bob went over to the cliff edge opposite and shouted to the other police for reinforcements.

That's about all. We made our way down the other side of the mountain and caught our rickety ferry for Aberdeen. But out on the deep water we were stopped by a police boat whose crew boarded, searched the hold, and checked the papers of both ship and passengers.

The chase was exciting, the refugee problem sad. The paper the next day said that they were not mainland Chinese. They were Vietnamese boat people, temporarily living in China, who had paid professional smugglers 600 dollars in Hong Kong currency per person. Hong Kong authorities considered them to have been resident in China long enough to be a Chinese problem and shipped them back. The twenty-five captured on our island were caught by the sharp eyes of waterborne marine police who spotted a strange junk in a cove.

On the way home we scouted out a jungle-and-rock route to Victoria Peak. As we dined in the elegant, round-windowed observatory restaurant and watched a blood-red sun sink into blue cloud gloom above the rainbow neons reflected in Hong Kong Harbor, Donna Kay murmured a long satisfied sigh, "My diary is going to get really great pages for this day!"

I don't keep a diary, but if I did there would be a special page for another Hong Kong experience, which was more productive of alpha waves than adrenalin: the time a friend and I stayed in a remote Buddhist monastery with a staff of two on Christmas Eve. Hong Kong has many kinds of walks, most of them peaceful.

JAPAN MOUNTAIN WALKING

"Are you trying to tell me that Japan also has mountains?"

"Yes, ma'am, I am." I've been trying for some time to teach Americans to lift their eyes above the smog of industrial statistics to the mountains that fill eighty-five percent of Japan. My passion for the Japanese, their Alps, *kanji*, and customs, generated by walking across their major islands, just won't quit. I know of no other way to support my habit of traveling in Japan's mountains than by inveigling paying passengers into following me through the delectable steeps of the Chubu Sangaku.

My involvement with advertising has mostly been writing travel articles and brochures. Although I've started no gold rush to the Hida range, my prose helped a couple of travel companies put me in charge of over a score of Japan mountain walks. Travel writing isn't easy. We must challenge the bold, reassure the timid, weed out the weak, scale the difficulties to reach an unknown clientele, and describe the indescribable. Our consciences counsel reporting the truth—but not necessarily the whole truth. It is a law of the universe that the whole truth can never be known. The trail to partial truth is bordered by thorns. We cover these prickles with euphemisms: "Expect some rain."

Let's attempt the slippery slopes of mountain writing. We'll look at some travel blurbs, dip into some diaries, peek at some letters, glance at this and that quotation, and make some candid comments.

I had made many solo trips in Japan hills but was still new at guiding there when I wrote the following account about my first paid trip.

There is a range of mountains in Japan so popular that even the most casual visitor with mountains on his mind will surely seek them. Before he has given up the search for maps in English, he will have memorized the five letters which spell Kita Alps. These magic symbols led me on several occasions to penetrate the steep, verdant hills of central Honshu, so, naturally, I was anxious to lead a commercial trip there. My chance came in September last year when our small group set out to walk across the Kita Alps.

In spite of my enthusiasm for all things Japanese and their mountains in particular, I worried that paying passengers might feel that a range without glaciers though named after the Alps might be overadvertised. The Reverend Walter Weston gave universal currency to the name when he wrote *Mountaineering and Exploration in the Japan Alps* in 1896. No doubt he used the term "Alps" in the sense of superlative scenery and meant no precise comparison with icefalls, cow pastures, or Matterhorns. Though in June the southeast monsoon rips off almost all the heavy snows of winter, leaving no glaciers among the misty cliffs and green, jungly steeps, the mountains have their own peculiar charm.

Even the Japan Travel Bureau was worried by my proposed trip. They had never heard of a foreign group walking from valley to valley right across the range. What would we eat? Can Americans eat Japanese food? With a flurry of letters back and forth across the Pacific, hotels were booked, schedules set up, and the trip was at last on paper. In due course, I stood in the immense confusion of Haneda Airport, Tokyo, promising my little band that somewhere out there were mountains.

Half our time in Japan was to be spent walking in the mountains, but the first half was given to general touring of the famous sights, so we had some familiarity with subways, sake, shrines, bean paste, bathing, and the sport of *besoboru* before we tackled the steep, forested base of our first Japanese mountain. When I woke at dawn in our roadhead hotel, the sound of liquid stole into my sleepy ears. Surely it was a defect in the plumbing. Poking my head out the window, I convinced myself that it was only last night's rain dripping from the eaves. It was hard to continue this self-delusion when I went out to the garden, however. I worried that my people might frown at walking in such a downpour.

They didn't frown. It was the first day, all was new, and surely it wouldn't rain all day. It did. It poured on our umbrellas, streaked down our slickers, and gushed into our boot tops all the way up the steep hill. It rained on every precipitous switchback, splashed on the soggy ground, and skidded off the slippery wooden steps that helped us ooze up an extra steep bit of trail. Rain shot from the water spouts of the small, partly open hut where we hung our steaming clothes and sloshed into hot noodles. A short lull as we reached the ridge top enticed some of us into climbing the fogbound granite top of Tsubakaro Peak. We were now above timberline and no doubt would have enjoyed a great view from the pinnacled peak had not rain and wind blasted us again. We spent that evening in the hotel-like quarters of a large hut, listening to the wind hurl solid chunks of rain against the stone walls.

After an early breakfast a few parties braved the storm, so we staggered out after them. Our course now lay along a narrow ridge above timberline. The trail was not too difficult but sometimes gave us pause when a steep section resorted to steel ladders that disappeared into the swirling mists above. Fortunately the fog, rain, and poncho-swirling wind all came at once and obscured what awful depths might have been below. Once we caught a ten-second glimpse of valley fields many thousands of feet below, but mostly it rained. In the respite gained in a wayside hut, eating hot lunches of rice around a stove festooned with our gloves and caps, we fell to arguing about whether we were in a typhoon. The hut master found enough English to inform us that we were not at the moment in the typhoon, which the weather reports warned us was near, but "under the influence of the typhoon." Apparently it just missed us, for which I give thanks to whatever *kami* is involved.

It did not rain every step of the way. We wore shorts while ascending Maeho, Okuho, Kitaho, and Nishiho peaks. Though not always fair, the weather was at least mild enough for bare legs.

Yari! This famous peak is mentioned in all the literature and pictured on souvenirs, modeled in clay, woven in tapestry, printed on napkins, stenciled on T-shirts. Its name means "spear," and it is sometimes called the Matterhorn of Japan, though far less grand than its namesake. (When Su read this, she exclaimed, "Quit apologizing. I was scared, and the final knife edge where the fixed chains stop just below the summit—wow!") We climbed it, but not in weather for wearing shorts. This one we climbed in wet, drizzling mist that was barely above the freezing point. It was the only one of nine peaks that gave us such a cool, damp reception.

So much for the glory of gaining a rock peak only a little above timberline, a peak whose solid, crystalline faces and ridges have little round white-painted spots for guidance and *kanji* characters that read, "Winter Road" or "The mountains are beautiful; leave garbage here." But we got there, and we did experience many of the emotions of mountaineers. We happily crossed the range accompanied by clouds.

There is much more to the Japan Alps than the actual peaks. We stayed in huts polished and shining like palaces. Thrice we had hot-spring baths in the mountains. One, I will never forget, featured a plate glass window looking out into a garden. By sliding around to the corner of the ample pool, I could look through the window, in another window, and right into the lobby. We strolled through dense but civilized forest. Civilized? Yes, a hotel appeared every few hours, complete with telephone, telegraph, TV, hot canned coffee, whiskey by the drink from a vending machine, and other amenities. In spite of all this, the steep-sided hills were mostly inaccessible by trail, and in 1966 I saw a wild bear. We walked along foaming rivers, up and down steep forest trails over tangled roots and barren rocks, and once, near the end of the trip, came upon an active volcano. We would have investigated the puffs of white steam at close range had not the posted warning signs prohibited.

All good things end one day. We came down the steep, leafy trail to jar our feet on concrete in the valley on the far side of the Kita Alps.

The Japan Travel Bureau had laid out a final treat for us. We were quartered in an old farmhouse this last night before boarding wheeled transport. But what a farmhouse—a 200-year-old dwelling preserved as a museum of art, a fitting scene for a great meal of Japanese cuisine served in almost Roman opulence. Our bath was a natural pool with both cold and hot springs, so the water could be tempered to the exact degree. We sat all in a row in this tree-shrouded pond enjoying a light mist in our faces, sipping sake, and dreaming of the mountain pleasures behind.

In the morning we boarded a bus for a few days of sightseeing by train and foot in Kyoto-Nara, but in spite of world-famous temples and elegant palaces, part of our minds and hearts will always remain in the steep, green, cloud-filled peaks of the Japan Alps.

This story sounds a little naive to me now, but only because I am reading it through a kaleidoscope colored by many other Japan adventures. If I wrote up a mountain walk today, I'd pick one of our new, more sporting routes, and I'd spend more space describing the flora and fauna. Especially the fauna. Why walk in Japan? To meet the Japanese.

Marco Polo reported: "Zipangu is an island in the Eastern Ocean some distance from the coast of Manji. It is of considerable size; its inhabitants have fair complexions, are well-made, and are civilized in their manners."

Their manners include each member of a walking party greeting us with *konnichiwa* ("good day") as we meet on forest path or rock ledge. They radiate unquenchable good will.

They are the kind of people who invite us into the office of the hut master for cocktails, hors d'oeuvres, and gifts; who spirit us into the kitchen to laugh and joke with the staff; who share their last crumb on a windy pinnacle hours from the hut; who take us into their homes in the city and stuff us with food and kindness. They may meet us on the trail six hours above their roadhead and press upon us a full bottle of wine to carry down-canyon. They exhibit such honesty as hotel employees finding a pile of coins accidentally left behind by one of our passengers and forwarding the money for delivery a week later in a mountain hut.

These cheerful extroverts do more than make us love them: they drive the poison out of us. (I don't know where the "inscrutable Oriental" is. I haven't found him in China either.) It is impossible for us to bathe in their laughter and optimism without upturning our own lips.

Our groups share fine cuisine with the Japanese in the polished-wood interiors of their cable-strapped, ridge-top huts, dining to the hi-fi sound of Western classical music. We go along with the evening amusement of giggling and laughing at the hut master's humorous speech, composing poetry and drawings for the guest book, watching weather or mountain safety lectures on color TV, and joining in community singing or stove-hugging storytelling. After wind-lullabied sleep we turn out at dawn for gang calisthenics followed by ritual sunrise photography. These doings are examples of their well-mannered civilization, but the quality of the Japanese that impresses us most, and no doubt affected Marco Polo's informants as well, is their boundless and contagious enthusiasm.

I've hinted that travel writers may soft-pedal weather problems. We travel leaders have to take care not to play the weather too *pianissimo*. In other words, there are no refunds for rain. Here is the way I wrote the brochure for a Shoji-Subashiri-Otome-Mount Fuji trip:

> Mount Fuji is known throughout the world for its beauty and for symbolizing the magic of mountains. Its graceful slopes seductively conceal an environment which can rout and destroy its suitors as effectively as any Matterhorn. The tall cone exposes a full 12,000 feet of mountain to contending currents of marine air that breed storms of ferocious power. Even in summer, to make the three-day climb from the plain at sea level to the sacred summit, spend an overnight on the crater rim, and walk back down to sea level is an enterprise to test the mettle of any mountain walker.

This is what happened to me the first time I climbed Fuji-san. I sought out a place called Miho near Shimizu, several days' walk from Fuji, because I had read this Japanese travel enticement: "If you have not seen Mount Fuji from Miho-no-matsubara, you have not truly seen it, and, once seen from here, Fuji-san will remain in your heart forever." As if the storm gods operate in cahoots with imaginative travel writers, a miraculous clearing showed me this sight one rainy evening. I vowed I would walk from the sands of Suruga Bay up and over the summit of Fuji-san and down to the sea again.

Next morning I started squishing along, first telling myself that it could not rain any harder. Then I tried the opposite approach. "Cheer up," I said, "it could be worse." So I cheered up, and sure enough it got worse. A few days later I reached the summit on hands and knees in a heroic crawl through the blast of a typhoon. I was the only one to gain the summit that day (some days eleven thousand pilgrims climb to the top), and the hut keeper gave me a medal for my feat. At the crater rim I found two fellows preparing to descend the Yoshida path, so I joined them to find the way in zero visibility, but, when we were knocked down, rolled, and in danger of being blown into the crater, we gave it up and went down the Gotemba side.

A few days later my feet dragged along the beach at Sagami Bay. I had completed my vow.

When potential passengers pin us down about weather we say "Well, uh. . . . " and search for ways of describing the unpredictable nature of the archipelago's storms without losing a customer in the process. Typhoons are supposed to favor certain seasons and areas. However, they sneak up out of pattern and attack the unwary. The fourth mountain I climbed on my first trip found me too dumb to know anything of typhoon warnings. When I returned from Mount Nantai, I bought the English-language *Japan Times*, which carried these statistics on the storm damage that day: "44 killed, 22 missing, 80 injured, 256 homes destroyed, 106,132 homes damaged, roads closed in 940 places, 37 bridges and 33 embankments washed away, 1,038 landslides, 6,000 train commuters stranded. . . . "

No wonder the priest of Futaarasan Shrine stared at me as I sloshed mountainwards through his gate that rainy morning. He could not imagine the ignorance of one totally unaware of typhoon warnings. Since I splashed happily back from the summit six hours later, still innocent in mind and unscathed of body, I could only have been protected by the same deity who, 1,200 years before, had befriended Priest Shodo, first climber of the mountain.

Here's a milder storm story, a page from a letter to Su written on one of my solo trips:

I was given this paper to demonstrate *kanji*, as the people are amused that I can write better than I can speak. Believe me, I can do neither well. It is 2:30 P.M. on a stormbound day. They do not run the lights in daytime in this snow-buried hut, so I write near the window, whose cracks knife me with cold blasts. There is a lull now, but I do not feel like walking in the soft new snow that fell last night and up to an hour ago. People drag in out of the storm with wet boots and socks; they throw their crampons on the stove to dry the straps. In comes another guy with hard hat, ice ax, rope, butane stove, completely soaked down jacket, bag of food, medical kit, set of hardware, more food, more hardware, two pairs of gaiters, clothes, a flashlight, and, of course, the usual wet socks, gloves, and boots and a pair of chopsticks in his shirt pocket. He dumps it all on the floor and falls asleep in a chair sitting up. Wonder where he's been? (Time out! The stove blew up!) I'm writing this in one of the upstairs rooms, where we huddle around a pot of charcoal. Yesterday? Well, I'll get around to it, but briefly. It was a great, if fatiguing day. Two peaks. One walkup and one fourth-class rock. Ice, snow, and a bitter wind, but, in spite of my general malaise and my usual dislike of anything the least bit technical in mittens and parka, I rather enjoyed it. The stove is going again. Supper is almost ready and the peaks down-canyon showed for a moment with blowing snow banners. Looks good for tomorrow!

Japan is not always stormy. There was one day of clear, hot, blue sky from horizon to horizon—except for one short shower. "No, we won't need to carry our umbrellas on a blue-sky day like this," I advised my passengers that sparkling morning. As we came up the steps from Sarusawa pond toward Kofukuji, the towering afternoon thunderhead spit rain at us. With habit-slicked automation, I drew out my folding umbrella and raised it above my head, then looked back to see every member of the group also unfolding umbrellas. By that time of the trip, they knew Japanese weather and they knew me.

Here is a startling quotation from a native alpinist who spoke to us on top of Spear Peak: "Yari is for beginners, but Gendarme, oh Jesus!" What was he doing, saying such a thing? Bad enough to crib our Christian expletive; worse to show he didn't know anything about beginners.

Beginners are the most difficult of all mountain animals to judge. I was driven to despair watching one fumble-foot on Frog Rock. Five days later she nimbly performed a ballet dance up Byobu Col. I've had to go back down to carry the rucksack of a paunchy passenger on the Sickle Ridge, and had him step on my heels with impatience going over Katsugo Mountain a week later. I've seen them in tears going up a ladder, and, the same day, talked them down a technical rock pitch, facing out, unroped, over great exposure.

Relying on this common tendency for the mountain newcomer to improve, I have been taking timid trampers up Gendarme, over the Panorama Course, across the "arduous and dangerous" (Japan National Tourist Organization's phrase) Hodaka Traverse, and up Mount Tsurugi. They do just fine, in any weather. They lead with their shoulder to keep a bulging rucksack free of the wall. When the road turns up, they stand straight in their toeholds and use their hands for balance. They don't even complain when the trail down goes crazy and tricks us through a maze of boulders and downed timber, and then dumps us, unguided, in a typhoon wash of cobbles.

But beginners, I say, are hard to figure. Every once in a while, I have members who can't eat the food. We gourmet dine our way across Japan, and they freak out and fuel their walking with western cookies and whiskey! Of course, breakfast is a critical moment for all of us in every clime. We emerge from our womblike blankets to face the hard realities of an uncertain day. It is only natural to beg for the kindest, softest, and easiest re-entry. A standard, familiar menu and the ritual "cuppa coffee" help to stiffen the will. But this trip, in radical contrast to others on the adventure travel list, does not feature Oriental types passing before you as if on stage, while you peer out of American tents over your British food. Walking through the Japanese mountains, we become, in effect, Japanese, for there is no other way we can do it. It is "really digging the culture, man," as the hippies say, and that is the essence of travel.

Here's a look at a page in my mountain journal:

Today's summit sojourn was a sort of real-life, three-dimensional enactment of a Zen painting. A dry cloud reduced the earth to six boulders on a precipice rim. Life was represented by myself, Barbara (now my favorite mountain traveler), and a middle-aged native couple who chatted in broken English and shared our rice balls and fish. They underestimated my education and became embarrassed when I caught them commenting about me in Japanese: "That old man has good health!" One dart of sunshine, three flakes of snow, much laughter, and good fellowship made the pinnacle top a temple. It already had a shrine. Why do we not recognize the holiness of mountain summits? In Japan the mountain summit is consecrated by a Shinto shrine, in Nepal by a Buddhist prayer flag, in Europe by a Christian cross. On American summits is a book in which to write one's own name!

No doubt when I wrote this, on one of the few filled-in pages of my diary, I was thinking of *sumi-e* paintings and had no profound Zen ideas in mind. But it may be that living with clouds while following mountain ridges can teach a Zen lesson about the mutability of the universe more insightfully than an afternoon's visit to a valley temple can.

All this talk of clouds, with their hint of storms, may be counterproductive to my usual purpose of advertising Japan to attract more passengers for our trips. I could plead that the August deep-green forests, the September varicolored flowers, the October scarlet leaves—all owe their existence to abundant precipitation. Maybe I should quote pages of statistics showing a probability of only twenty-nine percent rainy days in this season.

As I stuffed the cagoule deep in my rucksack on one of the seventy-one sunshine days out of a hundred and prepared to follow a mountain ridge, the hut keeper handed me a scrawled note. I quote it here because he puts in a plug for temple viewing, and also because, even though his English is fractured and unpunctuated, I cannot improve on his travel writing: "Please deeply see Japan that they are now and also old history merrily trip is looking forward to you."

19

What Am I Doing Here?

LAURIE ENGEL is enjoying a five-year introduction to outdoor adventure. She often describes how she reacted to this or that harrowing experience by asking herself, "What am I doing here?"

"Smoke talked me into going on this bicycle trip in India. I had ridden my daughter's bike around the block once. I hardly knew which end to get on. The first day I kept falling in the deep dust. We reached our destination at nightfall. We had only a thin reed mat on a concrete floor. Dinner was one hardboiled egg. And a rat ran across the floor, oh!"

Or: "We climbed all day up this steep mountain in the Minami Alps in Japan. They told us there would be a key, but, when we finally reached the hut just at dark, there was no key and no blankets."

She gets a lot of mileage out of the phrase "What am I doing here?" as she talks of the terrors of following me around in the far places of the earth. She is an expert storyteller, and her warmth, enthusiasm, and modesty captivate audiences of neophytes, who take courage from her bravery. The old hands laugh and empathize, because they too once wondered why they were there.

"What am I doing here?" is a thought that has occurred to many of us. No doubt it was wailed by an early explorer as he looked back from a mountain at a saber-toothed tiger patrolling the valley of his home cave. It is reliably reported that these were the words hurled by lookouts from the bows of the *Niña*, the *Pinta*, and the *Santa Maria* as they approached the rim of the world. It was whispered at a million cocktail parties last night. "What am I doing here?" was the problem of Job and may well be the main question mankind has to ask.

These words of alienation have rarely escaped my teeth, but recently this commonest of plaints has moaned through my tight lips in lonely tents in Nepal. Walking through the Himalaya can keep a professional leader happy for most of a decade, but there comes a night when the glow of a candle in an empty, empty tent is not enough. Love (spell it sex if you must) is as essential as air, and, like oxygen, is sometimes in short supply in high mountains. Two other necessities offered by civilization are practically unobtainable: hot showers and electronic hi-fi. Confucius said, "Music produces a kind of pleasure which human nature cannot do without"—and he could have added that it is not readily attained from the frozen bearings of a tape recorder nor through static-filled short-wave.

Yet it is not even the lack of these life-support systems that makes the long-gone leader mutter, "What am I doing here?" Rather it is the sudden realization that there is a world of hobbies, studies, diversions, and excursions that are not getting done. That he is not at play. That's it. But everyone works. "Yes," the temporarily disgruntled trek leader cries to himself, "but when does five o'clock come? Two months from now."

But, most likely, the third cup of steaming sweet *solcha* tea in the morning, a last pale star, and the first touch of sun on an ice spire will be all the answer he needs.

Is that what I am doing here? Taking the opportunity to enjoy low-latitude, high-altitude, morning twilight? Partly, along with a host of other reasons. Mountain climbers write articles attempting to explain their strange pastime, to tell what they are doing there. I have even tried it myself.

A multipage letter I wrote to Cheryl Arnold trying to explain what I was doing in a snow-spattered tent in the Palisades never got mailed. The crumpled pages shook out of an old rucksack the other day to reveal no great success in solving this old problem, which has been attacked in essay and book by the best of literary mountaineers with hardly better results.

Here are excerpts from that letter, leaving out some of the rambling through many ranges of the world and assorted reaches of the mind:

Thinking over some possible answers on the way up the slabs and ledges and chatter marks of the ice-ground stone yesterday, I remembered some recent feelings of peculiar satisfaction that happened this month in the mountains. It might be that these emotions resemble the "peak states" that psychologists talk about. It is a sudden, often fleeting, but powerful feeling that the present moment is one that is absolutely right, full, complete. Descriptions of *satori* that I have read seem to fit what I am trying to describe, although I would hesitate to ascribe anything religious to them. It is a realization in the bones, without cerebration, that the activity at the instant is the correct, fit, and proper one—a sort of gut feeling of profound belongingness.

These super impressions do not come often, or regularly, or on every trip, or anything like that, but I do experience them frequently enough to catch a hint that maybe they are an important clue to "Why climb?" That they do not have to be momentous occasions is proven by an instance on the climb of the day before yesterday. The peak was easy, so easy that it could hardly be called rockclimbing. It was little better than a talus slope, but two hours from camp my body settled into a rhythm that I can only describe as a feeling of being well-oiled. I whispered to myself, "Oh, how I like to go uphill."

Again, last week, Su's son Glenny and I were climbing a small mountain. (The summit register recorded only two ascents, those of David Brower in 1939 and Oliver Kehrlein in 1947, though surely Norman Clyde climbed it.) I noticed an unusually intense satisfaction in the sound of a carabiner as it snapped around the nut cord and the climbing line a split second later. A small thing; it happens many times in a climbing day. It means the right nut has klunked into the right crack, the belay is secure, the climber is safe, and the belayer is attached to the mountain. It is a small sound, a minor thing. Perhaps it is like the single, quickly muted cymbal clang which punctuates a phrase in a long symphony. Clang, and on with the score, but, having heard it, you know the rest will be right. Seldom do these things stand out in the memory. Yet probably they are the glue holding a vast edifice from crumbling into nonclimbing, though unnoticed in the general architecture.

As I search back along the winding trail of my career in the mountains, my memory spotlights special occasions. Rare ones stand out as if illuminated by a shaft of sunlight. The year 1947 was a good one in the Rockies and the Sierra. It was the year we made the first ascent of Mount Nevermind, and reached the bergschrund on the descent at pitch-black midnight after a two-rope rappel. It was the year I set a speed record climbing Mount X and Mount Y in a single day. Mostly I remember it for something that happened to me on the descent of Nez Percé, something that has never left me, though there is little to tell.

Gary was ahead; it was late in the day. The summit climb and rappel descent were over. The snowfield was easy; another hour of heel-plunging down the steep way would bring us into camp. There was that feeling—the feeling I have tried to convey—that I could walk down that snowfield forever. A sense of fitting securely into this place was so strong that it seemed my whole life's purpose was simply to follow Gary's footsteps down that declivity. Maybe it is a feeling of wholeness, a term we come to grips with in the words of John Middleton Murray: "For the good man to realize that it is better to be whole than to be good is to enter in a straight and narrow path compared to which his previous rectitude was flowery license!"

I can think of two other specific occasions when this feeling flooded over me. Skiing up through the snow-coned trees of Mount Hood on a winter's solo excursion with a heavy three-week pack. Another time, sitting in my tent on the lowermost slopes of Himalchuli, too content to read, to sleep, to listen to the radio, to do anything other than hark to a bell in the head that said, "This is it, this is it."

The letter raves on, but this fragment will do. No extension of letter or library is really going to answer the question of what one is doing in the mountains. Although responding to "Why?" is probably futile, I find it fun, as Laurie does, to recount anecdotes when "What am I doing here?" was a spontaneous cry in the wilderness.

Twenty miles is a good round number, a good, long way even in flat country. Ten miles out through the gently rolling Willamette Valley and ten miles home. A small mountain to climb at the end of the first ten miles. This mountain was really only a grassy hill, with a little volcanic cliff and a couple of groves of Douglas fir, but it had a *cave!* What more could a boy want for a fun-filled Saturday? A long walk, a mountain climb, and a wriggling belly-crawl through the mouth of the cave into its mysterious black room. In the absence of candles, it was explorable only by slow, cautious standing with outstretched groping hands. But I had matches. Matches and a jackknife—of course! Out I scurried to cut kindling for a fire. The perfect topper to it all. I would cook my lunch on a picnic fire in the cave. I lit the fire, impaled my hot dogs on a sharpened stick, and waited for some decent cooking flame to burst from the smoke. Smoke! "What am I . . .? Let me out of here!" I just made it through the narrow cave entrance.

On another occasion I no doubt asked myself what I was doing chasing that pie pan around, although I can't remember my thoughts after so much time. It was breakfast time in the Oregon Cascades, and, being the Oregon Cascades, it was raining torrentially. I was trying to make a fire on a small flat in front of my soaked sleeping bag. Anticipating the state of Oregon weather, I'd gathered a little stock of cedar sticks the night before, wrapped them in my parka, and stashed them in the driest bottom of my rucksack. In those days I carried a pocket knife, a hunting knife, a tin box of special dry tinder, and a bagful of Oregon wet-woodsy fire lore.

I made the approved cone of tinder, shavings, sticks, and big firewood. The fire ignited, but rain-ponded water rose into my tinder and put out the second spark. It was a desperate situation, but quick thinking saved the day. I remembered a pie pan in a former camper's debris and commandeered it for a floodproof fire base. Alas, it floated on the rising tide! But not before I had another fire started and was well on the way to melting grease in the frying pan.

To make a wet, bedraggled tale brief, I followed that floating pie pan around and around in a waddling squat in my raincoatless rags and tennies (Depression clothing), shaving cedar slivers to fuel the fire, on which I cooked a full breakfast of scrambled eggs!

When I first thought of writing about these reflections, I could recall no time when I complained, "What am I doing here?" Now I realize I have repressed the bad times. Or turned them into good times. And that is the point of Laurie's informal lectures. She is saying they turned out to be good times after all.

Right now I'm involved in two projects sufficiently complicated to wring from me that old cry: "What am I doing here?" But even the harder moments are part of the good life I once tried to summarize in a poem. A couple of lines:

> It's ice ax and blizzards and thunders
> and woodwinds and Venus and wonders

hint of the extremes encountered in pursuing mountaineering with an attitude at once pious and hedonistic. The unquoted punch line of the poem emphasized that if you seek mountains, and other high ground, in the spirit of picnic and pilgrimage, your rucksack of memories will ensure that you envy no kings.